A Zombie's Life

Italy's Whipping Boy Talks Life and Career

Giovanni Lombardo Radice, circa the early 1990s, in a portrait shot taken by Federico Riva

A Zombie's Life

Italy's Whipping Boy Talks Life and Career

Discussions on Deodato, Fulci, Margheriti, Lenzi, Bava, Argento, Soavi and a lot more

Giovanni Lombardo Radice
aka John Morghen

Midnight Marquee Press, Inc.
Baltimore, Maryland, USA; London, UK

Copyright © 2017 by Giovanni Lombardo Radice
Interior layout by Gary J. Svehla
Cover design by Aurelia Susan Svehla

Midnight Marquee Press, Inc., Gary J. Svehla and A. Susan Svehla do not assume any responsibility for the accuracy, completeness, topicality or quality of the information in this book. All views expressed or material contained within are the sole responsibility of the author.

Without limiting the rights under copyright reserved above, no part of this publication may be reproduced, stored in or introduced into a retrieval system, or transmitted, in any form, or by any means (electronic, mechanical, photocopying, recording or otherwise), without the prior written permission of the copyright owner or the publishers of the book.

ISBN 13: 978-1-936168-729
Library of Congress Catalog Card Number 2017907137
Manufactured in the United States of America

First Printing by Midnight Marquee Press, Inc. May 2017

Dedication:

To Mike Baronas who helped me accept my horror past.
If I hadn't met him, I would have never written this book.

To the loving memory of Lucio Fulci, Antonio Margheriti,
David A. Hess, Fiamma Maglione, Gabriele Di Giulio and
all the fellow actors and directors I worked with
who are now filming in Heaven.

Table of Contents

8	Chapter 1–Have You Ever Been in a Movie?
10	Chapter 2–The Family Beauty
15	Chapter 3–Curriculum Vitae
23	Chapter 4–Tom or Ricky?
26	Chapter 5–An Actor Prepares
29	Chapter 6–Memories
34	Chapter 7–Camera Rolling ... A Line to Go
44	Chapter 8–Movies, Drugs and Rock 'n Roll
47	Chapter 9–Yankee Doodle Went to Town
54	Chapter 10–Bulls' Balls, Cannibal Oral Sex and Sewers
58	Chapter 11–Parlor Games and a New Movie
60	Chapter 12–Zombie Love at First Sight
73	Chapter 13–A Drill Enters History
76	Chapter 14–A Greek Holiday to be Regretted for Life
79	Chapter 15–A Jungle Nightmare
90	Chapter 16–More Opera and a New Side Career
97	Chapter 17–The Greatest Loss

104	Chapter 18—Comedy, Drama and Romance
115	Chapter 19—A Deadly Impact and a Theater Comeback
129	Chapter 20—Falling in Love Again
135	Chapter 21—Theater Triumphs and A Pain in the Ass (in Outer Space)
143	Chapter 22:—The Airy Spirit of Horror
149	Chapter 23—A Role Can Change a Life
158	Chapter 24—A Church for a Movie and One in Which To Be Married
170	Chapter 25—Life and Death
178	Chapter 26—The Theater Years of a Not Ideal Husband
183	Chapter 27—How to Destroy an Escalator and Live Happily Ever After
192	Chapter 28—Freedom and Drama
198	Chapter 29—I Am the Third Fairy and Madness Is My Name
204	Chapter 30—I Only Sit on a Throne
214	Chapter 31—King of the Jews
223	Chapter 32—From Riches to Rags
229	Chapter 33—A Horror Comeback in Prague
234	Chapter 34—The Past Never Dies
241	Chapter 35—Que Sera Sera
247	Chapter 36—The Alphabet Game
256	Johnny, Johnny
260	Acknowledgments

Chapter 1
Have You Ever Been in a Movie?

On a Roman September afternoon in 1979 a skinny young man of 25, blue eyes and blond hair, is measuring the stage of the recently restored Teatro delle Muse (the Muses Theater), which is soon to re-open after many years.

The young man is worried and frustrated. It is apparent that the stage is too small for the imposing scenery of *Harlequin Educated by Love*, the 18th-century French play by Marivaux that he has presented in July at the Spoleto Two Worlds Festival, directing it and starring in the role of Trivelin, with white wig and a purple costume that had been created for Donald Sutherland in Fellini's *Casanova*. It hasn't been a success. Because of the scenery by Aldo Buti, reproducing a fountain with statues such as the ones in Versailles, with real water pouring out at the end of the play, the old and cavernous Spoleto church of San Niccolò has been selected to host the show, instead of a smaller space, where the subtle and refined Marivaux dialogue would surely have been more easily appreciated. Critics have been cold if not decidedly bitchy and the possibilities of presenting the play in the forthcoming theater season that in Italy goes from October to May are poor. Yet, if the play closes, it's a financial disaster. The Spoleto Festival's money didn't cover all the expenses. The young man has already sold the last of the family paintings and furniture that he inherited, and creditors are at the door. It is truly a hot mess.

Deeply concentrated in his measuring and gloomy thoughts, the young man has paid no attention to the small group of people who are chatting in the pit, show business people who have been invited to have a look at the renewed theater before its official opening. He didn't notice that a small blonde lady in her late 40s is looking at him intensively. When his pointless work is done he descends the few steps from stage, ready to go, but the lady stops him

Spoleto Two Worlds Festival, 1979: Johnny as Trivelin in *Harlequin Educated by Love* by Marivaux, with Marina Garroni as the Fairy

and asks him a question that puzzles him: "Excuse me, have you ever been in a movie?" His surprised expression makes the lady smile and introduce herself: "I am Annamaria Spasiano and I am a movie agent. If you are interested I would like to represent you. You have a great face."

The name doesn't ring any bells. He doesn't know that the lady is the mother of sexy actress Silvia Dionisio, or that Silvia is the wife of director Ruggero Deodato. Too focused on his stage world, the "movie mob" has never interested him and, in Italy, the two sides of stage business, theater and movies, have a tradition of being separate and not co-existing on friendly terms, the stage crowd royally disdaining movie people as "money vultures" and the celluloid world feeling the stage world to be filled with "old intellectual bores."

A youthful Johnny lights up

But money is exactly what the young man needs right now. So he smiles back at the lady and says that he is interested, sure. If some money can be earned he would be ready to walk on his hands wearing a red nose, let alone act in front of a camera. He answers a few questions. Yes, he speaks English. Actually he is trilingual since birth and can fluently speak English and French. Yes he has some photos to give her and of course a c.v. And yes he can bring the stuff to her office by tomorrow. She might have something for him real soon? That would be fantastic.

She gives him her card and he leaves, not knowing that his life is going to change forever.

That young man is me, Giovanni Lombardo Radice (affectionately known to most everyone as Johnny), soon to be known to the world of cult cinema as John Morghen.

Chapter 2
The Family Beauty

"You have a great face."

It wasn't the first time such a compliment had been paid me. As a matter of fact, beauty had been my ambiguous companion since childhood, becoming a half blessing/half curse, as when people gathered around my stroller in shops or gardens, making faces and weird voices to that exceptionally handsome little boy, blue-eyed and so blond to be almost white, features quite rare in 1950s Italy.

People are always ironic and skeptical when a beautiful person (man or woman) tries to explain that beauty is not always the flowered path to Paradise it's generally considered to be. What people don't understand is that the frightening quality of beauty doesn't depend on you. If you are, let's say, incredibly clever, only a rare disease, a tragic accident or extreme old age can take your brains from you. You can work with the intelligence that was given to you at

"You have a great face!" Giovanni Lombardo Radice (Johnny) at age 14

birth, expand it, direct it and increase it. It's a fortune you can spend being in control. And the same goes for an exceptional talent in music or in the arts. Not the same with beauty. You can wear it, and nothing else. You are valued, desired (at times *madly* desired) and admired for something that doesn't belong to your inner self more than a dress or a jewel and that can disappear for causes that are out of your control: a change in metabolism, hair falling, aging. And many a time, such as in my case, the beautiful person doesn't consider him- or herself beautiful. Groucho Marx stated that he would never have sought admission to a club that accepted members like him. In the same sense I was not in the least attracted by people who looked like myself.

But handsome I was considered, from the outside world and from my family, where beauty came from the side of my maternal grandmother, the Gherardini-Morghen: "You are a real Morghen," my grandmother proudly used to say, not foretelling the movie history her maiden name was going to have. My mother was a renowned and remarkable beauty, quite similar to Vivien Leigh, but she wasn't in the least concerned with her looks. She dressed soberly, never wore make-up and couldn't care less about her hair turning gray before its time, sarcastically despising women who "painted" themselves or dyed their hair. Nevertheless she was fascinated by beauty in others and quite concerned with mine. She got to the point of giving me appetite supressing pills, amphetamines, when, in pre-puberty, I tended to put on some extra weight. She herself was eating like a bird, her silhouette the only physical part of herself she cared about. Not surprisingly, anorexia got me, first at age 18, then with recurrent spells in different moments of my life.

Johnny's grandmother Adele Morghen

The marriage of Johnny's parents, Lucio Lombardo Radice and Adele Maria Jemolo, in 1946

Most families have definite roles for each individual member, like in old plays. There's the Clever, the Funny, the Clumsy, the Smart. I was the Handsome and what was asked from me was to keep being so. Of course I had to accomplish some family standards such as speaking at least three languages (a must from both maternal and paternal side), being polite in society, witty in conversation and well behaved at meals. But my shoulders did not carry the heavy intellectual burden that was on my older brothers, not always without consequence. Marco, the middle son, six years my senior, became a brilliant neuro-psychiatrist and a part-time writer, but Daniele, the eldest, born in 1947, cracked under the weight of what was expected from him as a first born. He fled home at 19, suffered many mental breakdowns and led quite a miserable life as a borderline schizophrenic.

My parents' marriage (Lucio Lombardo Radice and Adele Maria Jemolo), starting just after the war in Italy begun, had been a "misalliance," with the aristocratic Morghen and the hyper-Catholic Jemolo doing what was in their power to prevent their brilliant and beautiful daughter from marrying a mathematic professor to be, 10 years her senior and, God forbid, a communist. But love, born in the heroic days of the fight against Mussolini and the Nazis, in which they both had been active (my father being in jail twice), had been stronger than the family crusade.

Different they were and the marriage balanced on my father adoring my mother, like a frog kissed by a princess, and my mother allowing him to love her. Nevertheless, the incredible intel-

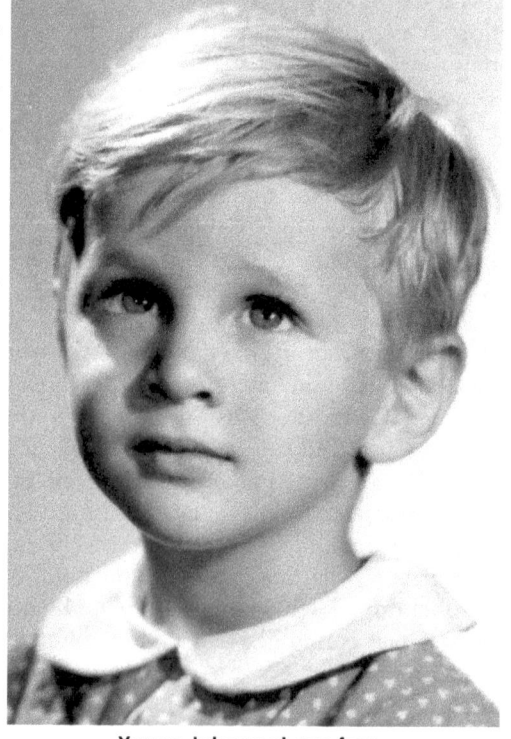

Young Johnny at age four

lectual standards that the two familes shared tied them down.

The Lombardo Radices were a Sicilian bourgeois family of lawyers and notaries that reached fame when my grandfather Giuseppe deviated from the routine and became a teacher, the first translator of Kant in Italian and the author of school reform that modernized the Italian system and is basically in use even today. In a conference tour he met my grandmother Gemma Harasim, a Slavic woman who was a teacher and an advocate for the female vote and female education. She traveled alone, wrote for newspapers and spoke eight languages, including Russian and Hungarian, a gift she was to pass on to my father. They had two daughters and a son.

Giuseppina, the eldest daughter, became a Greek scholar and a wonderful translator of Sophocles and Aeschylus. Laura, the middle daughter, was a teacher and the wife of Pietro Ingrao, a strong political personality in post-war Italy, the first communist to be President of Parliament. My father ... My father became "everything," a Man of the Renaissance (as was the title of one of his books). As a steady occupation he was a university mathematics professor, but he was also a politician, a pedagogist as his father, a translator, a journalist and a writer, winner of the prestigious Viareggio Award for his book about Kafka, Bulgakov and Kundera called *The Accused Ones*. He had out-numbered his mother by speaking 12 languages (eight fluently and four on a basic level). Always a rebel inside the Italian Communist Party, he had been a proponent of dialogue between communists and Catholics, a supporter of the Czech Revolution of 1969 and a protagonist in the European peace movement.

On my mother's side, her father, Arturo Carlo Jemolo, was a self-made man of incredible cleverness, who had become not only a famous lawyer (representing among others Fiat and the Bank of Italy), but a university professor and a respected moral authority, a Father of the Country, who had been one of the authors of the post-war Constitution and an important link between the Italian government and the Vatican, as a personal friend of Pope Paul the Sixth. He had married Adele Morghen, the last of a celebrated family of German engravers, including Raffaello Morghen, who is buried in the Florentine church

Johnny's maternal grandfather, Arturo Carlo Jemolo, during World War 1

Johnny, age 18, smokes a cigarette.

of Santa Croce along with Michelangelo and Galileo and who is well known for his etching of Leonardo's Last Supper. In the 19th century a Morghen had married Countess Adele Gherardini (my grandmother's grandmother), who was the last of a noble family that could claim as a member the Leonardo Monna Lisa (Monna Lisa Gherardini married to Messer Del Giocondo) and the Gherardini brothers who fought with William the Conqueror at Hastings in England, giving birth to the Fitzgerald family (Fitz-Gherard, son of Gherard-Gherardini). With my amused surprise, a few years ago a member of the Fitzgerald family sent me his greetings and the family coat of arms.

My mother had chosen a low profile. She had graduated in medicine but had then decided to work as a biologist. Her main aim in life was not to be bothered by reality and to lie in bed, smoking cigarette after cigarette and reading—her great passion. Every night, before bedtime, she used to read to me a chapter of a book, as she had done with my older brothers. And they were not fairy tales, but Victor Hugo's *Les Miserables*, Tolstoy's *War and Peace* and Dickens' *David Copperfield*. She also took me to the movies and she became the instigator of my passion for the theater, taking me to the Marionette Opera (The Pupi Siciliani) during the four years we spent in Palermo (from 1956 to 1960), the city where my father had received his first assignment as a university professor. In doing so she was quite brave. The Marionette Opera at that time was far from being the touristic attraction it is now and the building was located in a dark alley in the middle of the Palermo "Kasbah," one of the most popular and poor areas of the town, not a place for a lady to walk without male companionship other than the one of a four year old. The puppeteers warmly welcomed their little golden-haired fan; they allowed me backstage and presented me with a little puppet of Angelica, the beautiful princess who turned insane the proud warrior Orlando, the hero of the saga their puppets were representing. From there on my only toys were puppets and little theaters. At five years old I had no doubt about what I would later do in life.

Chapter 3
Curriculum Vitae

While prepping my c.v. for Mrs. Spasiano, I realized that, being only 25, I had already done quite a bit. But not everything had to be said.

My school career wasn't worth mentioning. I hated the whole experience and wished to be out of it as soon as possible. So I decided to "jump" a year and attempt to get my high school diploma at 17. But to do so I needed to have the best grades in all subjects and that was a problem. I was more than brilliant in Italian, History and Philosophy, but my Greek was awful and my ignorance of mathematics so gross that the previous year I had to take the subject again because I said that three divided by zero was three. Which in my humble opinion was perfectly true. If I have three pies and I don't share them with anybody they don't disappear, they stay three all the same. But apparently it didn't work that way.

As for Greek, I seduced the young romantic lady professor by using my exceptional memory to recite by heart some Sappho love verses in full metric, but the hairy and sturdy math professor was a harder nut to crack. So I decided to take the bull by its horns and talked to the man, saying that I knew I was an ass in his subject, but that I was already determined to have a show business career. What was the point of keeping me in school for one more year?

At that point Professor Arena (I will never forget his name) did something that at the same time was noble, clever and fully Catholic-Italian. He took the Bible out of a drawer and made me swear with my hand on it that I would never work with mathematics in my life. This done he gave me the grade I needed. And I did keep the oath. I couldn't teach mathematics to a six year old and can't make more than two plus two without a calculator.

My consuming passion for ballet, which I had studied for many years, would go as "dance" in the sports skills. Even if I kept studying the art form until I was almost 40, an injured back had prevented me from trying a professional career and I feared that ballet would have sounded too gay-ish. Nor was I to mention the diploma in sport physiotherapy I had taken in the dark days when I realized that

A young Johnny takes another puff.

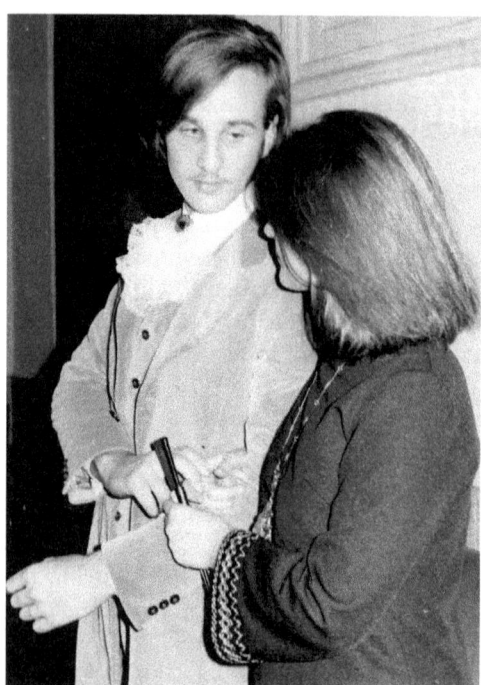

Johnny's theater debut, in 1970, age 15, with Marina Garroni in *The Rehearsal* by Jean Anouilh, with the French Cultural Institute Company

dancing was out of the question. I also thought that it wouldn't have been "professional" for an actor to include the two years I had worked as a journalist at *Sipario*, a monthly show business magazine, nor my experience at age 15 with the French Art Council Theater Company in Rome. That was too amateurish. But I mentioned my radio work as a host and director (an adaptation of *The Picture of Dorian Gray*, among other things).

I had been volunteer assistant director to Giorgio Strehler at the world renowned Piccolo Teatro in Milan and the name of this famous director could make an impression, but indeed my professional career had started when I joined the Turin State Theater for *Bel Ami*, a stage adaptation of the Maupassant book, in the almost extra role of the Marquis of Cazolles.

It happened quite casually, as many things in my life.

I was 18, out of school and jobless after the *Sipario* interlude. And I was escaping from a maddening love story. I had realized very soon that I was attracted to both boys and girls and never considered it a problem. At age 13, I had madly fallen in love with a friend of my brother, Marco, seven years my senior.

"T," I will refer to him so for privacy reasons, was fully heterosexual and quite a playboy, changing girl friends more easily than shirts. But something in the quite moving courtship of the little boy made us secret lovers. Quite incredibly our relationship lasted for life, with many ups and downs that I will have occasion to mention in this book but never reaching the state of us becoming committed companions. He was free and had dozens of women (but *never* another man or boy) and I was free and had many other love stories with both sexes, including the one that brought me to Turin and to my first professional engagement as an actor.

Corrado, nicknamed Dado, was a schoolmate twice the years my senior. He was a rich and spoiled kid, driving a roaring sport car and having a passion for horse gambling and an even more devouring passion for manipulating others and "owning" them. He was bisexual as I was and we started a love affair that was quite serious on my part, but just a game for him. Old story. He didn't really care about me, but he thought I was a nice object to possess and pleasant company for any mad ideas he might have, as when he suggested that we prostitute ourselves to finance a summer holiday. I was clay in his hands and incapable of saying no, no matter how crazy his ideas were. But during that holiday something cracked inside me and I realized that I had to escape as far away as possible.

Dado, when 19, got a 16-year-old girl pregnant and married her. It was a disaster and they soon split, with me taking care of the little boy whenever the child was supposed to be with his father. No changing diapers for flamboyant dandy Dado. I accepted the task quite willingly because I always had a passion for infants, but I assumed that he was no longer having sexual relations with his baby bride. I was wrong. On a sunny beach in the island of Ponza he told me he was going to phone his wife to say hello to his son and he returned with an ear-to-ear smile, saying that Grazia, that was her name, was pregnant again and that he hoped for a girl to be named Enrica, because it rhymed with "fica," the Italian word for cunt. I didn't say anything, knowing that arguing with Dado was pointless, but I had a vivid vision of a future of babysitting two kids while he was having fun with whomever, behind my back. I had to break with him and to do so I had to escape somewhere far away, not to be tempted by his mermaid chanting and strong sexual appeal.

Johnny played old father Aegeus in *A Midsummer Night's Dream* in 1976.

A face sprang to my mind and it was the face of Aldo Trionfo, a well-known director who was in charge of the Turin State Theater and an open homosexual. I met him at a Festival in Riccione while working for *Sipario* and had been the object of his close courtship. I honestly thought he was revolting. He was in his 60s, fat and with pronounced Jewish features that even the worst Nazi propaganda couldn't have imagined. So I politely eluded his attempts to corner me in elevators and vaguely thanked him when he said that I was welcome to join the crew if I ever decided to work with him in Turin. Now his words came back to me as an actual possibility when I considered working a thousand kilometers from Dado and his babies' diapers.

When we got back to Rome I told Dado I was out to buy cigarettes and jumped on the first train for Turin. Trionfo welcomed me warmly and asked

At age 16, wanting to look older

me to be his assistant for the season, which included a production of *Bel Ami*, a very avant-garde version of *Faust*, and other minor shows. But I didn't intend to be stuck in Turin and fulfill his lust for a year, so I answered that I wanted to be his assistant for *Bel Ami*, but also with a role in it, to experience a real theater tour.

The continuous traveling might work as a good cure to forget Dado.

It did. And it also started an entire new phase of my life.

The *Bel Ami* troupe was a huge one, counting some 30 among actors, dancers and extras, from 78-year-old Tina Lattanzi (the iconic, stagy and often parodied Italian voice of Greta Garbo) to a bunch of kids in their teens or early 20s, eager to take their place on stage for something more than a two-line role. I had always been interested in directing and was a huge Shakespeare fan, so I convinced some of them to join me in an ambitious adventure, staging *A Midsummer Night's Dream* in a small "off" theater in Rome, one of the many that had sprung up in the 1970s, with an entirely new generation of actors and directors that couldn't find a space on official stages.

My idea was of a Victorian version, with waltzes and hoop skirts and an emphasis on "class" conflict between the poor artisans and the rich and depraved aristocrats that doubled themselves in the fairy world. It was crazy, but full of ideas. The magic flower that forces love between people was treated as if it were a drug similar to opium, and the Puck character had been given to 12-year-old twins who could create the idea of the witty elf appearing and disappearing from side-to-side of the stage in a flash. It was a success, with extremely good reviews and a full house every night. I didn't get back what I had invested when selling some paintings and jewels I had inherited from my mother, but I was happy and excited all the same and so were the others, most especially after Saverio Marconi (the young actor playing Bottom) had been noticed in our show by the

Taviani brothers (esteemed movie directors) and cast as the leader in their new movie *Padre Padrone* (Father and Master) that won the Palmares at that year's Cannes Film Festival. Self-producing and not getting paid could indeed lead to something great.

We decided to keep going and set up our steady company, named Il Cigno (The Swan) after Shakespeare's theater in London.

The next production was another Shakespearean play, *Macbeth*, that doesn't have in Italy the same ill-luck fame it has in England (never quote it, never name a character and refer to it as "The Scottish Thing"). It was an even more eccentric version than *Midsummer Night's Dream* had been, all based on Freudean theories and depicting Macbeth and his Lady as two children suffering from an Oedipus complex and wanting to destroy the adult world embodied by King Duncan, Banquo and the others. The Witches were reunited in just one Mother figure, ambiguous and charming, leading the fatal pair to destruction. The musical score was provided by a selection of Mahler symphonies and the scenery represented a bedroom far larger than in reality, as seen through the eyes of small children.

It was quite expensive and my father became involved financially. Not only did he translate brilliantly the play into Italian, but he contributed to the budget by selling some paintings very dear to him: the big Attardi that had been given to him with the Viareggio Award and an even more valuable Guttuso, that the Sicilian painter had done for him when he was in jail under Mussolini.

From the Jemolo-Morghen family, who had opposed in every possible way my will to be in show business, I couldn't expect any kind of help at all.

As soon as I was out of school, my grandfather had officially summoned me to his office and told me that if I wanted to follow the family tradition and "be someone in life" I should take the diplomatic career and become an Ambassador, because: "You are good looking but you are not clever." On the other hand, if I wanted to disgrace them all by becoming "a clown" I was free to do so, but I wouldn't receive a penny. I told him that I wanted to be a clown and that was it.

Macbeth was a success too and led us to a prestigious contract with the Maggio Musicale, the celebrated Opera Festival in Florence. The whole company, including myself as a director, was hired for Luciano Berio's *Opera*, a complicated score vaguely inspired by the Titanic tragedy that involved actors, singers, the Swingle Singers Choir and the largest possible orchestra, which included rare ethnic instruments. It was a World Premiere and expectations were high.

Luciano Berio turned out to be the most pompous ass I had ever met, and his 1960s theater idea of people in black leotards wriggling on stage in nonsensical avant-garde movements didn't match my conception of ghosts from the Titanic tragedy. Quarrels were exploding every day and, at the dress rehearsal, conductor Bruno Bartoletti had one eye aimed at the orchestra and the other on Berio and myself, almost physically fighting in the pit.

Nevertheless it was a success, with a lot of young people attending and becoming the best box-office result ever for a modern opera.

We decided that for a time we needed to work on our individual careers. Personally, I felt that I had to improve my skills both as an actor and as a direc-

As Gratiano in *The Merchant of Venice*, directed by Giancarlo Cobelli, in 1978

tor. I hadn't been to acting school and I needed a Maestro. I found it in Carlo Cecchi, who had been Lord Henry in my radio production of *Dorian Gray*. Not even 40 years old, Carlo was already an iconic figure of the Italian stage as actor-director of his own company. I joined in the extra role of a servant in Molière's *The Bourgeois Gentleman* and just watching him night after night was the best training I could have asked for.

I then accepted a really weird contract from Ugo Margio, the craziest avant-garde director to be found, who wanted me to be Jesus in his theater adaptation of Milton's *Paradise Lost*. The show was to be presented under a circus tent in a Roman villa during summer, but the project slowed down to a crawl and when we opened, it was full winter. In my silk costume I was positively shivering, but it was fun, even if the golden spangles that covered my head were to be found on me for months to come. Giancarlo Cobelli, a famous director, saw me in that show and asked me to be Gratiano in his summer production of *The Merchant of Venice*. It was first rate stuff, with many stars of the Italian stage and Cobelli, a former actor and mime, proved to be an amazing teacher, even if a harsh one, with violent outbursts that could become physical, as when he threw a heavy marble ashtray onto the actor playing Bassanio, missing him (and me by his side) by an inch. While playing Gratiano, a comic role, I discovered that I had a real talent for making people laugh, a quality that I was to use a lot in my stage future but a talent that the movie world made a very scarce use of.

The Swan Company reunited in 1978 for a very different project than the Shakespearean plays we had previously produced. Our male lead, Saverio Marconi, had developed a passion for musicals (in later years he was to become number one in Italy), so he convinced us on a parody-musical adaptation of *The Girl Of The Golden West*. I wrote the text and the lyrics to the songs with Marina Garroni, making fun both of the Belasco original play and the Puccini opera.

Marina was also to star as Minnie, a role she was crazy about.

She was five years my senior and I had known her since school days. When I was 18 she had been the first woman I had sex with. A two-year relationship followed, with ups and downs and a magic trip to South America and to some theater Festivals in Colombia, Venezuela and Puerto Rico. I was there as a journalist, but I didn't miss the occasion to steal as much knowledge as I could from all the actors and directors I met there. I also added a language to my education, Spanish being quite similar to Italian and easy to learn. But I never was really fluent in it.

Girl of the Golden West proved to be a real adventure. We had joined forces with the Ugo Margio Company and (being obsessed by circus tents) he had found a small circus company that was to tour with us, presenting a triple bill: our *Girl*, his theater version of Bulgakov's *The Master and Margarita* and the circus show, with our actors used in the clown numbers. The tour was financed by the Campania District (the Naples area) with the aim of bringing theater into the most remote villages.

As Jesus in a stage version of Milton's *Paradise Lost*, directed by Ugo Margio in 1978

As Sheriff Jack Rance in a musical farce rendition of *Girl of the Golden West* by Puccini/Belasco, with Marina Garroni leading as Minnie (1978)

Suddenly it was like being back at the times of the Commedia dell'Arte, when thespians used to travel incessantly and created the entire job, from building the stage to performing on it. Early in the morning we had to pitch the circus tent, which implied taking away all the stones and debris from the selected area. By the time it was over we were ready for the first afternoon triple-bill show and an evening one then followed. Late at night it was time to unpack, sleep a few hours in some sordid inn provided by the local municipality and leave for the next destination. Never in my life have I felt so tired, every muscle aching, but it was thrilling. Our audiences had never seen a live show before and their reactions were genuine and overwhelming. I was Jack Rance, the sheriff, and portrayed him as a

Johnny, age 12, holds a lion club and lives to tell about it.

pompous and silly dandy, who roared as a tiger whenever provoked. Every morning, when I went to have breakfast in some dirty bar, a bunch of small children who had been to the show the previous night followed me, begging for my sheriff act and they didn't leave me alone until I had provided some tiger roaring and gun tricks.

It was time to get to more serious stuff. Patrizia Terreno (who had been Lady Macbeth) insisted we select *Svanevit* by August Strindberg, a somber fairy tale that I intended to stage as a veiled autobiography of the author.

Most unfortunately, we met the owner of an art gallery who claimed to be rich and willing to finance our production. He was the worst myth maniac to be found, all words and no facts. He indeed gave us a little sum to start things, but then disappeared in the middle of rehearsals, leaving me in the most impossible situation. Scenery was already there (but not even half paid) and so were costumes. We decided to keep going and I borrowed money from friends and relatives. But the stress got me all of a sudden and I went into a terrible depressive state, once more refusing to eat and unable to sleep. Lisa Canitano, whom I had been madly in love with in school days, helped me through this mess. She had been fascinated by theater, but decided not to take it as a profession and instead became a doctor. Freshly graduated, she gave me some strong pills to overcome depression, but made me promise in exchange that as soon as the show was over I would go to see a psychoanalyst to start therapy. I accepted. I knew that many burdens were on my brain and soul: a difficult family history, bisexuality and anorexia. I had to put some order into the mess or I risked the destiny of my brother Daniele.

Svanevit opened successfully, and when it was over, I was left with more good reviews, more debts and three sessions a week with Dr. De Pascalis, an austere strictly Freudian psychiatrist whom I was going to see for the forthcoming 12 years. He saved my life, but it has to be said that a great part of what I earned with my movie career went into his pockets.

This was definitely not to be mentioned in the c.v.

After *Svanevit*, the Spoleto offer to perform *Harlequin* came as a blessing. But once more I planned a too-expensive staging, as I already told.

The last paintings sold and more debt resulted.

Would Mrs. Spasiano bring some fresh cash into my derelict wallet? I didn't write that at the end of the c.v., but I sincerely hoped so.

She did and launched me in a new life-long adventure.

Chapter 4:
Tom or Ricky?

My new agent (my first as a matter of fact) kept her word. Her call asking me to meet director Ruggero Deodato came no more than two weeks after our first meeting. She was very professional and didn't mention he was her son-in-law.

The name brought to me vague memories of some scandal connected to his last movie and I remembered that my friend Luca Barbareschi had been in it. I tried phoning Luca, but couldn't find him. Always unpredictable and very rich, he was jumping from country to country and from a stage to a set, not forgetting to indulge in some wild nights, some of which I had also shared. No cell phones existed in 1979. If Luca wasn't answering his home phone there was no way I could reach him.

So I went to meet Deodato ignoring how controversial and successful *Cannibal Holocaust* had been. Nor had I read the script of *House on the Edge of the Park*, which Mrs. Spasiano had defined as "a thriller." I didn't know what to expect.

The meeting took place in the producer's office, Mr. Franco Palagi, who was an old Roman, small, bulky and with a thick accent. He was one of the foxy Italians who had profited from the Americans that arrived at Cinecittà to shoot epics such as *Ben Hur* and *Cleopatra*, helping with locations, transportation, extras and stealing what they could on the side; enough money to get into business themselves, producing low-budget movies for whatever style was popular at the moment: Spaghetti Westerns, Hercules movies (called "big sandals" for the shoes that were used in the films), the violent *gialli* and, after Dario Argento's success with his first films, gory thrillers and horror movies. What Antonio Margheriti used to call "the butcher filmmaking—paid by the kilo."

The other man in the room—skinny, nervous and with piercing blue eyes—was Ruggero Deodato, by then 40 years old.

Ruggero Deodato at his creative prime

After shaking my hand and offering me a seat, the two ignored me and started a quick conversation, totally obscure to me, even if I was the subject of it.

"Tom, Tom," Palagi was saying, "Classy, handsome ... definitely Tom."

"I am not sure," Deodato answered. "He has a crazy face. So skinny. He might be Ricky."

"Hasn't Ricky already been cast?"

"I can change my mind, can't I?" Deodato waspishly retorted.

What were they talking about? Who was Tom and who was Ricky?

"Then there's the English problem," Deodato added. "He knows it well. Don't you?" he asked looking at me for the second time since meeting.

"Yes," I said, "I do."

"See?" Deodato told Palagi. "The other doesn't."

So the movie was in English and there was "another."

"Ricky," said Deodato. "Most probably Ricky."

He gave me a script and told me: "Read it. You are going to be in this, one way or the other. We'll get in touch with Annamaria."

And that was it.

Walking out of the office, I was completely puzzled. I had expected a long and meticulous audition as the ones that were usual in the stage world. What if I were the worst actor on Earth? What if my knowledge of English was a lie? Was my face the only thing that mattered?

I was to learn that yes, it was. After one movie or two, what you had done would be considered, but your looks would always come first.

The Italian movie industry had been quite solid in the 1930s, under the Fascist dictatorship, producing mostly period films and sophisticated comedies. Skilled theater actors were employed and had become movie stars, such as Vittorio De Sica. Even the wonderfully beautiful Alida Valli had been a student at the National Cinema School. Looks had their importance, but not without a solid professional ability.

In the post-war renaissance all this had been swept away by the new school of Neo-realism, with its crude, life based stories and the habit of taking the actors from the street, to perform exactly what they were in life. A bunch of masterpieces came out of the New Wave, movies to stay forever in cinema history, such as *Shoeshine* or *The Bicycle Thief*, but the acting profession suffered a terrible blow and never recovered until quite recently. Theater actors were mostly confined to the humiliating (if rewarding) task to give their voice to the unskilled street actors. Dubbing became, and still is, a wealthy industry, increasing its income with the frequent use of foreign actors and, later on, with the vast amount of T.V. series coming from the U.S.A., Great Britain or Germany.

One movie after the other, some street actors became good professionals and could use their own voice, but many disappeared, at times tragically, leaving their places to new muscular lifeguards and curvaceous girls fighting at the Miss Italy beauty contest.

I was to elaborate all this in years to come. For the time being I had to be satisfied that Mr. Palagi and Mr. Deodato were happy with my looks.

Back at home (a huge apartment I had inherited from my mother and that I recently had decided to occupy, sharing it with "T") I immediately read the script. Twice.

My reactions to the story were mixed. It was an interesting plot, quite well written, but with far more sex and violence than I was used to, not being in any way a fan of "genre" movies. I was in love with period films, movie renditions of classical literature, Hollywood evergreens such as *Gone with the Wind* (that I almost knew by heart) and occasionally some good thrillers or ghost stories. In the script that was in my lap (as my mother before me, I used to live in bed and do whatever from there) there was no Hitchcock and no Baby Jane, let alone Scarlett O'Hara. But somehow it worked and, most importantly, the Ricky guy that had been mentioned was a great role and perfect for me. Not so Tom, who was important in the story but rather dull and uninteresting.

A recent photo of Ruggero Deodato

"T" came into my room, craving his dinner but not wanting to say so (a typical attitude of his) and I gave him the script to read while I cooked (an art I was pretty good at). In front of a mushroom risotto he summed the situation in his usual few words way: "Do it. There's a lot of cunt in it." The idea of meeting sexy actresses was very appealing to him and he knew I wasn't jealous of his Casanova adventures. As long as I was his only "boy" he could fuck as many chicks as he wanted. Chewing the second course, a Woronoff filet, he came out of his harem dreams and agreed that Ricky was definitely the best role for me.

And, with my great joy, Ricky it was, as Annamaria Spasiano announced to me by the phone, along with a money offer that was far from generous for movie standards, but not bad for an absolute beginner and princely if compared to the meager stage money I was so used to earning.

Shooting was to begin in a month.

Chapter 5
An Actor Prepares

Overwhelmed by happiness for getting the role, I didn't spend a moment thinking about the "other" that was supposed to be Ricky before I stepped into the project. Only later on, on another set in Savannah, Georgia, I was to learn that the "other" was Michele Soavi.

For the time being I had other priorities and the first one was being prepared for my role as best as I could.

It wasn't my absolute first time in front of a camera. At age 16 I had been an extra in *Non Ho Tempo* ("No Time Left"), a movie on the life of 19th-century French mathematician Evariste Galois, pushed by my father who had participated as a consultant to the screenplay and who had also been cast to play a high school math professor. On another occasion he took me on board as one of the students in some documentaries about mathematics and science that he was shooting for the Italian State Television. But these experiences hadn't prepared me for such an important role as Ricky.

I was a devout follower of the Stanislavsky method that emphasizes living the character, connecting him as much as possible to personal experiences. But

I was also very intrigued by the zoomorphic approach, a technique much in use in English acting schools, based on the study of animal behavior and deciding what animal your character is. Stanislavsky and Lee Strasberg advocates had adopted it many times, such as when Marlon Brando, in *A Streetcar Named Desire*, portrayed Stanley Kowalski as an ape, grabbing things with a twisted hand for example. The body comes always first when studying a character. Find his body, his muscles, his gait, his physical "rhythm" and more than 50 percent of the job is done.

What animal was the frail and neurotic Ricky?

After much thinking, I discarded birds that had first tempted me and selected a lemmings, those North American rodents that can stand like men and are at the same time shy and aggressive, with sudden and incomprehensible suicidal spells that make them jump into the void by the hundreds. I went to the zoo and watched them for an entire morning, trying to reproduce their alerted sideglances, the nervousness and the quick movements. People were staring at me as if I was mad, but I couldn't care less.

But there was also a "class" thing about Ricky that had to be studied. He was obviously of very low extraction, but wanting to show off, thus imitating his father-friend Alex. John Travolta immediately came to my mind as the perfect iconic figure that someone such as Ricky would have tried to imitate. *Saturday Night Fever* had hit the box-office only three years earlier and I remembered it well. I would have liked to watch it back more carefully, but videocassettes had yet to arrive in Italy, so I had to rely on my memory of that so unforgettable way of walking, hips and shoulders separated from the rest of the body. For days I walked through the apartment in a John Travolta gait, with the Bee Gees music playing loudly, for the faint amusement of "T" who was used to my weird actor training.

Giovanni Lombardo Radice as Ricky (left) and David Hess as Alex play a high stakes game of cards.

Ricky's body was almost there; it was time to start working on the inside, on what "made him tick."

The strongest point that I had to work on was his relationship with Alex, his violent friend who was a rapist and a murderer. Ricky seemed to be totally dependent on Alex. In my imaginary biography of the character (something that Stanislavsky heartily invites actors to do), he probably was the only son of a weak mother, maybe a prostitute or a junkie, growing up with no father figure and bullied by other boys from his poor suburb. Alex had been the first and only one to care for him, hiring him to work in his garage and protecting him, thus probably fulfilling a need for affection of which he was most likely incapable of living in a man-woman relationship.

Was there something homosexual in their friendship?

I couldn't imagine that in decades to come the question would have been asked a million times by fans and journalists. But I did think about it.

In my opinion any strong human relationship has something "sexual" in it, but this doesn't imply that actual sexual intercourse occurs. Women tend to be quite openly physical in same-sex friendships. They kiss and hug, they walk hand-in-hand and often have the funny habit of going to the toilet together, one refreshing her make-up while the other pees. Men are less warm and open and tend to express affection for their friends with slaps on the shoulders or rough playing in locker rooms or showers that might include slaps on the ass and in the lower regions, but surely not pecks and caresses. In both cases real sex hardly ever occurs and at times sadly so. I met quite a lot of women and men who spent their lives in a perennial struggle with the opposite sex, despising it and always complaining about "women" or "men," only tied to either just by fucking, and having (at the same time) a special warm and open life-long relationship with a friend. I am quite sure they would have been much happier if they had "jumped the fence" and added sex to the many things they were sharing with their best friend: passions, tastes, habits. My ex-wife, a woman with a sense of humor, used to cry out loud during marital crises: "Why wasn't I born a lesbian?"

Summing things up, I was convinced that in the Alex-Ricky relationship there was some sort of physical attraction, but I was pretty sure they hadn't had sex together.

Dependence was the key word and that was something I knew quite a lot about.

For the greater part of my life I depended on some strong man figure, with an obvious connection to my bisexuality, but with wider shadings than just sex roles. I am a dreamy, unrealistic sort of individual, not at ease, if not clumsy, with the practical side of life. I don't drive (never got a license); I can't fix anything from electric to hydraulic (even changing a light bulb can lead to a disaster); if I try to hammer a nail into a wall I am sure to twist the nail, destroy the wall and hammer my thumb; technology puzzles me and it took me ages to adjust to the Internet, that I still use at 50 percent of its potential. All these are typical "man" skills and I always managed to have a man by my side, coping with them, and not always a lover. "T" was the archetypal incarnation of the father-lover-maintenance man, but in the last 10 years I have been living with a Romanian guy, not even remotely my sex partner, who has an impossible temper, scolds me every day because I am untidy, but helps me with the dogs (who recognize him as the real Alpha Male in the house), thus allowing me to leave for a movie or a convention at short notice. He can fix whatever from T.V. sets to washing machines, not to mention that after six months of living with me he became a computer genius, not having seen one previously in his life.

But at that point of my life, neither "T" nor the many less steady "strong" men I had shared bits of life with were in the least comparable to Alex. Not dandy Dado nor the refined, cultivated director and set designer Beni Montresor, with whom I had had a short liaison at the time I was preparing *Macbeth*.

Had I ever meet someone like Alex in my life? Not necessarily a rapist or a murderer, but someone lower class, with a bossy attitude and a criminal record of some kind?

It took me a while to dig into undesired memories, but the shrink sessions were starting to work. Yes, I had met someone that I could picture as Alex.

Chapter 6
Memories

In a hot spring late afternoon of 1970 I was biking on the hill road leading to the Villa Borghese, the largest park in central Rome, where I had spent many a day in my childhood sailing little boats in the lake or biking around. In a meadow where dog owners used to take their pets and thus was named Dogs Valley, my mother had often let her beloved dog Archimedes run wild.

Now my mother was in a Swiss hospital, with my father by her side. In 1969 she had suddenly come home from work all yellow in her face, from what looked like a bad case of hepatitis. It was pancreas cancer. She underwent surgery but the tumor was too big; there was nothing to be done. Only my father, who bravely decided not to tell anybody, not wanting her last months to be spent in a gloom and doom atmosphere, had known the fatal diagnosis. Officially she had pancreatitis that could be cured. Her parents put all their money and strength to have her treated by the best doctors, which only resulted in prolonging her suffering. Being a doctor herself, I am pretty sure she knew she was going to die, but she pretended she was going to be cured and gulped whatever placebo was given to her, her perennial cigarette lit and a book in her hands. She died in June of 1970, at the youthful age of 44.

I was 15, with my parents both in Switzerland, I was completely master of myself and also free from school because of the Easter holiday. I was at home with only the company of my brother Marco, all busy with his university studies and his love story with the girl he was to marry a year later. The faithful Sabina, our

Villa Borghese was the park in Rome where Johnny spent many happy times during his childhood {photo is part of the park's promotion for tourists].

The Renaissance villa that houses the Etruscan Museum, at Valle Giulia

housekeeper, devoted to my mother as to the Virgin Mary, was cleaning the place and cooking our meals, but surely not interfering with my whereabouts.

My few friends were on vacation somewhere with their families and "T" was deeply involved with a new girlfriend. I was alone and bored, so I decided to take my bicycle from the cellar where it had been neglected for a long time and have a ride. But I was out of shape and the climb to Villa Borghese was a hard one. So I decided to stop and rest, lighting a cigarette, a secret habit I had taken since I was 13.

I stopped by the huge flight of marble steps that faces the Museum Of Modern Art, in the area called Valle Giulia, because of the nearby Renaissance villa that hosts the Etruscan Museum, built by Pope Jules The Second. I sat on a step and closed my eyes, enjoying the sun on my face.

A voice startled me: "Have a fag for me?"

A skinny dark-haired boy about my age was standing at my side, smiling, with a soccer ball in his hand.

I gave him a cigarette, but instead of lighting it he put it in his shirt pocket. "Wanna play?" he said in a thick Roman accent, bouncing the ball.

"I am no good," I answered.

"Me neither," he answered blinking an eye.

It was a lie. He was obviously well trained and managed to master the skill of passing the ball closer and closer to some bushes at the side of the flight of steps. But I didn't realize he was doing it on purpose, as I was too concentrated on not looking like a perfect ass while kicking the ball with my duck dancer feet.

A final kick sent the ball into the middle of the bushes and the boy went to retrieve it. But after a few seconds he yelled, "Come and help. I can't find it!" I stepped into the vegetation and found him in a little glade, surrounded by bay plants. The ball was at his feet and he was smiling. For sure something weird was going on, but I didn't have to wait long to understand what he wanted. He came close to me with a funny smile and put a hand on my crotch: "You're cute," he whispered.

Never in my life had I experienced such a rough and quick approach. I didn't know about gay cruising places and the very idea of open-air sex was new and frightening to me. But nevertheless I was aroused and my dick was stiffening under his touch. He took my hand and guided it to his already full erection. "But someone could see us," I whispered. He shrugged his shoulders and made a face that meant don't worry, starting to unzip my pants. But at that point a vibrant male voice called "Sergio!" with a commanding note. It was obviously the boy's name, because he snorted and half mouthed "fuck," while the voice called again: "Sergio, come here!"

"My cousin," Sergio explained, "I have to go." He found his way out of the bushes and I followed, zipping up my pants. A tall and powerfully muscular boy in his late 20s was waiting for him, dressed in tight low-waist bell-bottoms and a bright red wide collared shirt, opened to reveal a thick gold chain and a hairy chest. "We were playing soccer," Sergio said apologetically. The other didn't answer but pointed to a big expensive car, waiting on the street. Sergio sighed and muttered "che palle," the Italian slang expression literally meaning "my balls" to indicate that you are bored with something. He then put up a smile and went down the stairs, waving to the driver of the car, a formal-looking man in his 60s. The other boy blinked at me and said this was his uncle in an explanatory way. The scene was quite clear: an under age hooker, a pimp and a John, but at that time I was still a Snow White innocent about such matters and the situation just seemed peculiar to me. I smiled uncertainly at the older boy, fully realizing how attractive he was, even if dressed in a tacky way that my mother would have summed up as "to be hanged." His skin was brown and his long black curls were surrounding a face that could have belonged to a Roman emperor, with piercing black eyes, aquiline nose and turgid, sensuous lips. A scar on one cheek completed the pirate picture. "I am Nando, Sergio's cousin," he said. Nando, shortening for Armando or Fernando, was the most typical Roman name to be found in the working class, perfectly matching his looks and outfit. "Johnny," I shyly muttered, automatically introducing myself with the nickname I was called by the family, who made fun of me looking like John-John, President Kennedy's son. "You were playing five-against-one, uh?" he said smiling ironically and pointing with his head toward the bushes. It was the first time I heard the expression, but, feeling guilty, I immediately knew what he meant and blushed. "I must go home," I said, avoiding his eyes, and I grabbed my bicycle.

Nando's laughter followed me: "Come back, we are always here."

I did.

In the following days I biked to Villa Giulia every afternoon, warmly welcomed by Sergio and Nando who had nicknamed me "il biondino," the little blond. Sergio didn't make other sexual passes. Maybe that first afternoon had been just a momentary spell or, most probably, Nando had warned him against it. I wasn't in the least disappointed, because the one I was strongly attracted to was Nando, to whom I was driven as if by a magic spell. I played ball games with Sergio, and Nando at times joined us, both of them making good-natured fun at my lack of ability. As with many lower class people, raised with the laws of the street, they weren't asking questions about my family, my life or me. They lived day-by-day and had accepted me as something that just happened. I didn't ask

The Piazza del Popolo in the Villa Borghese park

many questions either, only learning that they lived in the Magliana, a southern suburb with a bad reputation, where Mussolini had "deported" the ones living in the Coliseum area when he decided to raze an entire neighborhood to the ground to build the large Empire Road.

Every afternoon some "uncle" would stop and take Sergio for a ride that lasted from 15 minutes to half an hour. After a while, even if naïve, I made two-plus-two deductions about what was going on, but didn't ask questions and pretended not to notice the money that Sergio was passing to Nando after each encounter. And Sergio was far from being the only one dedicating himself to the oldest profession in the world in the Valle Giulia area. After sunset, as the evening shadows were growing longer, a small army of young men, from 15 to their late 20s, were taking possession of dark corners, leaning against light poles or trees on the street side, waiting for clients. In a few years, when Dado decided to pay for our holiday by hooking, I would have been one of them. More than one elder man driving an expensive car was slowing down, staring at me with tempting glances. Once one of them signaled me to approach, but Nando hurried to his car and spoke to him, making him drive away. I wanted to look "grown up" in Nando's eyes, so when he came back I said, "I could do it too, you know."

"What?" Nando answered.

"What Sergio does," I said blushing.

Nando looked at me with a somehow sad expression and asked, "Do you need money?"

"No," I said, caught on the hoop, "but …"

"Then you don't need to do it," he interrupted me, walking away.

I blushed again, that time from joy, thinking that he cared and wanted to protect me. Not that he didn't want to have any kind of problems by messing with a upper-class kid, as I obviously was.

Nando had his own business too on the Valle Giulia steps, and I couldn't tell what it was. Cars were stopping for him too, but not to take him for rides. He leaned through the window, always with his right hand in his pocket, had brief conversations with the driver and then shook hands. I was too far away to notice that with this swift gesture that he was at the same time handing over a little package hidden in his pocket and receiving money in exchange. But one evening, while sitting beside me, Nando spotted a police car coming up the hill. He stiffened, and with a quick move, took something from his pocket and put it into mine, whispering, "take your bike and go for a ride. Don't come back if the cops are here." I looked at him with puzzled eyes and he urged me, "Go!" I took the bike and pedaled away. Watching back, I saw the police car stop by Nando. I biked in the direction of the zoo, only a half mile away, and arrived in front of the main entrance, but it was already closed. Sitting on a bench, I carefully surveyed the area, making sure that no one was around and searched my pocket, finding a small plastic bag, containing some 10 even smaller sealed bags with white powder in it. I had seen enough movies and T.V. to know that it was a drug of some sort and not the weed I had already experimented with. I was scared and proud at the same time, because of the trust Nando had placed in me. I was putting back the bag in my pocket when I saw the police car slowly arriving. I froze. Had they seen me with Nando and were they now looking for me? Cold sweat started dripping on my back. What if they stopped and searched me? But they passed by without even looking at me. I sped back to Nando, who was anxiously waiting. I got close to him and blinked, feeling very much like Bonnie and Clyde. He put his hand in my pocket and got the bag; "good boy," he said, blinking back. At that point I was overwhelmed with adrenaline and passion and dared whisper, "I love you. I'd do whatever for you." He didn't laugh, as I had feared he would. He looked me in the eyes, with a somehow melancholic expression and caressed my cheek in the sweetest possible way: "Johnny, Johnny …, " he sighed. "If only you had been a girl …"

The following morning my parents came back from Switzerland, my mother reduced to just skin and bones and wanting to die in her bed. I didn't go back to Valle Giulia for a long time and when I did, there was no trace of Nando and Sergio. I was never to see them again.

Chapter 7
Camera Rolling ... A Line to Go

With my "actor bag" packed with a prairie dog, John Travolta and personal memories, I was ready for my first day in a movie, on a late October day.

The "House" of the title (*House on the Edge of the Park*) was a villa in the Olgiata, a very classy residential area 20 miles from Rome. Iron fences surrounded it and security appeared at every entrance. Villas were in every style from modern to fake Victorian and for the most part had a pool, as the one we were going to use. Many years later I was to film in a very large mansion in that area, built by a lunatic millionaire, that featured some original wood panels from Versailles, all plated with gold and with complicated decorations. In another one, in the early 1990s, Countess Alberica Filo Della Torre was murdered in one of the most mysterious criminal cases Rome had ever seen. Our "House" was a two-floor large villa, surrounded by a big garden and with a huge basement where make-up and the costume department had been established, along with a big kitchen where a cook was to prepare our meals, a solution that I guess was cheaper than the usual "food baskets" that are normally in use on Italian movie sets (with a choice of "red basket" with tomato sauce pasta, "white basket" with butter and parmesan rice or pasta, and "fruit and cheese," always my favorite).

Giovanni Lombardo Radice, as Ricky, wins the card game and possibly the lady as well.

I met the rest of the cast and had positive vibes from the very beginning.

I was happy to see that David Hess, already in his Alex costume, was quite similar to the Nando of my teenage memories: older, chubbier and shorter, but definitely in that line. He welcomed me warmly, complimented me on my English and hurriedly left to chase Ruggero Deodato, all busy with lights and furniture moving. "Ruggero, Ruggero, I had a wonderful idea!"

"David, don't break my balls!" Deodato yelled back at him.

This was a scene I was to witness literally every day in the next three weeks. The other two male members of the cast were about my age: Gabriele di Giulio (a striking handsome guy, tanned and blue eyed), who was to be

Howard, and Christian Borromeo, who was Tom, the role I prayed not to get. The female cast included Annie Belle, a sexy little French girl as Liza, Lorraine De Selle, a classy brunette, as Gloria and Marie Claude Joseph, a very beautiful black woman from Martinique, in the minor role of Glenda. The three girls were enthusiastic with the fact that I was speaking French, most especially Annie, whose English was not very good, and Marie Claude, who didn't speak a word of it.

Encouraged by the fact that my fellow actors seemed to be nice people, I changed

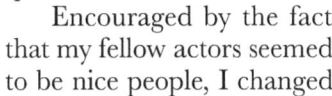

The laser disc sleeve for the EC Entertainment release of *House on the Edge of the Park*

into my Ricky clothes: jeans and a tacky long-sleeved t-shirt, with a bright colored eagle on it. I then had a look at the horrible fake-leather jacket I was supposed to wear and thought, if the foxy plot I had invented in my mind worked, I wasn't going to be able to live with that jacket. I had seen it a few days before at a costume fitting I had and thought it was completely wrong. It was shapeless, heavy and made me look awkward. Apparently there weren't any other choices. But I didn't resign myself and went to have a look in the fashion district. In the window of a classy shop in Condotti via (the most expensive shopping street in Rome) I saw a black leather jacket that was just perfect: tight, waist short and with big padded shoulders as the fashion of the time required. It cost a fortune, but I bought it all the same, my tricky plan already devised.

That first day I took it out from my rucksack and I went looking for Deodato, taking the other cheap one with me as well. He was discussing something with the production manager, a little man called Masini, and Deodato looked at me, asking if I needed anything. I showed him the two jackets, saying that I got the beautiful one from a friend of mine who owned a shop, with permission to wear it, but I required guaranteed insurance if it got damaged. Deodato of course agreed and so did Masini. A week later I made a small cut on one sleeve with a knife and showed it to Masini, saying that one of the girls probably had stepped on it with stiletto heels while it was on the floor after my striptease scene. He grunted and swore, but gave me the money and the jacket was mine to wear in real life, especially if a disco night was calling for it.

Thus all costumed, I was ready for my first scene, where Alex and myself were arriving at the house with Tom and Liza, and also ready for my first lesson in what is the main activity of an actor on set: waiting. We had a rough

On set: David Hess left and Johnny right; "David Hess proved to be the best possible partner I could have prayed for."

positions rehearsal and then the crew started working with the lights, always the longer part of filming. With time passing I was increasingly nervous and all sorts of fears were assailing me. What if I wasn't able to stop on the right mark? What if I tripped on the four steps I had to descend? What-ifs seemed never ending. I decided that a dose of my special medicine was required and got into one of the bathrooms, carefully locking the door. I took out a small box from my pocket and made a line on the washbasin shelf with a small amount of the white powder. I then rolled a banknote and sniffed it, enjoying the bitter taste down my throat.

Cocaine had made its first appearance in my life only very recently, but had already become a habit.

I had never been much interested in drugs. I had suffered from some sort of juvenile alcoholism that had been slowed down by a gall bladder operation when I was 18, but marijuana and hash, very popular with my generation, had never looked really attractive to me. I had smoked, of course, at parties or with "T," who loved the stuff and was always more inclined to love making after a joint, but I had never bought it myself or felt addicted in any way. Then, the previous summer, while I was in Spoleto, my brother Marco and "T" had decided to try cocaine in a very peculiar way. Along with some other people they had financed two drug-dealing guys for a trip to South America and were paid back with a considerable amount of the purest Colombian cocaine on the market. "T" was always ready to experiment with something new, and the drug that had attracted even Sigmund Freud fascinated Marco. I had been always very scared of "hard stuff," but "T," sharing my apartment, wanted to get me into the adventure. Unable to refuse him anything, I tried the white, yellowish powder and was immediately conquered by its appeal. It didn't slow you down as pot did, a feeling I never cared much for, but instead it made you feel like a lion, as though you were master of the world and ready for whatever action

David Hess (Alex) looks nasty alongside the striking Claude Marie Joseph.

was to be. In years to come I was to find out how momentary the sensation was and how easy it was to get psychologically addicted to that feeling, snorting line after line to have the feeling return. But when I started to shoot "House" I was at the beginning of my coke trip period and just thought the thing was a blessing, also considering that there was plenty of it at home, already paid for and the best on Earth.

Returning with self-confidence, I had my movie christening, hearing for the first time the "silence ... sound ... camera rolling ... action" sequence of events. All went well and we moved further to more difficult scenes.

Being familiar with stage acting, it was a real blessing for me that my first movie was somehow "theatrical." The main action, almost 3/4 of the movie, occurred in just one room, thus allowing Deodato to shoot in sequence instead of the usual jumping from set to set to film out of chronological order. I could follow the character almost from beginning to end without the complicated task of shooting out of sequence, first filming a scene that was last in the script or the other way round.

David Hess proved to be the best possible partner I could have prayed for. He was always encouraging, friendly and full of a contagious energy. I trusted him and relied on him as Ricky relied on Alex and that helped a lot with our on-screen relationship. He was often bitching with Deodato, but I soon understood that it was a sort of "act" between them, a "macho" dance to decide who was in charge. Deodato was the director, self-assured and very much in command, but David was undeniably the star, recently crowned by the success of Wes Craven's *The Last House on the Left* that had largely inspired our movie, something I ignored at that time. And he wasn't the kind of actor happy with just doing his best work. He wanted to have a say on every aspect and was often changing the dialogue or creating new ideas, some of them really good, as

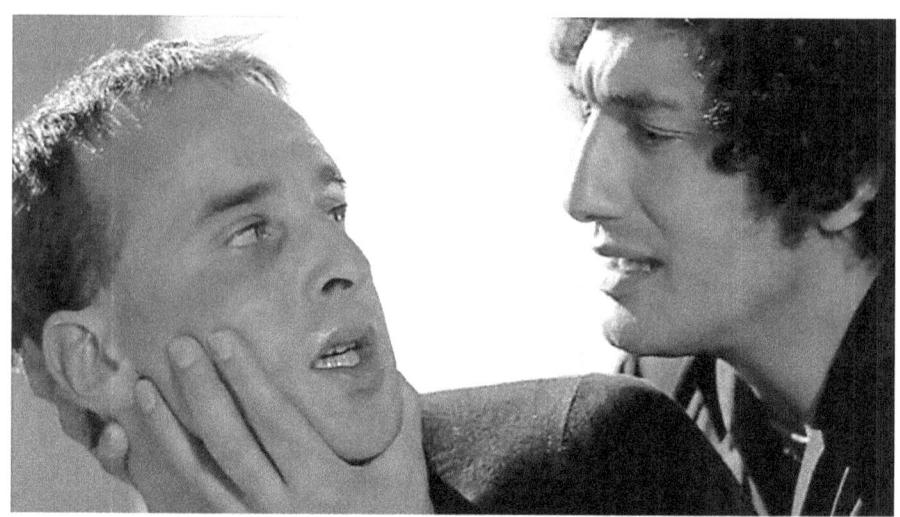

Ricky, left; Alex right

when he decided to recite "Little Miss Muffet" while threatening Gloria with his razor, thus turning a nursery rhyme into a nightmare. But Deodato's main problem was the lack of time. He had only three weeks scheduled for shooting in the villa, which was almost the entire movie, and he was often pissed with David's demanding requests, no matter how good they might be. And David wasn't the only one he was shouting at. The whole crew was reproached daily in high-pitched tones for not speeding along fast enough or for chatting too much. But he always added something funny to his scolds: a joke, a personal remark, a funny nickname, and the small bunch of technicians adored him as the crew of a ship trusted its captain. I was to meet some of them in other movies, as it happened with Enrico Lucidi, the almost six-feet-tall cameraman, often forced to fold himself in two for the unusual angles Deodato required. Claudia Florio, heiress of one of the most influential families in Italy, was both assistant director and continuity person. I got on friendly terms with her, as well as with Marcellino, a little electrician not taller than a 10 year old and who was to almost save my life while shooting *Deadly Impact*. And Rodolfo was the handsome property guy, who would constantly throw a pack of Marlboros on the table or turn a whisky label toward the camera, thus getting paid on the side for hidden publicity, a customary habit, as I was to learn.

Photography was in the capable hands of Sergio D'Offizi, a brisk man of few words, always impeccably well dressed as were many in his profession. Watching the movie back with the experience I have now, I must say that he did miracles, considering the short time he had and the gap of shooting on location, which always complicates things, especially with the positioning of lights. *House on the Edge of the Park* has spotless photography and at times is very effective, as in the kitchen scene with Alex and Liza, apparently only lit by the open refrigerator.

Step-by-step we got to my "striptease" scene, which is now a YouTube favorite because of my funny, stupid way of dancing. It cost me quite a lot to dance that bad, considering that I had studied professionally for many years.

Ballet is very different from disco dance, but I could have danced much better all the same. But the point was that, in my opinion, Ricky had to move awkwardly but at the same time thinking he was a real blast on the dance floor, thus ultimately making a fool of himself in front of his audience, without realizing it.

The first big problem arose in the poker scene. Four of us were sitting at the table and I was the only one who could both play poker and speak English. Borromeo spoke good English but didn't play poker, Di Giulio played poker but his English was very poor and Marie Claude couldn't make heads nor tails of either. By then I had realized that she barely knew what we were

shooting. She wasn't an actress, but the owner of a hotel in Martinique that Deodato had met shooting on location. Our Latin lover director was currently bedding her, even while he was in the middle of a love affair with Francesca Ciardi from *Cannibal Holocaust*. That was the reason for her being in the movie, displaying her ebony tits for the joy of the crew.

Deodato's routine was to shoot a large shot of the entire scene, called a "master," then close-ups and special angles if needed, and this is what he intended to do with the poker scene, even if it were quite long. As usual there was no time for rehearsing, but disaster was at the door. At each take something wasn't working because either the wrong card was put on the table or a line came out incorrectly or at the wrong time. After some 12 takes, Deodato was on the verge of hysterics and Palagi, who was on set that day, was sweating bullets thinking about the waste of film. At last I took Deodato aside and asked him to let me rehearse the scene for 10 minutes. He agreed and I took command using all my stage director skills to make each cast member understand what he or she was supposed to do, talking in Italian with Christian and Gabriele and in French with Marie Claude. It worked and the "master" was finally completed. Deodato's esteem toward me grew by leaps and bounds. With a few exceptions, Italian directors are generally technically very good but they are not skilled in directing actors, and most times they don't speak languages other than Italian,

Even though *House on the Edge of the Park* was deadly serious, the movie required Johnny's character Ricky to do some goofy things.

so problems may arise when actors are bad actors, foreigners or both. Always tactfully, I was to use my theater credits as a director in many a movie to come.

Another problem of a different nature arose in the scene when Ricky, instigated by Alex, had to attempt to rape Gloria.

Annie Belle had gone through her long sex scenes with David, seducing him in the shower and then making rough love on a bed. She hadn't any problems either in being stark naked in front of the camera or in being manipulated by fellow actors. After the scene David bragged that he had actual sex with her, but it was hard for me to believe it. You might be a ladies' man, but if you are not a professional porn star I don't think it's that easy to have an erection surrounded by crew members and floodlights, and I'm not sure either that Annie would have allowed him to screw her for real. She was very open-minded and not by all means shy, but, as she told me in private, she didn't find David attractive.

With Lorraine it was a different story. She was more lady-like than Annie and did mind parading her graces in front of everybody. If needed, she could show her tits, but she was determined not to reveal her bush to the camera. In the script it was black on white that I had to tear off her panties, but what was to be seen was left to the director's choice. And Deodato wanted to see pussy. Lorraine was too smart to openly refuse, but at each take she was whispering to me to hide her privates with my elbow or raise a leg not to be in full sight, hoping that, being in a hurry, Deodato would have resigned himself to have on camera just her sexy ivory tights with red suspenders. She was wrong. At each take Deodato kept screaming, "Put that fucking leg down," and was especially mad at me, shouting, "What are you doing with that bloody arm? We want to see pussy! Stick it up your ass!" Finally, caught in between being a gentleman and a professional, I chose the latter and proceeded in forcing her down and exposing her most secret jewel.

But when we shot our sex scene in the greenhouse, it was my turn to play hide and seek with my dick and not because I was shy, but because at that time Italian censorship could tolerate full female nudity but not exposed penises. It helped a lot that it was a cold night and the greenhouse roof had been removed to position lights. My absolutely average endowment shrank to baby size. Before getting into the greenhouse, Ricky runs after Gloria, who manages to escape to seek help and, at the first take, the entire male crew was laughing to tears. I had lost control of my duck dancer feet and apparently I resembled Charlie Chaplin chasing a chick in an unusual punk outfit. During my entire career I had to think about my feet whenever they were in sight of the camera and try walking or running putting them straight.

Then, while the greenhouse was prepared for the scene, the most bizarre meeting took place, with Deodato summoning screenwriter Gianfranco Clerici and myself to discuss in what position Ricky and Gloria should be having sex. Missionary? Doggy style? Should she lie on her back with her legs on my shoulders? Someone casually passing by would have thought of some very serious congress of pimps or brothel owners. We finally agreed her on top of me, thus emphasizing her power over the virgin Ricky. Apart from hiding my dick, I didn't have problems in shooting such an intimate scene, but I understood that making love is an almost impossible part of the identification process, becoming really difficult to separate one self from the character during the physical act. It was really cold and, in between takes, Lorraine and I tightly hugged under some blankets, speaking French and making fun of the situation.

As the days went by, we actors had become friends, with the exception of Christian Borromeo, who was always by himself and didn't encourage any kind of relationship other than the professional one. I didn't try very hard to break the ice, I must say, because I felt something creepy in him as if he was carefully hiding something, like being a terrorist or a spy of some sort. Just fantasies of course, but that prevented me from trying to get familiar with him, even if respecting the fact that he was quite a good actor.

With the others it was a different story. We were often shooting from late afternoon to two in the morning because of the light outside, but whenever we were working in daytime and had the night free Annie, Lorraine and I were going out and having fun, Gabriele and David joined us only at times, Gabriele being involved with some private cunt hunt and David being tired or wanting to stay with his wife, who had followed him to Rome and was in the movie too as the rape victim in the opening sequence. We generally had dinner at my place, which was the largest and most comfortable, and then went out to some disco. A great lover of Italian food who was happy with my cooking, David was at times sharing the first part of the program, devouring huge portions of pasta and then skipping the dancing part. Not so "T," who hated disco clubs, but was hunting Annie as a dog is hunting a juicy bone and thus being very generous with our cocaine. I had found out that the others, with the exception of David, were sharing my passion for the white magic powder and lines were

Giovanni Lombardo Radice (left) and director Ruggero Deodato conduct a "Q&A" session at a recent horror film convention.

going down our nostrils without remorse along with large amounts of alcohol. We didn't know that some of us were to pay sky-high prices for that juvenile nonchalance. Annie was to become an alcoholic and a drug addict and, as I was recently told, fought hard to survive, but not an actress anymore as her beauty was gone. And Gabriele Di Giulio died a few years after the movie wrapped from a heroin overdose. I was to fight hard myself in the future against cocaine, a false friend that had turned into a monster.

And cocaine was to cause the funniest accident I had while shooting *House*. One evening I had realized that I wasn't needed on set for a while, so I went to the bathroom for my usual snort. But what I had with me was a "rock" that needed cutting. I had a razor blade with me and started the operation on the washbasin marble shelf. But, out of the blue, I heard Clauda Florio calling me with her stentorian voice: "Ricky! Where is Ricky? On set! Immediately!!" Most obviously Deodato had decided to include me in the take. I sped up and, doing so, caused the rock to split all around into hundred of fragments. I desperately snorted what I could and collected the rest with my finger that I then licked carefully. I hurried on set ... But instead of the line I was supposed to say, only a sort of "Mgbbmgnnnn" came out of my completely anesthetized mouth. I was literally incapable of speaking and everybody was staring at me with a puzzled expression. I mimed that I had eaten something hot, but it was hardly believable even when I recovered my speech and said it had been a chili. Someone giggled and made snorting gestures and I realized that my secret had been known by almost everybody. Only Deodato's hurrying to resume shooting took me out of embarrassment.

Time was running and the film was almost completed, with Deodato growing more nervous with a tendency to scream as the end approached. And this caused minor problems for me, such as not laughing in Annie's face when she was delivering her dialogue using a French accent that made Inspector Clou-

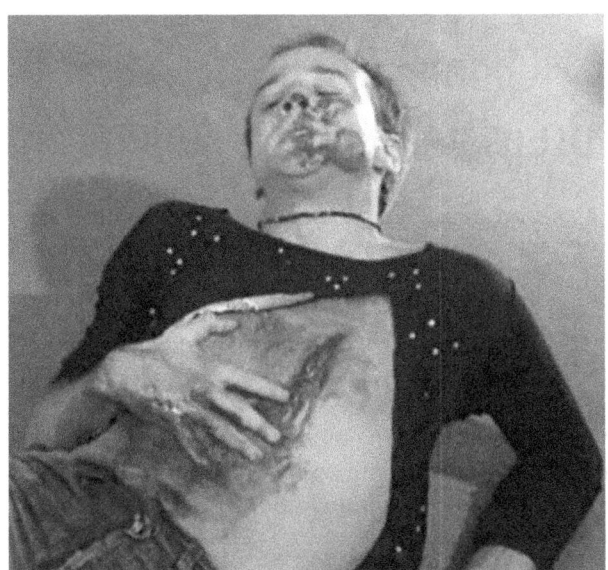

Like all good villains, Ricky comes to a very bad end by the end of the movie.

seau sound like Laurence Olivier. If she had to say: "For curious people with a knife in their hand, I only feel pity"; what came out was, "And fir kiriòs pipòl vit a nif in der end I only fil pitì": hard to stay serious.

Brigitte Petronio, as Cinday, arrived to be tortured by David. She was a skinny girl of few words, just perfect for the role of the sacrificial lamb. The insistence on the razor on her small tits was excessive and, even watching the movie now, it is, in my opinion, the worst part of the movie.

As Ricky, I was trying to stop Alex and he was stabbing me, only to repent immediately and show all his affection for his buddy. Bleeding in David's arms I was astonished by his ability to cry on command, something that I could never achieve unless concentrating for a long time.

We finally said goodbye to the villa and moved elsewhere for the few scenes outside: Alex and Ricky in the car with Tom and Liza, and our first meeting with them in the garage. The EUR area, built by Mussolini in futuristic architecture, provided skyscrapers that could pass for American if seen in the distance from a car window. Some exteriors without actors were to be shot later in New York.

The garage scene was my last and I went under Tom's car to fix it, which was stretching "let's pretend" to the limit for one who couldn't tell a screwdriver from the Virgin of Fatima. All went well and we parted with lot of hugs and kisses.

Annie stayed in Rome for some time and I occasionally met her, at times with Lorraine, whom I kept seeing for a long time as a close friend. We were similar in many respects, both mixed blood and multilingual, cultivated and somehow snobbish gypsies. She was a theatergoer, a classic music lover and a very independent individual as I was, and we both loved to have an occasion to speak French. I was to see quite a lot of her in years to come, going to dinner or to a play, and saw her even more after she got engaged to Franco Scaglia, a brilliant journalist and television producer.

David left for America and I wouldn't see him for many years. And, as it happens in the movie world, I lost track of the others.

More movies were going to be in my future.

Chapter 8
Movies, Drugs and Rock 'n' Roll

Quite happy with my first movie experience and with some new friends, I got back to my usual life, not really sure if I were to have a future in the celluloid world.

Nowadays I live almost as a hermit, always home and seeing nobody, and I am surprised if I think back to how intense my social life was in my youth. I had many friends, mostly connected with the stage world, and we used to meet every night in one house or the other or, in the good season, in the outdoor cafés in the Navona Square or at the Pantheon where, surrounded by the beauties of Roman architecture, we gossiped incessantly and inquired about new jobs. In that crowd I was nicknamed the Afghan Greyhound, with a touch of envy for my slender body and the upright dancer posture. I was also renowned for my skill with languages and that got me my first T.V. job, as the English secretary of an oil company that was secretly involved with suspicious trades. It was somehow a comic role, one of the few I was to get, and I had to speak Italian with a heavy English accent; the title of the miniseries was *Crude Oil Is Dangerous* and it was directed by Enzo Tarquini, who, later on, was to be very important in my screenwriter career.

A recent friend of mine was Alessandra Panelli, a young actress, three years younger than me, and the daughter of one of the most famous comic duos in Italian entertainment, Bice Valori and Paolo Panelli. We had shared a house in Spoleto during the Festival and one night she had tended to me as a sister when I got back home utterly drunk, vomiting all over the place. I couldn't imagine that 10 years later we would have married and had a son.

Alessandra was a sweet girl with simple tastes and, if she drank or smoked pot, it was just to be sociable. Not so were many of the others, who had been overwhelmed, like me, by the coke tsunami that seemed to have fallen over the Italian showbiz world. Everybody was snorting it and thinking it was classy and trendy, not in the least comparable to "trashy" heroin. But it was also very expensive, as "T" and myself had found out once our South American supply was over. It was too late. We were already dependant on that sensation of omnipotence that made you laugh at hunger or fatigue and we had to cope with the cocaine that was on the Roman market, not half as good as the primo stuff we were used to and now often badly cut with amphetamines or even marble powder that made your nose bleed. The "downs" were sudden and frightening, leaving you frustrated, anxious and only wanting to have more. We were running out of funds, so "T" started picking on his parents' money and his wife had followed him, giving "T" free access to their bank account to pay home bills or taxes. But we were aware that that money had to be repaid, so "T" had a very clever idea. His parents owned a country house with some land, covered with olive trees and vines. In a clear sunny spot "T" built a greenhouse and planted marijuana that grew fast and incredibly well, giving us pot to sell. Pot

Johnny played the part of Charlie Bukowski in *Cannibal Apocalypse*.

was much cheaper than cocaine, so the process of refunding "T's" parents was slow also because some of our income was used to buy more coke for ourselves. But it was working and our "customers" were increasing every day. "T" was in charge of the planting and picking and I helped with the complicated process of drying the leaves and did most of the selling, often biking through Rome with my rucksack full of pot. At that time penalties for dealing with "light" drugs such as marijuana or hashish weren't as hard as they are now, but nevertheless being found with a kilo of stuff could lead to serious consequences. I was just lucky and was never stopped, which was somehow a miracle considering that those were the days of The Red Brigades and terrorism of all sorts. Rome was positively packed with police, but maybe, in the cops' eyes, terrorists weren't supposed to ride a bike as I was.

But my new pusher career was interrupted by another call for a movie, no more than two months after *House on the Edge of the Park* had been completed.

It was a movie by Antonio Margheriti, also known to fans of genre movies as Anthony Dawson, the American name he had picked up when he realized that translating his name into English as "Daisy" could lead to gay misinterpretation. Many Italian genre movies tried to "mask" themselves as American for the international market, and actors, directors and even crewmembers were asked to adopt a stage name that sounded Anglo-Saxon. It was so for this new movie I had been asked to be in (to be released as *Cannibal Apocalypse*) and, hating the idea of having a completely fake name, I translated Giovanni into John and picked up my grandmother's surname of Morghen. My father's mother had a foreign family name too, which was Harasim, but Morghen sounded more theatrical to me, with its reminiscence of Morgan the pirate. With that name I was to appear in many movies to come.

As it had happened for *House on the Edge of the Park* I wasn't asked to audition for the role of Charlie Bukowski and, as a matter of fact, I don't even remember meeting Margheriti before shooting. It probably happened, but it must have been very brief. He had quite surely heard about me from Deodato or someone else involved in *House*. The genre movie mob was a narrow one and they all knew each other; the news about a new young actor, speaking English and with an interesting face, was easily spread.

I don't remember meeting Margheriti, but I sure remember reading the script that had been provisionally titled "Cannibals In Town" and thus made me laugh from the very beginning with the image of a bunch of cannibals shopping in a mall, half naked and with a bone in their nose. When I finished reading the script I wasn't laughing anymore. It was the worst piece of crap I had ever set my eyes upon. The whole idea of cannibalism as a disease that could be passed from one person to another seemed to me utterly ridiculous and the amount of blood and entrails involved made *House* look like a movie to be shown to virgin nuns. In recent years, watching the movie once again for interviews or DVD commentaries, I changed my mind about the story and realized it had a metaphorical side I hadn't considered at the time, connected to the disease being started by the Vietnam war, thus stating that violence comes from violence. It was also somehow prophetical, because the AIDS epidemic was to start only a few years later. What I focused on from the initial reading was just the indulging on gore and splatter that had been strongly recommended by producer Maurizio Amati, a younger member of a family that owned many movie theaters in Rome and had relatives in all corners of B-productions. The screenplay was by Dardano Sacchetti (a very professional screenwriter) and by Margheriti himself, but I was told later on that Maurizio Amati had put his hands in it too and he was surely far from being Marcel Proust.

I found it awful, but, of course, I agreed to be in the movie; it was another addition to my resume. My psychoanalyst had considered my coke habit as Freudians always face things: a Sphinx expression and the "what it makes you think" question. But he had increased my sessions to four a week, to be paid even if I was elsewhere for work. With shrink bills and coke buying, my need of money was constant and the sum I was offered by Amati was more consistent than what I had been paid for *House*. But it wasn't the only reason. Charlie Bukowski hit me at first reading as a great character, even better than Ricky. He was at the same time weak and cruel, melancholic and crazy, tender and frightening. There was a lot of acting material there and insights to work with.

I signed the contract and, by the end of January 1980, I was on a plane to Atlanta, Georgia in the U.S.A.

Chapter 9
Yankee Doodle Went to Town

I traveled alone, because the rest of crew and cast had already started shooting on location. During the long overseas trip I tried to identify with a wild cat, the animal I had selected as an inspiration for Bukowski. I also thought about Atlanta, that was the hometown of Margaret Mitchell and her classic novel *Gone with the Wind*, a favorite of mine both as a book and a movie, to the point that I have a portrait of Vivien Leigh proudly displayed in my living room.

Of course I wasn't expecting a pre-bellum Peachtree Road with ladies in hoop skirts sitting on their porches, but I wasn't prepared for the big ultra-modern city Atlanta had become, all skyscrapers and malls. I was very curious about lifestyles in the American South, with all the tales about racism I had heard contradicted by the fact that Atlanta had a black mayor. As soon as I arrived I was to realize that some problems between the races did indeed exist.

I wasn't immediately needed on set and I was nervous and fully awake because of the jet lag, so I decided to have a long walk around to see what the city looked like. It was late afternoon and I walked for a long time, watching buildings and parks, with nowhere special to go, just allowing myself to be led by instinct and a very good photographic memory to find my way back to the hotel. At some point I started realizing that white people were more and more rare and that the majority of men and women were black, but I didn't really think about it until, in a narrow alley that had attracted my attention, I found three black guys bigger than life blocking my way. I smiled, but they didn't smile back and addressed me in a way that the was nowhere near "nice."

"Whut the fuck are ya doing here?" one aggressive male asked with a heavy accent. I answered that I was just having a walk, but they didn't seem to believe me and got into a "no white shit here" that I found most worrying.

"I am a tourist," I said, and "I just arrived."

"Tourist, uh?" one said with a skeptical grin. "And where the fuck from?" I said I was Italian and that caused an uproarious laugh. "You look Italian as my ass looks white," the taller of the three said, towering over me. I started sweating cold bullets, but I remembered I had my passport with me and I produced it. They didn't seem familiar with the document, but at least they realized it wasn't American. They looked at one another, uncertain as to whether to beat me up or believe me, then one of them had a genius idea and told me, "You Italian? Then sing!" I was speechless, but I realized that, in their idea of an Italian, if I wasn't black-haired and with a moustache at least I should sing. After all I was an actor, so, at the top of my lungs, I got into "O Sole Mio" ("It's Now or Never"), the most Italian thing I could think of. They adored my rendition of that classic, positively rolling with laughter and smacking their sides in delight. Suddenly they became friends with me, patting my back and insisting on buying me a beer. Sitting in a pub they explained to me that it was the black area and no white man was going there unless in search of trouble. We chatted for a

John Saxon as he appeared in *Cannibal Apoclypse*; Johnny described him as "politely cold."

while and then they let me go, not without singing one more song. I selected an old Roman ballad about a man in jail seeking revenge and translated the lyrics for them. The idea was probably familiar to them and they were moved almost to tears. We parted with big hugs and my solemn promise not to return there if not with the company of a black friend.

On my way back I went into a liquor store just in front of the hotel and I bought a bottle of whisky. Crossing the road a police car stopped me and I was severely scolded because the bottle was not in a bag as a state law required. Once again I produced my passport to prove I wasn't local and apologized. The United States was indeed a different country.

When I met my fellow actors, I realized that no party time was to be expected. John Saxon was politely cold, Elizabeth Turner royally distant and Tony King seemed absorbed in never-ending fitness exercises to keep his bodybuilder physique in shape. I thought he was very attractive, but he looked straighter than Fifth Avenue and had by his side a black woman as attractive as him. No chance of foul play. Anyway they were all many years older than me; Cinzia De Carolis, who was about my age, had already left after shooting her scenes. The only one who was friendly was Venantino Venantini, a usual presence in B-Italian movies, who was there with his son Luca, who also had a role in the movie, was a very beautiful child and not at all whimsical as children actors often are.

But even if good company had been available, I didn't have time to enjoy it. The filming schedule was entirely different from *House on the Edge of the Park*, with filming starting early in the morning and going on for 12 hours, mostly on street locations with no comfortable couches to relax on between takes. My first days on set were devoted to the movie theater/supermarket sequence, that saw me as the only protagonist in every take, starting from the cinema, where, in a cannibal fit, I had to bite a girl's tits. I only pretended to as she was a minor and her breasts couldn't be exposed. From there on it was endless running, jumping, rolling and shooting. I soon realized that I had to be in good shape, cutting out drinking, eating properly and going to bed no later than 10 to get seven solid hours of sleep. Fortunately make-up and costumes were in the hotel, so I only had to get up and go next door. On the other hand, the bad thing was that, to

Johnny plays a crazy Vietnam cannibal veteran who becomes a killing machine in the mall.

undo the make-up and change back into your clothes, you had to go back to the hotel, no matter how dirty and disheveled you were. But America is a big democracy, maybe with a touch of "mind your own business" to go with that philosophy, as I witnessed one day, when I took the hotel elevator with some other 15 people, being covered in very realistic stage blood. Nobody moved a muscle or stared at me, let alone asked if I were okay. For one moment I thought of pretending to faint to see what happened, but I was too tired for such pranks.

The supermarket scene was very long and difficult and required many special effects, which were in the formidable hands of Gino De Rossi, nicknamed "Big Bomber" for his love of explosives. We had a mixed crew, half-Italian and half-American, and the American Big Bomber helpers were speechless when, with some wire and a few nails, they were creating in two hours what they had estimated was worth two days' work. Communication between the Italian side and the American side of the crew was difficult, because the Italians didn't speak English and the Americans did not speak Italian. The Italians thought that speaking slowly with infinitive verbs would solve the problem, so the sound man could be caught saying in Italian to his assistant, with a voice used for infants or by Apaches in Westerns: "Actor speak too low ... Raise volume!" Many a time I had to intervene translating bits of information or teaching the American grips the basic Italian words of their trade, but there was never a chance that the Italians would bother learning 10 words of English.

I brought some coke with me from Italy, but I was trying to use it as little as possible, because I was afraid of the sudden "downs" I had already experienced.

Nevertheless, one day, during the supermarket scene, I felt very tired and in need of a good snort to keep going. The mall we were using was huge and I carefully selected the toilet at the other end of the area where we were shooting that day, not wanting to be interrupted by members of the crew or, even worse, by one of the policemen that were always at our side, as it is customary in the U.S.A. when shooting outdoors. So I walked through deserted aisles of soap power and gardening tools and reached the most remote area labeled "Gents." No one was in sight, so I started the usual procedure of making the lines and cutting the powder if some stone were in it. While I was busy with my work, I glared into the mirror and froze, paralyzed with fear. One of our policemen was standing at the door. In a second I had visions of being shamefully arrested, ruining the film and my future career, with local newspapers headlined: "Italian actor convicted for coke dealing." But the policeman shyly smiled and produced a joint, asking me, "Do you mind?" The poor guy was there for the same reason as me, so I relaxed and went on, politely refusing to share his pot. God Bless America!

I resumed shooting, doing everything a crazy Vietnam cannibal veteran is supposed to do in a mall; I shot dead a motorcyclist and the security man in attendance and then got drunk and sang my personal rendition of "Yankee Doodle" to his corpse, thus allowing the police captain to say the immortal line: "He'll be singing through his ass by the time I've finished with him." At the end of the scene I was attacked with gas grenades, and John Saxon stepped in, suggesting to me that I piss on it and then surrender; I accomplished that but not without biting a policeman, played by Antonio Margheriti's son Edoardo. The cannibal virus was on its way to infect the world and we could move on to the rest of the movie.

Charlie Bukowski's dazed glaze

Day by day my second director fascinated me more and more. Margheriti was a perfect gentleman, always impeccably dressed and never shouting, but he was self-assured and perfectly in command with a detached attitude that had more than one shade of irony about what we were doing, something I greatly appreciated. He often made jokes about the script and the gore in it and he never posed as a Maestro, but downplayed his work saying he was selling movies "by the kilo." Maybe it was true but he was indeed a fantastic shopkeeper, with a great ability in action sequences and a supreme respect for the acting profession. He was one of the few Italian directors I met who imposed silence to let an actor concentrate. He seemed to like my work and I respected him deeply, but not without a touch of affection, as if he was an uncle, one of those nice and witty uncles that make Christmas dinners bearable even if you get human flesh instead of turkey.

As shooting proceeded my social life improved a lot with the arrival of May Heatherly, who was playing the infected nurse joining the cannibal army composed of Saxon, Tony King and myself. She was there mainly because she lived in Spain and there was a share of Spanish money put into the movie and another week of shooting in Madrid after we finished in Atlanta. The poor thing arrived one night, famished and jet lagged, and Maurizio Amati thought that the most chivalrous thing to do was to make heavy passes at her. I diplomatically rescued the damsel in distress and we immediately became friends. She was a very cultivated woman, officially engaged to the son of the Spanish Ambassador to the Vatican in Rome, and cannibals and gore weren't her cup of tea as they weren't mine. But our disdain for the subject matter was nothing

Saxon and Johnny in the mall. Saxon's extreme hate for the movie showed with his being icily cold with whatever Italian was in sight, according to Johnny.

when compared to John Saxon, whose hate for the movie showed with his being icily cold with whatever Italian was in sight. She was taking the whole thing as a good sport and with a sense of humor. She was the perfect person to chat with on set or dine with.

But by then I had made another friend, one of the stuntmen who was a member of the motorcycle gang that had tried to stop me in the supermarket. Later we would have an epic night fight involving our cannibal army in the streets of Atlanta. He was a boy about my age, tall and with long blond hair, looking aggressively punk on his motorbike, and being charming and sweet in real life. He was into smoking grass, but didn't say no to some of my coke. One Sunday he took me to Stone Mountain, a park with the largest high relief sculpture in the world, the Confederate Memorial Carving, depicting three Confederate heroes of the Civil War: President Jefferson Davis, Generals Robert E. Lee and Thomas J. "Stonewall" Jackson. My *Gone with the Wind* southern heart was beating fast and, sharing a joint, he laughed to tears when I said that we were "stoned in the face of Stone Mountain." As many Americans he was crazy about my European sense of humor and he had something very childish in him that appealed to the eternal baby in me. In the company of real babies we took the little train that was running through the park and at the end of the day he presented me with a drawing of "Sherman crossing the Tennessee below Chattanooga" that has been in my many houses ever since, surviving removals, along with a little Confederate flag. I was often at his place after work; I met his girl friend and even slept with him in the same bed. He was attractive, even if not really my type, but I didn't try any kind of seduction, not being sure of his reactions and not wanting to spoil our friendship.

Not wanting to depict my younger self as Mr. Nice, it has to be said that I had found a way to have sexual relief in a local gay sauna, the first I saw in my life, the very idea being miles away from 1980s Italy. The Roman Catholic upbringing in me was very shy inquiring about such things, so I entered a sex shop in deep embarrassment and whispered something to the clerk about "clubs in town." He gave me a sarcastic look as if saying: "I know your sort sister" and sold me a sex guide to the town, where every sexual inclination was included. The sauna was far from big and less than clean, but I was fascinated by the free and open sex in every corner and enjoyed the Turkish bath cleaning my skin from cannibal blood and street dust. The crowd was mainly middle-aged and bearish, definitely not my scene, but occasionally some nice guys were there. I was very attracted to black boys and never have had sex with one, but apparently blacks who attended had a sort of gay apartheid phobia and were only coupling with other black guys. Nevertheless I managed to get into some satisfactory action that improved my mood and made me more of a Southerner by intimately knowing some locals, even if Rhett Butler wouldn't have approved.

Lurid poster art for the American release of *Cannibal Apocalypse*, under the title of *Invasion of the Flesh-hunters*

After the street brawl with the motorcycle gang, our Atlanta days were rapidly coming to an end, as our escape would lead us to the city sewers that were being rebuilt at the Rome studios awaiting our return. On our way we stopped at a gas station, not in need of gas but to savagely kill the owner and tear him into pieces. Cannibals do have their own priorities. The last take depicted us running away from the gas station and, one second before shooting started, the prop man gave me a plastic bag with blood dripping from it. I asked what it was and he answered: "Bits of the attendant to take away." The camera was rolling and action called, and I couldn't restrain hysterical laughter while running with my cannibal picnic bag. Fortunately it was a long shot and the camera couldn't see my face.

Chapter 10
Bulls' Balls, Cannibal Oral Sex and Sewers

Before going back to Italy we were to spend one week in Madrid, to justify the production being a Spanish co-production. On the plane I had a nice chat with Margheriti, who told me funny stories about the Peplum movies he had done, with gladiators so rubbed with oil as to be ready for a barbecue: "Let the steaks in!" he would say to have them on set. I told him I liked his tie and he took it off and gave it to me: the man was a living blessing.

It was my first time in Spain, because, as my parents before me, I had never wanted to finance the Franco dictatorship with tourism incomes. But Franco had died in 1975 and the country was finally free, now under the reign of King Juan Carlos, who was a champion of democracy and was adored by his devoted subjects. Madrid was electric and it showed at every corner, with the peoples' wish to make up for all the years lost in fear and repression. There were discos and gay bars and porno cinemas where I saw the most fantastic version of *Cinderella*, who instead of a special shoe had a vagina that could sing and laugh and Prince Charming had to copulate hard to find the rightful owner, following the advice of the Good Fairy, who was an outrageous black drag queen.

But I also went sightseeing, at times alone and at times with May, who lived there and introduced me to local habits, such as eating bulls' balls as a delicacy. I can't say I loved them, but the paella she cooked for me at her place simply

Johnny as Charlie Bukowski, looking handsome for a zombie flesheater

Johconquered me. In the Prado Museum I enjoyed more spiritual pleasures, almost becoming a victim of the Stendhal syndrome in front of the never-ending display of paintings by Velasquez, Goya and El Greco. I bought a reproduction of a painting by Goya, an ugly and sad little infant in a pink court dress, with a bird in her hand.

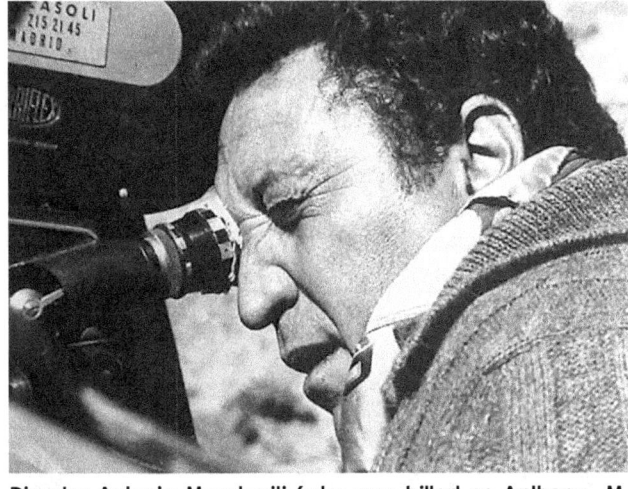

Director Antonio Margheriti (who was billed as Anthony M. Dawson in America) sets up a shot.

Our shooting in Madrid was concentrated on the hospital scenes and it was for one of them that May Heatherly, almost in tears, sought help from John Saxon and myself. The nurse she played was having a love affair with the head physician and, when the cannibal virus infected him, she was supposed to bite off his penis while performing a blowjob.

It was too much even for May's sense of humor and she didn't want to do it. So Saxon and I, for the first and only time acting as buddies when not in front of the camera, talked to the director Margheriti and convinced him that it was indeed pushing things too far on the road of bad taste. He agreed and she bit off his tongue instead, with the appropriate profusion of stage blood.

When shooting my exit from the hospital for my first break, Margheriti, with his usual understatement and humor, paid me a great compliment by scolding the cameraman for bothering me about my exact position when in front of the guardian at the gate: "Leave him alone and follow him," he said. " Can't you see he is doing a Marlon Brando act?" I was decidedly in love with the man.

The Spanish week flew in a flash and we were already on our final plane for Rome.

On the first day at the studio, where we were going to shoot the long sewer sequence, a mystery that had intrigued me from the beginning of the shoot was finally solved. Since Atlanta, I was wondering why John Saxon was always first in the make-up morning schedule. He was the star and stars are generally supposed to be last, allowing them an extra hour of sleep.

On that cold winter morning I arrived on set before my call-sheet time and went to the make-up room to ask where my dressing room was. John Saxon was there and the make-up man was carefully arranging what was left of his hair on his forehead, filling the empty spots with black shoe polish. They didn't see me and I silently tip-toed away, swearing to myself that if I were to lose my hair, as indeed happened, I would accept my fate without submitting to such a humiliating procedure.

Tony King and Johnny play prisoners of war in Vietnam who are fed human flesh, while being held captive in a pit.

The sewers sequence proved to be a hard nut to crack. The corridors were narrow and smelly because of the stagnant water, and as soon as the lights were on, the temperature rose to a sweaty hell. We were all wet with perspiration, crippled because of the low ceilings and easily irritated. We had stage blood constantly on us and one evening I found poor May Heatherly in hysterics, trying to clean it from her legs with a Lady Macbeth desperation. ("Away damned spot!") She was going to an Embassy reception with her in-laws and the bloodstain was visible under her stockings.

We were supposed to fight rats and they arrived in crates full of the white- and red-eyed dirty things. I positively refused to come anywhere near them and a prop leg was built to show me kicking them away. Then the day arrived to photograph my death, a bazooka blowing away my stomach with the camera zooming through the hole. It was a complicated special effect and I shuddered with fear when Big Bomber insisted we do it at the end of a very tiring day of work, instead of shooting it the next morning as wise Margheriti was suggesting. But Big Bomber won the deal and I found myself lying on my stomach on a wooden board and grabbing the sewer bars with my hands, a dummy of my body hanging from my neck, filled with explosives that an excited Big Bomber kept adding more and more to. It was brilliant and very realistic, but I was terrorized, thinking of the many accidents that had occurred with explosives in movie history, from Brandon Lee dying to people losing an eye. As much as I was stretching my head upwards, my face was still only a few inches from the little bomb exploding in my fake stomach.

Feeling like a French nobleman under the guillotine, I prayed to God, the Virgin Mary and All Saints, asking forgiveness for my sins and awaiting my destiny. It went well, but the expression of fear and desperation in my dying eyes was absolutely real and should not be attributed to my acting skill. Strangely enough, many years later, when I saw *Death Becomes Her* I didn't recognize the homage that Robert Zemeckis had paid to my death doing a similar effect on Goldie Hawn.

My last days in the movie were devoted to the pit sequence at the beginning at the story, when Tony King and I were war prisoners in Vietnam and fed with human flesh. I had expected the worst cut of meat to be used for me to chew, but with my great surprise I was given a wonderful filet. When the day was over, I spotted the production manager carefully cleaning it and taking it home for dinner. The next day another juicy filet arrived and I played a trick on the poor man by taking it myself. When it was time to go home he was looking for the steak everywhere, but he couldn't ask anyone where it was, as not to be caught.

I thought that my work in *Cannibal Apocalypse* was over and I said farewell to the rest of the crew who had a few days of work ahead of them, shooting exteriors in the Manziana woods, which in Italian movies was the magic place that could become everything, from an English forest to the Amazon, and now it was Vietnam.

But one afternoon, maybe two weeks after my death scene, I got a call from the production manager saying that they needed me for a "fegatello," literally meaning a roasted pork liver, which is the phrase used for small details that are left behind to be shot after the movie is over. I asked what it was and he said it was the small detail of me biting the girl's boob. Shit, he was right! We hadn't done it in Atlanta because the girl was a minor. "Hurry up!" he said. "Take a taxi and we'll pay you back." I did, but the traffic was heavy because of some accident that had occurred and it took me forever to arrive at the studio. When I got there I entered the shed and saw an old prostitute sitting on a chair in the middle of nothing, with a light on her. She was naked from the waist up and was covering her flabby breasts with the make-up prop already applied with a half-open raincoat. When she saw me, she fully opened the raincoat and said in a heavy Roman accent, "About time! Are we gonna do that munch?"

"Good evening," I politely answered, then leaned on her and viciously attacked the prop tit, filled with stage blood.

Now the movie was completed for real.

Chapter 11
Parlor Games and a New Movie

Being unemployed and with no future plans, I resumed my drug-pusher activity that increased as fast as "T" was growing more and more marijuana plants, the greenhouse expanding to airplane hangar proportions.

The demand was incessant and I tried to accelerate the drying process by using the kitchen oven. The poor thing got crazy stoned and exploded, fortunately not with me in front of it.

But one day, out of the blue, "T's" parents arrived for a short surprise visit and made the strongest possible demonstration of bourgeois hypocrisy. When they saw the greenhouse, "T" was forced to tell them that it was marijuana. I cowardly went inside, but I could hear from a distance their outraged complaints about the lack of morals and the abomination their son was throwing on their good name. A silence followed: "T" was explaining what had happened (without mentioning our coke addiction); he had taken money from the bank account and was refunding it with the marijuana.

Next morning, when I met "T's" mother at the breakfast table she politely asked me about the plants as if they were roses. did they need a lot of water? Were they growing fast? Holding in laughter I thought that Karl Marx had his reasons when saying that everything the ruling class does is for money purposes and even morals and religion kneel in front of the god of Gold.

My social circle was expanding too and it produced a wonderful twist when I was introduced to director Duccio Tessari and his wife, actress Lorella De Luca. Duccio was one of the kings of the Spaghetti Westerns, being the creator of the Ringo saga that had pushed Giuliano Gemma, a former stuntman, into stardom. His wife Lorella, fawn eyes and the prettiest little nose in Italian cinema, had been one of the most popular "girls next door" of the Italian Neorealism comedies. In their personal life they were warm, friendly and very interested in young people in the business and they had the ritual almost every night of hosting an "open house" after dinner, where show biz people met to play parlor games or poker or just chat and gossip. I became a frequent guest and I was introduced to the giants of the Italian movie industry. At the Tessari evenings you could meet actors such as Vittorio Gassman, Paolo Villaggio, Monica Vitti or Giancarlo Giannini, directors as big as Sergio Leone and Dino Risi and tycoons like Franco Cristaldi, who separated from Claudia Cardinale and was proudly parading his new conquest, actress Zeudi Araya, who had the most beautiful woman's ass I ever saw in my life.

I also met iconic actor Gian Maria Volontè, and with the complicity of coke, we became friends. He was a real myth for my generation, the most versatile and unpredictable actor on the Italian scene, passing in a flash from Westerns to deeply engaged political movies. He was also an open supporter of the Communist party and had sided with the student's rebellion in 1968.

His addiction to cocaine was even worse than mine and, being very rich, his supplies were royal. Whenever I arrived at his place in Trastevere, a ski run of white power was always waiting on the sitting room table and we passed hours sniffing and talking. I was always alone with him and I was mesmerized by his charisma and strong manly sex appeal. He was a notorious womanizer, but it was quite obvious that, in some way, I attracted him too. I was too shy and intimidated to make open passes, but we got to hug and even lightly kissed. It has also to be said that, while affecting me differently from many people, cocaine did stimulate a need for sex in me but at the same time made me partly impotent. And being hugged and kissed by a man like him was already a dream.

Monica Vetti was one of many veteran celebrities that Johnny met at the regular after-diner "open house" parties hosted by director Duccio Tessari and his wife.

Too concentrated about my crush for Gian Maria and with studying the stars at the Tessari evenings, I didn't take much notice of a big ruffled man with a beard, who was not very talkative and seemed shy, if not at war with the world. But that man was Lucio Fulci, and he was probably looking at me quite carefully, because in a few weeks he was going to offer me my third movie role and probably the one most cherished by horror fans: Bob in *City of the Living Dead*, also known as *Gates of Hell*.

Chapter 12
Zombie Love At First Sight

I didn't audition for Fulci, as I hadn't for Deodato and Margheriti either. When I met him at the production office, he said that he had had good reports about me and changed his mind about the actor he had previously decided to cast as Bob. Once again I was stepping into somebody else's shoes. Considering that Giovanni Masini was production manager, I thought that it probably had been him pushing me, after the good result of *House on the Edge of the Park*.

Fulci was very brisk and, inquiring about him, I was told that he was famous for his bad temper and for mistreating people on set. I also remembered that I had seen one of his movies, *Seven Notes in Black*, and found it pretty effective. A good director with a bad temper ... it was a challenge I was ready to face.

My reactions to the script were once more mixed. It wasn't as good a story with as solid a plot as *House on the Edge of the Park*, but neither was it a piece of crap like *Cannibal Apocalypse* had looked at first reading. Zombies were new to me, as I hadn't seen either the Romero movies or any others dealing with walking dead people, but after *Cannibal Apocalypse* I was already familiar with blood and gore, even if in *City of the Living Dead* it was a different kind of splatter, more related to ancestral fears and old legends.

I formed the opinion, which is still with me, that these horror stories I had bumped into were the adult versions of childhood fairy tales. If you forget about Walt Disney (always a favorite of mine) and consider the original versions of the stories written, for example, by the Brothers Grimm, you'll see that there's a great deal of horrible things occurring. In *Cinderella* one of the stepsisters cuts off her heel to fit into the crystal shoe and, at the end, birds peck out the eyes of both of them. Cannibal bogymen are frequent in literature and in many stories the hero fights against devilish presences, including skeletons and corpses rising from their graves. Of course the difference is that fairy tales are read or narrated, not shown on screen in every disgusting detail, leaving it to children's imagination to sort out the visions apt to exorcise their fears by identifying with the hero of the story. As Bruno Bettelheim acutely points out in his wonderful book *The Uses of Enchantment: The Meaning and Importance of Fairy Tales* (which I strongly recommend to all horror fans), a fairy tale must have a happy end in order to achieve its aim, which is to demonstrate that growing up is a hard fight (symbolically represented by monsters, magicians, witches and all the rest), but a worthwhile one, because it is rewarded at the end by a serene and fruitful adulthood.

Anyway, money apart, what got me into doing the movie was once again the appeal of the character I was to portray.

Bob was very much in the line of Ricky and Bukowski, a frail victim crushed by the world around him, but he was a more ancestral and beast-like version of the whipping boy: the village idiot, alone and rejected, living like an animal and possessed by frightful visions. Insightful acting material was definitely there and

Italian Fotobusta for *City of the Living Dead*, featuring Johnny (left) and Catriona MacColl screaming her head off in the center.

the physical side of the character once again became prominent. I decided he was a rat, a sewer rat similar to the ones I had refused to approach in *Cannibal Apocalypse*, and as much as I considered them repulsive, I intended to become one of them.

The news that we were going to film in Savannah had struck me as pretty funny, considering I had just got back from Atlanta. Being twice in the same remote part of the world in the space of a few weeks is not a frequent event, but I liked Georgia a lot and the perspective of hearing so soon again that magic drawl was appealing.

So I found myself again on a plane, this time sitting beside Fabrizio Jovine, the actor playing Father Thomas, the devil-possessed priest whose suicide was the start of the story. On the long flight I had the impression that he was somehow politely courting me, but I might have been wrong because no further passes were made in Savannah. Anyhow he was pleasant company and chatting with him and smoking (still allowed on planes in 1980) helped me through the long journey.

This time I arrived tired and jet-lagged and I just wanted to go to sleep. But in the hotel corridor I met a spirited bearded young man, who introduced himself as Carlo De Mejo, who I knew was the son of beautiful Alida Valli. He looked quite uneasy and asked me if I knew where in the room he could find tissues, the most bizarre question to ask in an American hotel, where tissues and soap bars are positively everywhere. He then disappeared, as though floating in a world of his own, which was, as I later understood, very much his attitude toward life.

Next morning I went to make-up and stopped at the door, thunderstruck. Perfect beauty was in front of me, embodied in Antonella Interlenghi, who was to be my closest partner as Emily, the only one in the village to care for poor Bob. All was shining in her: her delicate skin, the green eyes and the ruby lips. I felt like kneeling and reciting Romeo's words when he first sees Juliet (from Shakespeare's *Romeo and Juliet*):

Oh, she doth teach the torches to burn bright!
It seems she hangs upon the cheek of night
Like a rich jewel in an Ethiope's ear,
Beauty too rich for use, for Earth too dear.

I didn't recite any immortal lines but shyly introduced myself, conquered by her nice classy attitude as by her beauty. But my devout contemplation of that miracle on Earth was interrupted by a boy with a bony face, curly hair and pale blue eyes who addressed me saying: "Ah, so you are the asshole stealing all my roles!" He was Michele Soavi and, as it had happened with Ricky, it was he who had been Fulci's first choice for Bob. I clumsily apologized, but he laughed and patted my back, saying he was joking. He didn't care much about acting and was much more interested in being assistant director to Fulci for this movie, since he wanted to be a director himself. It was the beginning of a great friendship, one of the stronger I had in my life.

"Ah, so you are the asshole stealing all my roles!" Director/actor Michele Soavi (not quite the youthful boy) introduces himself to Johnny.

Watching Michele more carefully I remembered his face. I saw him in a movie called *Small Lips*, with a pun on "lips," the word used in Italian to name one's mouth as well as the vagina's labia. It was a period, romantic/erotic film very much like *Lolita*, focusing on the burning passion of one man for a teenage girl. Michele was a Gypsy acrobat who was making the man jealous. I had been struck by his performance and thought he had charisma and a great face. It was a pity he didn't care about acting. As I found out when I got to know him better, even if he wasn't planning on a future of stardom, he was quite vain, in a boyish charming way and very proud of his resemblance to James Dean that he tried to imitate, driving the same car and motorcycle and always dressing in denims and leather bomber jackets.

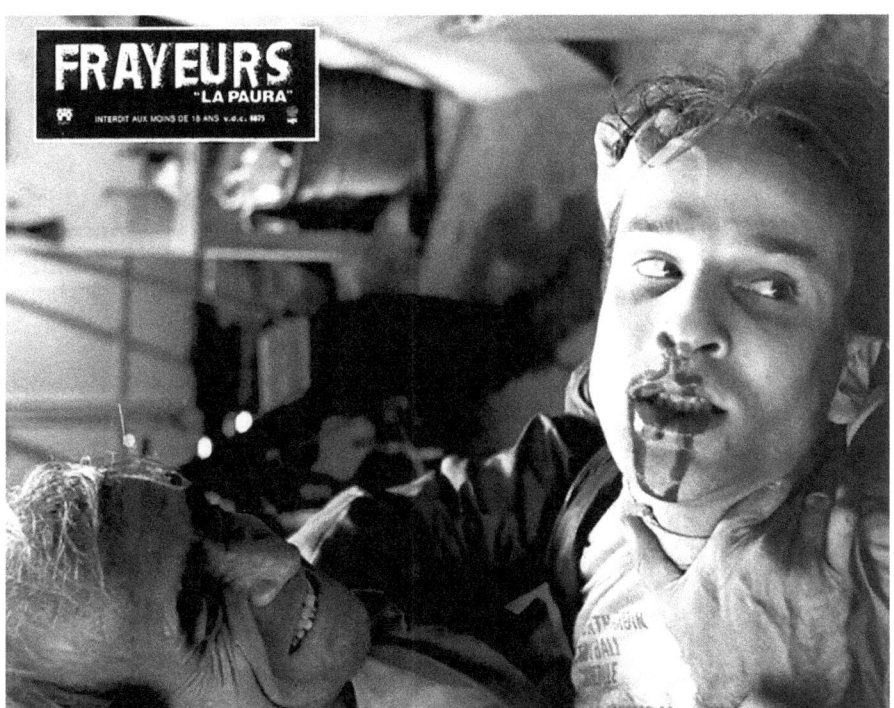

A French lobby card for *City of the Living Dead* feturing Johnny's fateful meeting with a power drill.

I also found out something that he was trying to hide as much as possible from the movie world: his rich and influential family. He was the son of refined novelist Giorgio Soavi and, even more important, his mother was Lidia Olivetti, a surname that in Italy was indelibly tied to whatever tape machine was in sight. Michele's grandfather, Adriano Olivetti, had been a prominent and surprising personality in post-war Italy, an openly leftist industrialist who was also a respected intellectual and patron of the arts. He had married Paola Levi, who was the sister of Natalia Ginzburg, the most famous Italian woman novelist and a renowned translator of Proust.

His family was quite the perfect match with mine and, as it happened with me, he had refused that kind of legacy to devout himself to something entirely different. But I never thought of hiding my ancestors, while he carefully did, not to look a spoiled brat in front of producers, crewmembers and directors who had started from nothing. I could see his point: my family was tied to intellectual and blood aristocracy and it was rare that movie people might know them, while Michele's family was rooted into a financial and industrial power that everybody knew about, having used an Olivetti in their life. But even if we had different perspectives about accepting or refusing our family heritage, the same breeding was a strong bond between us. There were indeed differences. If I had been a terrible student in some subjects, I was anyway quite cultivated in history and literature and I could use three languages, while Michele's refusal of his origins had brought him to be quite uneducated except for those disci-

A stunning Italian locandina for *City of the Living Dead*; artwork by Enzo Sciotti

plines that interested him. For instance he knew some painters such as Munch or Chagall and some writers such as Poe and Lovecraft, from whom he gathered his authentic passion for the horror world. Being Fulci's assistant hadn't been a casual choice but a conscious step toward what he wanted to achieve.

But this goal, and much more, was to happen in the future. That very first day our chat was interrupted by the costume department, calling me for a fitting of the prop hunchback they prepared for me. I didn't know about it and I thought it was a terrible idea that risked making me look like Marty Feldman in *Young Frankenstein*. I asked them to wait a few minutes while I went in search of Fulci, even if I was afraid about his reaction. To create a problem the very first day with an aggressive director is not the wisest recommended behavior on the set. I found him and I shyly told him that the hunchback was in my opinion too stagy and that I could walk myself in a weird way. "Show me," he said briskly. As part of the personal training I was continuously doing, I had recently studied Richard the Third, elaborating a sort of "stiff" gait, my left shoulder slightly twisted upwards. I paraded that way in front of Fulci, waiting to be kicked in the ass, but he just said, "Okay, no hunchback," and resumed what he was doing. In walking away I heard him mutter to his faithful assistant Roberto Giandalia: "And they say theater people are no good ..." Maybe that first step hadn't been in the wrong direction.

So wearing Bob's rags but without looking like the Hunchback of Notre Dame, I started wandering in deserted streets and half-destroyed houses, making love to a plastic doll and witnessing horrible images such as a hand coming out of a wall or the sudden appearance of a putrescent baby corpse.

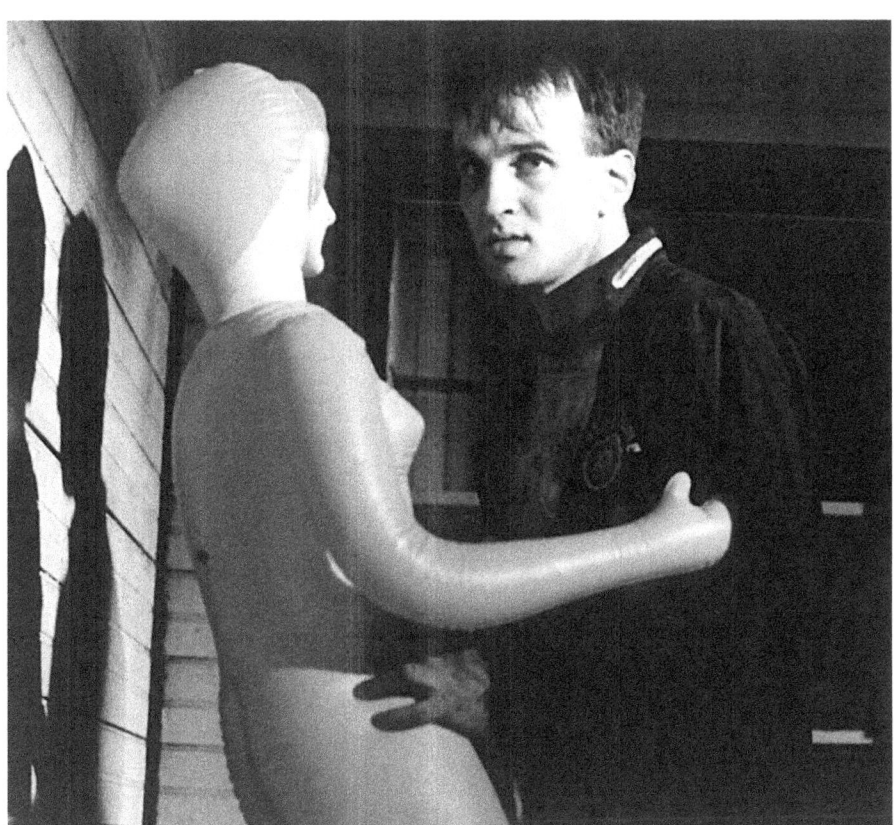

The outcast Bob (Johnny) turns to rather unusual sources for companionship.

Savannah, Georgia is one of the oldest cities in the U.S.A and its 19th-century buildings are much admired and considered "antique," an idea quite amusing for one who was passing every day in front of the Coliseum. It is anyway a very nice place, with a real downtown and some interesting pre-bellum houses and inns in the harbor area. But it was spick and span clean and freshly painted, not in the least giving the idea of the fading ghost-hunted village depicted in the movie. So a lot of stage fog was used, provided by big noisy machines, and the photographer had the challenging task of creating the needed Gothic atmosphere of fear and sorcery. Sergio Salvati was in charge of effects and he did a wonderful job of turning bright and touristic Savannah into the gloomy place where Salem had once been. He liked me a lot and was the first real Maestro I had on set, teaching me some crucial points about acting in a movie.

In *House on the Edge of the Park* I played Ricky as if I was on stage, mostly relating to my partners and reacting to them, and in *Cannibal Apocalypse* my attention had been mostly dedicated to action and movement. In *City of the Living Dead* I was alone quite a bit and I had to express my feelings and inner thoughts to no one in particular, thus needing to create a relationship with the camera as if it were my partner in the scene. Salvati taught me where to look, how to create different spaces and distances in my eyes, and he was indeed of great

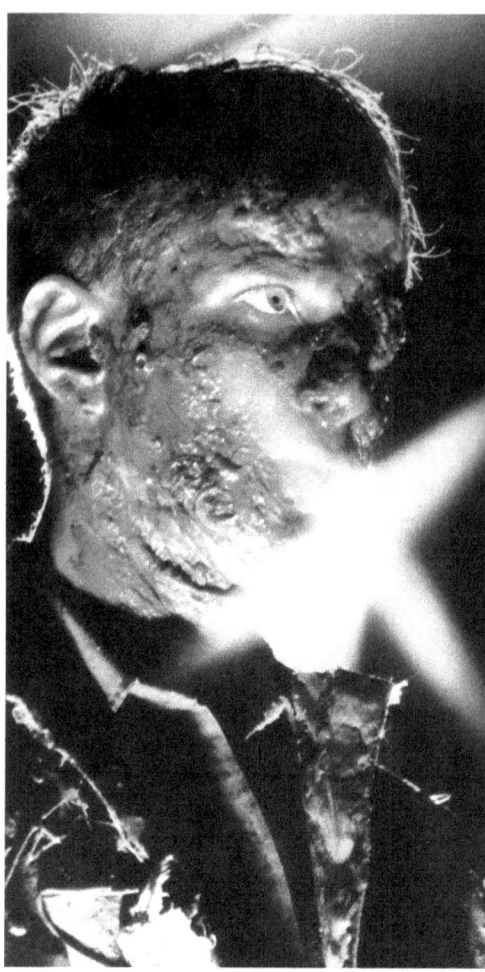

Bob returns as one of the ungodly living dead.

help in the developing of my skills as a movie actor.

While wandering about foggy Savannah-Salem, I had to be haunted by the vision of Father Thomas hanging himself, and during the scene I had my first accident.

We were shooting at night in a pedestrian underpass in a park that had obviously been a shelter for homeless people, because all the dirt and rubbish in the world was there without our art department bothering to recreate it (green- eyed and handsome Rodolfo Ruzza was again the prop man). Walking on that floor of debris during the scene, I stepped on a huge rusty nail that easily went through my gym shoe and into my foot. I was brave and didn't stop, thus growing in Fulci's esteem, but when the scene was over I was taken to the local hospital emergency room to get a tetanus injection. It was an occasion that differentiated Italy and the U.S.A., all favoring the latter. The hospital I went to was clearly not intended for the well-to-do and an old tramp, much in need of a shower, was in the waiting room; maybe he was the same one who had been living in the underpass. Nevertheless the place was spotless and the organization as good as in the best Swiss nursing home ever. I got my injection and was given treatment, cleaning solution and bandages for a week. Thanking everybody for their kindness I thought of Italian emergency rooms, old, dirty and packed with people waiting for hours, at times without a chair in which to sit. Once again God Bless America, and this time for real.

But the United States also had a few shortcomings, like a certain tendency to follow the rules by the book and being frightened of whatever small changes might occur in pre-scheduled patterns, as demonstrated by a Savannah waiter that I could easily have strangled.

After one or two nights shooting I had been invited to join Fulci and Salvati for a late dinner, a great token of esteem from a director who considered actors mostly as pains in the ass. There was only one restaurant open until late hours

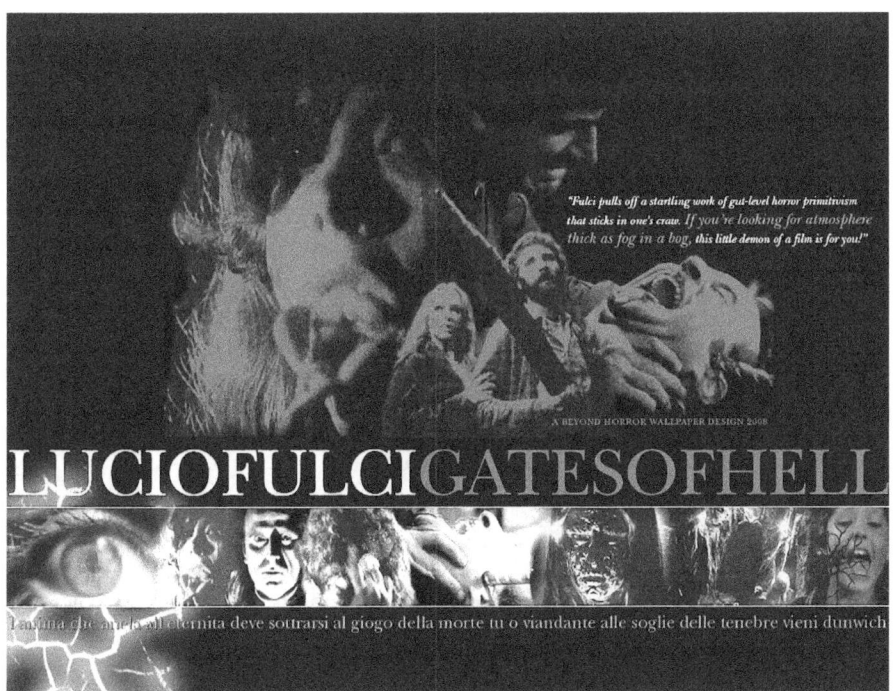

Lucio Fulci's *City of the Living Dead* saw release as *Gates of Hell* in the U.S.A.

and the menu was in the typical flowery prose of many American diners, calling a salad a "slim and trim garden path" and chicken wings "crispy and lively hen house best." What sounded like the simplest food was a filet mignon with mushrooms, but if the meat was indeed very good, the mushroom sauce was awful, so the second time I asked for the filet without mushrooms, starting the following conversation:

> Me: I am having the filet mignon, but with no mushrooms, please.
> Waiter: (Puzzled) I beg your pardon?
> Me: Just the filet, medium, without mushrooms.
> Waiter: (Almost outraged) I don't think we can do that, sir.
> Me: Sorry?
> Waiter: The filet mignon comes with the mushrooms.
> Me: Okay, but I don't like them; so if you could please just don't add them.
> Waiter: That's impossible.
> Me: Why?
> Waiter: Because you pay for the mushrooms, sir.
> Me: (Fighting to stay calm) Yes, I pay for them, but I don't want them. It's my choice.
> Waiter: (Icily cold) I'll get your order.

Needless to say, the filet arrived with the fucking mushrooms on it. So I took my knife and pushed them out of the plate into a paper napkin, almost shouting: "Is it that complicated?" When I saw Jack Nicholson in *Five Easy Pieces* experiencing almost the same series of events, I was comforted by the fact that native born Americans did find that attitude maddening.

If Fulci was very nice and polite with me, I did indeed witness his famous bad temper explode on more than one occasion, and it wasn't the half ironic shouting of Deodato, but heavy cursing and throwing objects at whoever caused his rage. These were manly production people and, during one filet mignon dinner, Fulci explained his attitude to me, thus revealing that even if his rage appeared to be very realistic and frightening, his exploits weren't entirely coming from real anger. "You are a theater director?" Fulci continued.

> So one day you might want to direct a movie. I'm giving you this tip. Production people must always be kept in a state of tension, otherwise they relax and you don't get want you want. The very first day you must shout like mad for no matter what, like screaming—This fork smells! Even if it is nothing but nonsense, it does not matter. And you must keep doing so every three or four days to keep them in suspense. They'll work like mad to prevent you from making a scene.

I never had the occasion to put his advice into practice, but I thought it was a clever trick. Soon though I found that his fury could nevertheless be real.

Studying Fulci more closely I felt a certain pity for him, because he was clearly not at ease with life and was rather unhappy. Crew members didn't like him much because of his shouting spells and they mocked him behind his back for his untidy appearance, getting to the point of saying he smelled, something I state wasn't true. From set gossip I learned that his wife had committed suicide because of a cancer diagnosis that had later proved wrong, and one of his daughters had suffered a serious back accident falling from a horse. So he had some reasons not to face life with a happy smile and, in addiction to personal tragedies, he was suffering as critics rejected his work as being mere B-movies. He proudly told me that he was held in high esteem in France and considered a Maestro, and that he hated the snobbish intellectual Italian movie reviewers. He was proud of his career that had started out as being assistant to Luchino Visconti, and he wanted to be acknowledged as an artist. He would be, but unfortunately, after his death, it is too late for him to be aware of the iconic status he holds nowadays.

My role in *City of the Living Dead* wasn't as extensive as the previous

Catriona MacColl continues to scream her head off as she is pursued by another member of the living dead.

ones, so I had many free days and enjoyed the company of my new buddies, who were just as free as I was, mostly shooting at night. As it happens in movies, I never met the actors I wasn't working with such as Christopher George, Catriona MacColl or Janet Agreen, but I was always with Michele and Antonella, and the little gang included a young production assistant called Ian and another Italian boy working as assistant director whose name was Ranieri Ferrara Santamaria. The five of us were always trying to go to the hotel pool even if sunbathing had been strictly forbidden as unbecoming for professional zombies, but at times we managed to avoid the close surveillance organized by the make-up department and happily splashed in the water.

Ian was of Puerto Rican ascendant, openly gay and very funny. There were no gay clubs in Savannah, but he knew all the discos and bars and did his best to keep us amused. On the other hand Ranieri was a pain in the ass: a spoiled brat who was the nephew of a very famous lawyer, trying to make up for his lack of personal charm and physical beauty by showing off his wealth. He didn't like Michele and myself any more than we liked him, but he was with us because he had a crush on Antonella, who was cruelly making fun of him and calling him La Rana (The Frog), making a pun on his unusual first name. At times I felt sorry for him, as he was the perfect portrait of a loser and I wasn't surprised when, a few years later, he died from a heroin overdose. His death started a great scandal involving many Roman rich kids, including Edoardo Agnelli, the son and heir of the owner of Fiat automobiles.

No heroin was used in the Savannah days and no coke as well. I tried curing myself of the habit and didn't carry any with me. But if "heavy" stuff wasn't on the scene, pot was our constant companion. Ian always had some and Antonella liked smoking grass more than anything else; she used all her feminine charm to get it. It wasn't an uncustomary sight to see her on set fol-

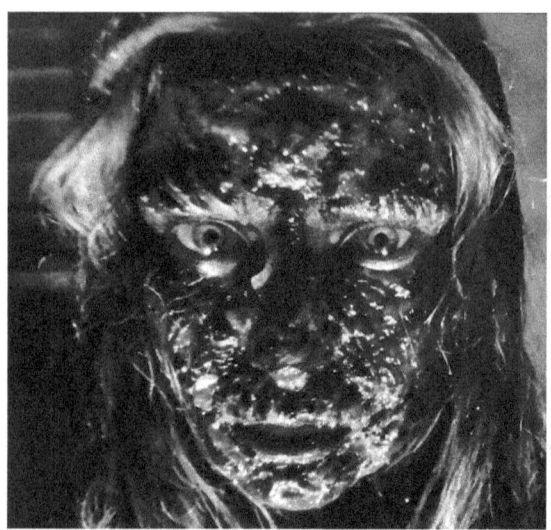

Intense blood-soaked make-up makes the living dead look memorable in *City of the Living Dead*.

lowed by black pushers who resembled the worst Hollywood cliché, all flowery shirts, bandanas, muscles and golden chains and they were totally bewitched by her in the manner of the rats from the Pied Piper of Hamlin. Michele adored pot too and couldn't live without it, this being his mutual bond with Antonella, whom he wasn't crazy about as I was, finding her whimsical and moody, as she indeed at times was. If there are Hollywood Princesses, she was the real Cinecittà Princess, the daughter of two famous actors, educated in exclusive boarding schools, attended by servants and nannies and dressed in high *couture* since childhood. Strangely enough at 20 she was already the mother of two daughters, having married at 15 with an Italian aristocrat. One of her daughters was to follow her path, making her a grandmother at 36. But the little girls were in the capable hands of some French Mademoiselle and she was wildly enjoying life with endless energy. At weekends she was constantly flying to New York where she had friends and caused a turmoil on set not arriving on time one Monday morning; she was also once arrested for indecent behavior when caught sunbathing topless. Poor Giovanni Masini had indeed the worst time of his career with her. In later years she calmed down and I could have some nice chats with her, but in the Savannah days I was just madly infatuated with her looks and accepted whatever mad behavior she might exhibit.

But Michele also interested me. The more I knew him the more he looked to me like a mix between Peter Pan and Puck in *A Midsummer's Night Dream*, an airy spirit whose hectic behavior was an exciting shock for someone basically lazy and dreamy as I was. And I also found him sexually very attractive, with his little agile body, all bones and nerves. I wrote a poem where I described him as "a Botticelli Mars painted by Kandinsky." Once again quoting Shakespeare, I could have said: "Two loves I have, of comfort and despair …"

But there was no drama going on. We were young friends and, most of all, deeply concentrated on our work, even if it caused some stress, as it happened to poor Antonella when it was her turn to be faced with Father Thomas' ghost, causing her death out of fear.

City of the Living Dead is renowned among horror fans for the wide use of worms. In a famous scene they arrive by millions, crashing the windows and flying onto the faces of Catriona MacColl, Carlo De Mejo, Christopher George

and Janet Agren. At the end of the day the bloody things were in every corner and everybody was hysterical. Someone (probably Christopher George) was really pissed with Fulci and made him taste his own medicine by putting worms into his tobacco bag; he didn't take it with a sense of humor. I hate worms and insects as much as I hate rats and considered myself lucky not having scenes with them, but I was on set when it was Antonella's turn to have them spread on her face, mixed with dirty mud, by the zombie hand of Father Thomas. She came to one of my dirty hideouts to comfort me, but hearing a weird noise I unkindly escaped, leaving her alone.

The scene was carefully described in the script, so she knew what was happening, but at the very last moment she went into hysterics, screaming at the top of her lungs that she didn't want to do it. What followed was out of a Nazi movie. Two portly grips seized her by force and kept her on the floor while the camera zoomed in on her face and the disgusting mush was spread on her face, now distorted by fear. No Academy Award-winning actress could have reacted better than she did.

By the end of our Savannah shooting days, another episode, probably the funniest in my whole career, saw Antonella featured prominently.

We were to shoot the scene in which the bad guys of the village (and among them Venantino Venantini, who had killed me) had to face their zombie revenge. Make-up started at eight in the morning and went on for six hours, with the final touch of marmalade to create the idea of decomposing flesh. At the end of the procedure we couldn't even open our mouths to eat, drinking was possible only through straws, and if there were a bee or a wasp in sight, attracted

by the marmalade, we were indeed to have problems. So Antonella and I sought refuge in a van, waiting to be called on set. To make our condition more miserable, our clothes had been buried in the dirty ground for days and their smell was awful. We waited for an hour, then one hour more … no one arrived. We were on the verge of tears and Antonella had an idea: "Why don't we smoke some grass to relax?" I agreed and a joint was made with the grass she had and awkwardly smoked through lips half sealed by zombie make-up. But that time some satanic pusher or Father Thomas provided the grass, because it was as strong as LSD and totally freaked us out. We were staring at each other in our zombie make-up, yelling like mad or laughing in hysterics. It went on for some time, then we finally calmed down and returned almost to normal. But another two hours had passed and my patience had run out. It was sadistic and unprofessional to keep us waiting in those conditions for hours. So I opened the van door, ready to make my first "star" protesting scene on a set. And I found myself facing a young woman and a small child about six years old, who looked transfixed at me and started yelling, "Mommy, mommy, the Creature, the Creature!" and wasn't satisfied until I agreed to hold him for a personal picture, all the fury gone.

When we finally were called on set, we found an entirely new Lucio Fulci awaiting us. As, most directors, he wasn't interfering much with the acting and just made approving or disapproving noises, not always easy to be told apart. But that day he was hopping up and down in excitement and his instructions were continuous and detailed, "Zombies don't walk that way!" or "Zombies stare like this! … They stretch out their arms this way!" Apparently he had seen them and knew all their habits as if they were some old and dear relatives. We carefully followed his instructions and that terrible day was finally over, as was our stay in Savannah.

Chapter 13
A Drill Enters History

I had three weeks before resuming shooting in Rome, so I decided to go to New York and visit my good friend Livia Aymonino, who was living there. She put me up in her nice bohemian apartment in Greenwich Village and I had a very good time with the Italian colony that had settled in the Big Apple. Livia had been in charge of organization in my theater company and was a real sport, with always a sarcastic comment on her lips. We went to fashionable clubs and discos including the mythical Studio 54 and I explored some new gay areas such as dungeon clubs that I didn't find particularly appealing. I really couldn't see why fucking should be more enjoyable among pools of vomit and smashed beer bottles. But my female attraction was tickled by again meeting Alberta, a

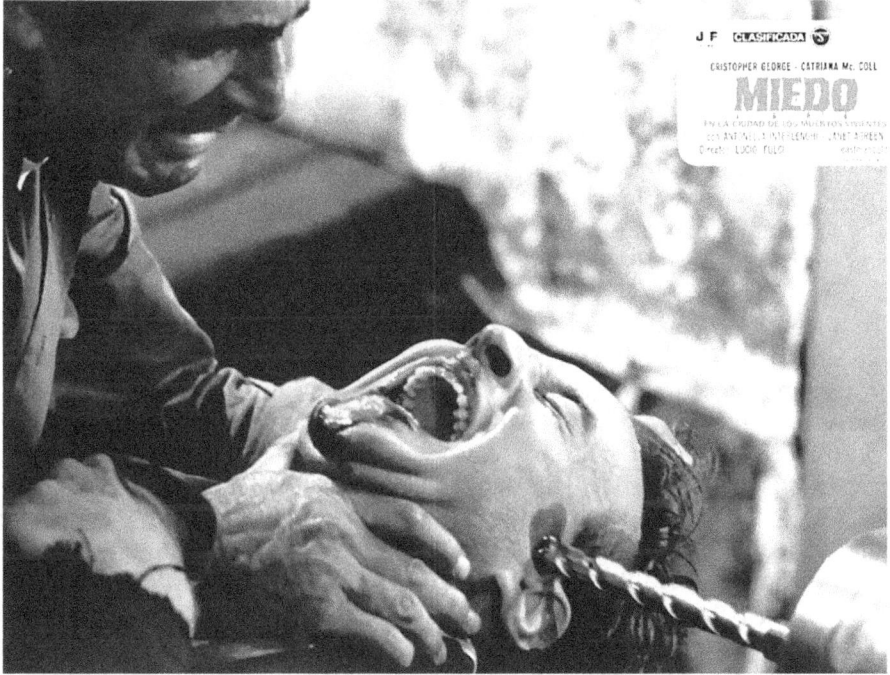

Bob (Johnny) gets drilled by Mr. Ross (Venantino Venantini)

gorgeous friend of Livia whom I had tried bedding one night in Perugia, when we were touring with *Macbeth*. I hadn't succeeded, not because she wasn't willing to go for it as much as I was, but because I had encountered the only Puritan hotel concierge in Italy, who didn't allow her to my room and didn't mellow when I offered him a tip. Alberta was now working in New York and we courted and petted an entire evening, first in a restaurant, then in a club and then she invited me to her Uptown apartment, but thankfully not to see her butterfly

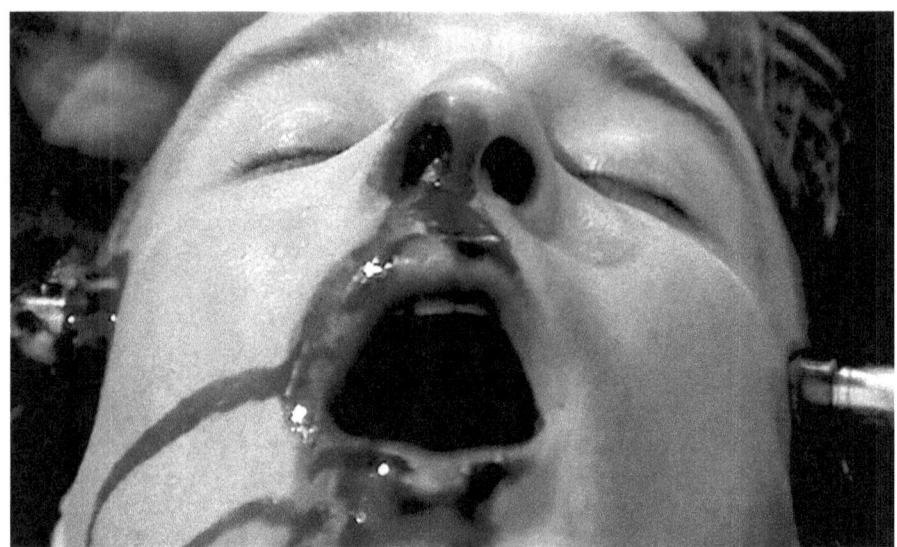

collection. However when we got there and started kissing she suddenly said that she didn't feel like going on. I was speechless and for a moment I saw the point of view of some rapists, even if I have always considered it one of the most repulsive possible crimes. At three in the morning I tried to get a cab on the street and my opinion on women's tantrums and whimsical behavior didn't improve a bit.

My only interior scene in *City of the Living Dead* shot in Rome was my death. Poor Bob, who is suspected for all the weird things happening in town, takes shelter in a garage, falling asleep in a car. In the morning the owner's daughter arrives and offers to share a marijuana joint. But her father (played by Venantino Venantini) surprises them and shows his severe disapproval by using his huge electric drill and pushing it through Bob's head.

I wasn't very worried about the scene because I thought that the worst part of it had already taken place with the plaster casting of my head (I had done this before leaving for Savannah). It had been a career martyrdom never to be forgot. Giannetto De Rossi (not to be mixed up with his almost twin Gino De Rossi—Big Bomber) was making the cast and he had covered my head with plaster, leaving just enough space for me to breathe through a straw. It took more than one hour, and as the plaster was solidifying, I felt more and more suffocated and almost went into hysterics, telling Giannetto afterwards to keep the cast in a well-guarded safe because I was never ever going through such an ordeal again, not even if asked by the combined creative force of Fellini and Visconti.

But the scene had its problems all the same, the first one being the girl playing Venantino's daughter. She was a Miss Nobody, but for some reason she behaved like a star and started complaining about this and that since early morning. That was the occasion for Fulci to show what he was capable of when in a real fury. He started yelling at the girl, calling her all possible names, from whore to piece of shit, and literally kicked her off the set: "Get another one!" he screamed at the top of his lungs. "Get whoever! It won't be worse than this slut!" After 10 minutes Miss Nobody was kneeling in tears at his feet, begging to be pardoned, and the first part of the scene was finally completed.

Then Venantino stepped in, his big hands grabbing and pulling me from the window I was trying to reach. This proved more dangerous than the drilling itself. "Let's pretend" definitively wasn't his favorite game. He was pushing me toward the bench where the drill was and a further problem arose, because the bench was too low. This time Fulci had to thank not only my theater credits but also my many years of ballet training. Only by arching my back in what is technically called a cambré did I manage to have my back on the bench, thus being in the proper position to have my head drilled.

Since I started answering interviews about my horror past or chatting with fans, the most frequent question has been: "How was the drill effect realized?" This was so frequently asked that I recently started warning journalists that if they were to pose the question, I'd bite their head off instead of drilling it. As I always say, it was indeed quite simple. I had a sort of little "pillow" attached to one side of my head, filled with stage blood and with make-up to match my skin, and that was where the drill entered. I was then splitting stage blood from my mouth (which was disgusting but not difficult) and screaming like a pig as one would be in such a situation. When the drill was coming out at the other side of my head, the prop head so painfully achieved was used. And when I was dying with my head pierced, a grip was turning a fake drill point on the other side, the edge never in sight. It was very long and shot from many camera angles, so I was tired because of the awkward position I had to maintain and pissed at Venantino using all his force to keep me down, but I was not in pain or afraid. I felt that Fulci and the crew were very excited and conscious that they were shooting something that was to be one of the movie's stronger moments, but maybe not even they were aware that that drill would become quoted and cherished for decades to come as one of the most worshipped instruments of death in horror cinema history. Generations of fans would remember when they first saw the scene, how impressed they were and, of course, would remember me as the one who was drilled. So, all in all, thank you drill, you got me into the hall of fame.

Chapter 14
A Greek Holiday to be Regretted for Life

With *City of the Living Dead* completed, I was unemployed and with no theater engagements either, the Swan Company gone forever because of its debts. So I resumed my usual life, living with "T" and sharing with him the ups and downs of our coke addiction and the continuous need for money. I realized that coke wasn't the blessed remedy I thought it was, and from time to time I tried quitting, but I couldn't face the depression and lack of energy that followed. What could be found on the drug market during these times was bad quality, and one night I collapsed and went into a sort of coma that could have been fatal if "T" hadn't promptly injected me with a tranquilizer.

I kept seeing Fulci occasionally at the Tessari evenings, and I invited him home to a party, where he had a chance to demonstrate that great sense of humor. Shortly after *City* had opened I had got a poster from the production people and hung it in the bathroom, while theater posters were proudly displayed in the living room. Fulci went to pee and came out yelling: "People, people, I am in the loo!"

My first three movies opened in 1980 almost simultaneously and were shown for a short period in cinemas that were far from first rate. Reviews were short and disdainful, but in some I was mentioned as "an interesting new actor" or "an amazing and impressive face" and that was okay with me. My theater friends didn't see them and were mostly unaware of this new side of my career. My poor father tried to watch *House of the Living Dead*, but he couldn't make it through to the end. Considering that he had a bad heart, I dismissed his apologies and forbid him to make further attempts.

Summer arrived and, as usual, I went for a lonely holiday. "T" hated the sun and the heat and considered my love for sunbathing a sort of perversion. That year I selected Greece and more specifically the Northern islands of Skopelos and Skiatos, more difficult to reach and thus less invaded by tourists, half of them gay. Even if I loved having sex with men, I wasn't enthusiastic about the so-called gay lifestyle and was very bored with queens and sissies of all sorts. Furthermore, having been to Greece before, I knew that the gay obsession for it as a paradise of Mediterranean manhood was just crap. If in old times Greece had been the cradle of homosexuality as a recognized and legalized behavior, the Turk invasion and the later homophobic predominance of the Christian Orthodox religion had swept away old habits, and Greek men were the straightest to be found. So the search for sexual adventures always ended with a melting pot of European gays from all countries fucking each other in bushes by the beach with no Greek in sight.

My summer trips were based on traveling just with a sleeping bag and a small rucksack, ready to set wherever I liked, a beach or a pine tree wood. Thus equipped, I took a plane for Athens and then a bus leading up North. If I had known what the results of that holiday were going to be, I would have quoted

A recent photo of Skopelos, Greece

Iago when talking about the row between Cassio and Montano: "And would in action glorious I had lost/Those legs that brought me to a part of it!"

One of the first days in Skiatos I went to buy something in a pharmacy and met two Italian girls who were trying to explain something to the doctor in broken English. The man himself wasn't an Oxford graduate and so they were getting nowhere. I inquired what the problem was and the older girl, named "L" (privacy again ...), anxiously explained to me that her younger sister was allergic to bee stings and had forgotten to bring the antidote; if she were to be stung she could die. With English and a few Greek words from my disastrous school past, I related the problem to the doctor so the girl could buy the medicine. We got to be friends and they put me up in the little house they had rented. "L" was also in show business and we found out that we had mutual friends in the business. When the Greek holiday was over we went back to Rome together and kept seeing each other, which led her to meet "T" and fall in love with him.

I was mildly annoyed because I had always wanted to have little in common with "T's" girlfriends, but I didn't worry, considering that since our story had started, more than 10 years before, I had seen legions of girls and women pass by his bed and fall into oblivion. Furthermore "L" was uncommonly unattractive, engineered toward fatness and with teeth that needed be taken care of by a skilled aeronautical engineer. But, like many unattractive women, she had an iron will and she was determined to nail "T" for life. He was by no means in love with her, but he was weak and passive, very much the character played by Keith Carradine in the feature film *Nashville*, summed up by his wonderful song, "I'm Easy." In future years "L's" fight to conquer him would lead to great changes in our lives and I was to regret not leaving her and her sister to their dire fate in that Greek pharmacy, to be killed by all the bees on the island.

Fall arrived and I started to be very worried with my finances, with no work in sight and my bank account shrinking by the day.

Annamaria Spasiano had retired and I had now a new agent, namely old Giuseppe Perrone, a gay wreck from the 1950s, but as a matter of fact his assistant Pino Pellegrini was in charge of everything and he called me one day saying that Umberto Lenzi wanted me for his next movie and had a script to read, with the not encouraging title of *Cannibal Ferox*.

If I had mixed reactions to the scripts of my first three movies, my thoughts after reading Lenzi's effort in screenwriting were adamant: It was a sordid piece of shit. Not only was it full of atrocities, but also it indulged in a sort of racist portrayal of natives, only faintly masked by the fact that their brutality was stirred by the white men's mischievous behavior. But the more disturbing thing was that it didn't relate to fantasy as *Cannibal Apocalypse* or to old legends like *City of the Living Dead*, but it pretended to be "real," thus connecting with the disgusting "documentaries" by Gualtiero Jacopetti, an openly Fascist director who had been on trial in the early 1960s for the hideous contents of his movies.

Not only was the script revolting, but Lenzi was offering me the role of Joe, who once again was the frail friend of the bad guy, just a pale and uninteresting version of Ricky, Bukowski and Bob. The leading male role, Mike Logan, was also very flat, but at least it would have been something new and perhaps a way not to be typecast for life as the perennial sacrificial lamb.

My final decision was to ask Pellegrini to tell Lenzi that it was the leading role or nothing and that I wanted three times the sum the production had offered. Even if I was broke, one half of me was hoping for rejection, but my offer was accepted and I was tied to the project and bound to leave in a couple of months for the far away destination of Leticia, in the Amazon. I was only mildly comforted by the fact that Lorraine De Selle would be in the movie too, in the leading female role of Gloria, the young anthropologist who was going into the jungle with her brother and a friend to prove that cannibalism didn't exist. She had to witness this with her own eyes, the scientist's instincts also aroused by the sadistic behavior of Mike Logan, a pusher who had fled from New York for the Amazon in search of emeralds.

Chapter 15
A Jungle Nightmare

There's an Italian saying that goes, "Morning will tell how the day will be." If it is true and the *Cannibal Ferox* [aka *Make Them Die Slowly*] morning was to be considered by the plane trip to Leticia, black stormy clouds were indeed gathering. To save money the production had booked our trip with different low-cost flights, with the grating side effect of having us encounter layovers that lasted almost three days. Flights were: Rome to Paris; Reykjavik to Toronto; New York to Caracas; and Bogota to Leticia, for a total of seven different planes and a few hours waiting for connections here and there. The ordeal started one January morning of 1981 in the Rome airport, where I met the cast and crew. Danilo Mattei, who was playing Gloria's brother, openly admitted that he was into cocaine and that he had high hopes about finding the best possible in Latin America, considering that we were going right into the middle of the coke golden triangle. I had thought about it too and shared his expectations, but Giovanni Masini, who was again production manager, joined us and looked us straight into the eyes, saying: "Boys ... I know you and I know where we are going; I'll watch you closely." He had worked with me in two other movies and probably the same thing happened with Danilo, and his allusion was quite clear to us both. But we thought that it wouldn't be impossible to elude his watchful eyes.

On the first plane for Paris I sat next to Umberto Lenzi and had a first taste of his egomaniacal and bombastic personality when he involved me in a parlor game of his invention, a movie trivia quiz with questions such as: "Who was the cameraman in Sergio Leone's *Fistful of Dollars*?" He of course knew all the answers out of an obsessive mania about movie credits and he was always winning and delighted about as excitedly as a six-year-old would be. From Paris on, I carefully avoided being anywhere near him and watched from a distance as some other martyr was drawn into the game. I was also informed by crew gossip that we were facing a very embarrassing situation, because Garibaldi Schwartze, the still photographer I knew from *City*, was the constant companion of Lenzi's first wife and jealousy was apparently still there. If our director was to involve me again in his demented quiz show, I would ask him who was the still photographer in Lucio Fulci's last movie.

Plane-by-plane and airport-by-airport, we were

Director Umberto Lenzi

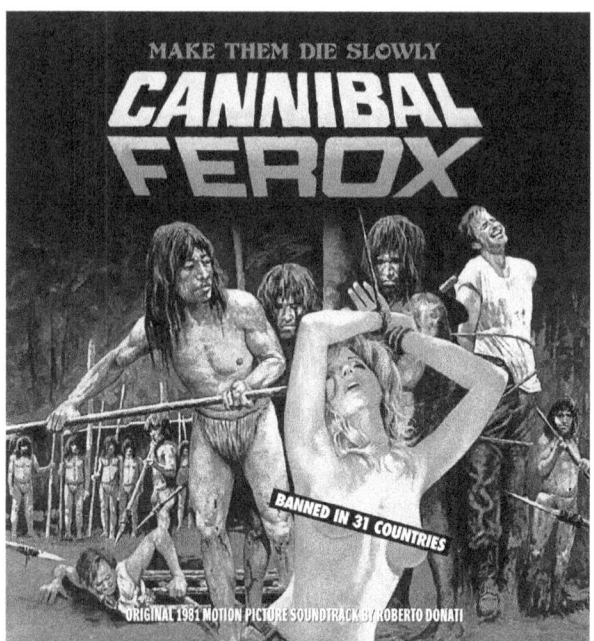

Cover art for the CD release of Roberto Donati's musical score for *Cannibal Ferox*

more and more disheveled, sweaty and utterly confused, mixing up day with night, breakfast with dinner and toeses with roses. When in Bogota we could have been a bunch of zombies, which would have made Fulci happy, and on our last small plane to Leticia I could only see a bed in front of me. When we finally arrived I didn't even glance at my whereabouts or at the hotel: I saw a mattress, collapsed on it and slept for 24 hours, not being needed on set for the first few days. But Lorraine, Danilo and Zora Kerova (who played Pat, Gloria's friend) did work the next morning, as did the whole crew. I know that working in a mine is much harder than making movies and far less paid, but being an actor has at times its wearisome shortcomings.

When I woke up to inspect the place, I immediately realized that my happiness relied on working as much as possible, because nothing around me was promising a nice time off.

Leticia was the last outpost of civilization, before thousands of miles of thick jungle in Colombian territory, existing right at the boarders with Brazil and Peru. But civilization was indeed too big a word to describe it; it was reachable only by plane or by water, which is to say the murky and yellowish Amazon River on which shores it had been built. Real houses were few and far between and most buildings were plate or wood huts facing on the three or four dusty streets that crossed each other. But these streets, quite strangely, were busy with traffic produced by huge Jeeps and costly motorcycles. No shops were to be seen, just a sparely furnished supermarket, no bars, but a porno movie theater and a casino, both in creepy cabins, stared back at us. The contradictions were easily explained by the fact that the cocaine business was making people rich and able to drive luxury vehicles or gamble and bet, but they had nowhere to go and no way to spend their money apart from parading in the streets and driving as if they were in Le Mans. There were of course different gangs of cocaine dealers and their favorite sport was to shoot each other as soon as the heat was somehow mitigated by sunset, in a sort of sick ritual that could be contemplated from the porch of our hotel, as if in the first row in a theater. Almost every evening there

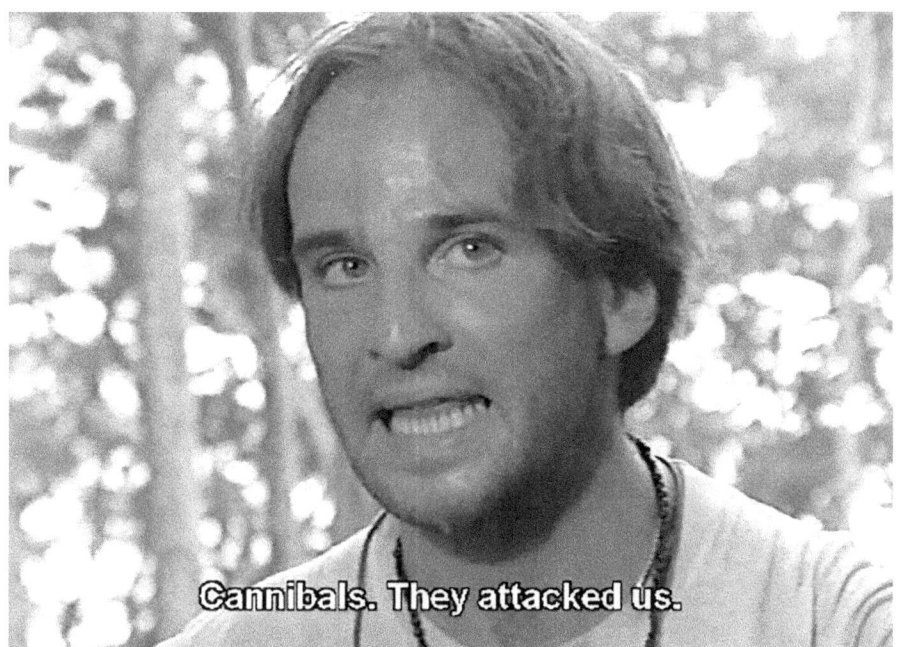

Johnny was baffled when trying to find nuance in his character of villainous Mike Logan.

was some running, shouting and shooting that didn't seem to bother the locals, who were not involved. A real war was then actually happening in the hills just outside of town. Peru and Colombia were quarrelling over some territorial boarders and bursts of machine gun fire could be heard in the distance, with the occasional flash of a small bomb. Such a delightful little Paradise, indeed.

Our hotel was a one-story building quite in the style of an ancient Rome villa, with a large inside porch circling a green-yellow pond that had the pompous and undeserved name of "swimming pool." It was dirty and dilapidated and run by lazy waiters who seemed happy with having "no" for an answer to whatever question was asked. Do you have any cooler Coke? No! Can I have a toast or a sandwich? No! Is there a way to have hot water in the room? No! This last question wasn't indeed very frequently asked, because the heat was overwhelming and no air-conditioning was in sight, so a cold shower was appreciated, but it would have been more so if the running water hadn't been so intermittently weak with low pressure.

Waiting to shoot, I stayed mostly in my room, reading a book or going through the script, wondering what the fuck was I to do with the character of Mike Logan, if you pardon my French. He was a bad guy, full stop. No insights, no shades, nothing. I tried thinking of some great villains portrayed in Shakespeare's plays, like Aaron in *Titus Andronicus* or even Iago, but it was of little help. Their lines were composed by a genius and not by Lenzi, and there's quite a difference in saying. "Oh, beware, my lord, of jealousy!/It is the green-eyed monster which doth mock/The meat it feeds on" versus "Shut up twat!" This was of course Mike Logan's favorite phrase for the gentle sex. Even

Johnny states that for the role of Mike Logan he worked out in the gym to be more muscular and that he let his hair grow, coloring it a more aggressive blond tone.

the animal naming game was no fun; Mike was some sort of feline, not noble enough to be a lion but surely as cruel as a tiger. I decided to focus on the fact he was a coke addict, something I unfortunately knew a lot about. I didn't cut off people's cocks when high on coke, but I could transform my own nervousness and neurotic behavior into his spells of sadistic fury. Or at least I could try to do my best. Having known two months in advance about my engagement, I had time to work on my appearance. I had worked out in the gym so my chest and arms looked more macho-muscular and I let my hair grow, using chamomile to turn it from my natural honey color into a more aggressive blond.

So, some three days later I tiger walked to work, arriving almost by night time because the jungle locations were three or four hours away by boat. We had to begin shooting as soon as possible, forced to stop before the afternoon rain started pouring, typical for that time of the year, but something the production supervisors hadn't foreseen.

In my contract there was a clause saying that I would have the "star" treatment "due to my being a leading actor." I dismissed it as pompous and ridiculous and now wondered what the fuck it meant considering I was exactly in the same boat as the others, from nightmare trip to terrible hotel. But on that first day, the special treatment materialized in a diminutive Colombian lady, who stood behind me with a sun umbrella and a warm smile. I never liked to be waited on more than necessary and abhorred the idea of that sort of personal slave, so I thanked her and told her not to bother, but only to call her back after an hour, almost fainting from heat and perspiration. The humid hot climate in the

Amazon was something I never found in any other part of the world. It was like an invisible cloud getting into your throat and making it hard, not only to move, but even to stand erect. And the heat was not the only problem! Insects of all sorts were everywhere, on the ground and on the trees in the form of worms of all sizes or in the air as bird-sized mosquitoes, famished for blood. We were showering in insect repellent every couple of hours, but some sting or bite was nevertheless always there, making us hope that the malaria therapy we had started a week before leaving was effective. The repellent was nevertheless useless for worms and we were frightened when told that there was a special kind, as little and stingy as a needle, that fell from the trees and could get under your skin and then into your bones, deforming them. That was the reason for the crew wearing hats, but that was of course impossible for the actors, so we just avoided being under trees as much as possible, which made the little lady and her sun umbrella a blessing, because standing in the sun waiting for everything to be ready was indeed torture. There were of course also invisible dangers such as snakes of all sizes, and each time I had to lead my way into wild bushes with a machete (one of Mike Logan's favorite activities), I was crossing myself hoping that the noise and stick hitting on the ground, provided by the crew before shooting, had scared away whatever form of wild life.

These were, as a matter of fact, the only occasions where Lenzi's incessant screaming activity could have been of some use. The man was shouting at whomever and for whatever from morning to dusk and his outbursts weren't the half ironic insults of Deodato or the Biblical wrath of Fulci, but a vulgar and heavy cursing that involved God and all the Saints and could become annoyingly personal, with reference to height, weight or one's mother's sexual habits. The Italian crew had worked with him before and was used to it, so they just sent back half-mouthed curses and kept doing their job, but the locals, most of them working in a movie for the first time, were taking him seriously and were in a total state of terror that led them to even worse results. The sound assistant, who was so insulted the first time he was late in saying "Partito!" (camera rolling), realized that to prevent being reproached again he had to say the word at the top of his lungs, with consequences that I will relate later on.

All in all, the Amazon was the un-friendliest spot on Earth, created by God in a moment where he was severely pissed with humankind. Lenzi was the worst director I ever had … and the mix was lethal. As I said once in an interview, you can bear to shoot in the Amazon if directed by Kubrick, and you can bear to be directed by Lenzi if they are shooting in a five-star hotel in Saint Tropez, but do not let the two meet.

Anyway Lenzi didn't dare shout at me and our professional relationship was coldly polite. After a few attempts to involve me in conversations, stating the fact that he was as influential a director in cinema history as John Ford, he had backed in front of my smiling silences and had left me alone until the day he approached me saying that the next day I had to kill the pig.

Many cruelties to animals had already happened, demonstrating that Lenzi, who was by the way the only author of story and script, was indeed a sadist. I wasn't on set the day a tortoise was killed and then eaten, and neither was I on set the day a sort of local mongoose was supposed to be gulped down by an anaconda, but the events of this last scene had been told to me by the shocked crew. The snake wasn't hungry, but, just to make Lenzi happy, it had condescended to open its mouth and take the little prey in, without harming it; it would have been satisfactory to leave it at this, but Lenzi wanted to witness death, so he had insisted, until the cameraman called "cut," to keep shooting the sequence.

The killing of the little pig that had fallen into the same trap as Gloria (Lorraine character) was included in the script to show that Mike Logan was himself a sadist, rescuing the girl, but wildly raging on the little animal with his machete. Not in my worst nightmares I had thought it would happen for real. So when Lenzi told me about it I thought it was a joke. But he insisted, quoting the script, so I understood he meant to kill the little pig and I told him that he could consider himself lucky that we were in the midst of nowhere, or I would have called the animal protection people right away. Our first public row ensued and it ended with him saying that Robert De Niro would have done it, and me answering him that Robert De Niro would have kicked his ass all the way back to Rome.

Danilo Mattei, who was into a most annoying macho man trip, volunteered to be the slaughterer (stunting my hands), but at the end the killer was the special effects guy, Big Bomber, who seemed to be tied to whatever movie I was acting in. But from Pigs Paradise the soul of the little animal was crying for revenge and I accomplished its wish, even if not by choice. When later on we were to shoot my close-ups during the killing, I had to plunge my machete (a real big cutting thing) into a plastic bowl filled with stage blood and Big Bomber was holding it, but in the most stupid way, with both hands cupping underneath. Grinning with sadistic fury I went for the bowl with all my force, cut it and got into Big Bomber's hand, almost severing his thumb. It was quite a serious wound and he was taken to the local hospital, which was probably more risky than the cut itself; I had been there before, because during one of the never-ending flights one of my ears suffered from changes from pressure and became "stuck," but seeing the unhygienic conditions of the place and medical instruments, I simply cried "miracle!" and ran away, waiting for my ear to unplug by itself.

A big discussion followed the pig accident, with Masini stating that my scruples were hypocritical because I hadn't complained about the moccocoi (a big worm) eaten alive by a native in another scene. Weren't worms animals as well? My answer to that was that eating worms was a local habit, disgusting to us, but well established locally, while killing a little pig just for the sake of Lenzi's cinematic genius was butchery, and I have to say that the majority sided with me.

The relations among the actors were good, but nowhere near the camaraderie that I experienced with *House* or *City*. Walter Lucchini, the guy playing Joe (the role I had dismissed), was a dancer and totally inexperienced as an actor, his English was quite basic, but he was humble and easy going and I could talk with him about dance teachers we have had in common or the ballet world in general. Zora Kerowa was also very good natured and pleasant company, but she had started a sex thing with Danilo, and when not on set, the two of them were mostly in a bedroom shooting a private movie of a different sort. My real set anchor was Lorraine, but in recent years we quarreled quite a bit, after she became a producer and I had to deal with her as a screenwriter. But I will always be grateful to her for the good company and the French bitching and gossiping during *Cannibal Ferox*. What we mainly had in common was the mutual dislike for Lenzi, who had arrived at the point of almost throwing her into the river to shoot a scene she had asked to postpone because she had her period. Unfortunately I wasn't on set that day, otherwise I would have used my "star" status to stop him. The only problem was that she was scared of every insect in sight and called me day and night because there was a spider or a lizard in her room. I instructed her to circle her bed with repellent, as I was doing, and hope for the best.

Cover art for the laserdisc release

Another comforting feminine presence was Fiamma Maglione, who was there with multi-purpose tasks such as playing Mike Logan's New York girlfriend, composing the music score for the movie and being the companion of Mino Loy, the producer who was also there. Fiamma was a quiet, warm woman with a sense of humor and endless patience that showed, not only in personal relationships, but also in her constantly embroidering complicated patterns. I told her I could knit because my grandmother taught me when I had a broken leg as a child and I was dying of boredom, so she tried to teach me how to do needlework, but it was just too difficult. Mino Loy also proved to be a nice gentleman and pleasant company and it was with them and with Lorraine that I spent the little free time I had, mostly some late evenings and Sundays spent around the so-called pool. Lorraine had nicknamed me Naughty Mike and was teasing me by asking, "What's Naughty Mike reading?" or "What did Naughty Mike have for breakfast?"

Shooting was very tiring because of the weather, the mud that covered us and the long hours spent in the boat going back and forth from locations. We all gathered for dinner in the hotel, which consisted only of rice and chicken and chicken and rice: no vegetables, no fresh fruit. After 10 days of chicken, Lorraine stated that next day she was going to lay an egg. And lunches on set were as well unexciting, consisting with a variety of only three or four sandwiches,

An autographed photo of Johnny from *Cannibal Ferox* as the cannibals are about to tie him up, before they tear him apart.

half of them going to the little crowd of starving children that gathered in front of us every time some food was in sight. We had a lot of local extras playing the cannibal tribe and their situation was disgraceful due to the exploitation their land and their lifestyle had suffered. They were poor as hell, dressed in rags and many of the adult men were alcoholic. The younger ones, such as the good looking guy who was playing the chief of the tribe, seemed to hate us and I couldn't but agree and would have said so if I could communicate in their language. But they spoke a local dialect only faintly similar to Spanish, and even if they had lowered their defenses, talking about complicated matters would have been impossible.

Their poverty was so terrible that they were more than keen to give one of their children to the first European or North American asking for custody, hopefully out of a good heart, but not necessarily so. One day, during a lunch break, I was walking from one of the two villages that had been built for the movie to the other, on a path in the jungle that ran for maybe half a mile. Midway I spotted a little girl about four or five, all alone and desperately crying. I tried asking where her mama was but she didn't seem to understand. She didn't look hurt, so I took her in my arms and reached the village I was directed to. Half the "tribe" was there, many of them women, and I asked who were the parents of the little girl. Nobody answered. So I walked back the half mile to the first village and repeated my question. Once again silence. I insisted and didn't know what to do, when finally the little girl outstretched her arms toward a woman who was trying to hide behind a tall man. It was obviously her mother and she quite unwillingly embraced the girl that she had perhaps hoped I could adopt.

Another unpleasant accident occurred when I had to deal with the Indio playing the native who had guided Mike and Joe into the jungle to find emeralds in the river. Pissed with the fact that not a single stone was found, Naughty Mike, after a good snort of cocaine, attacked him and tortured him, first by pecking at his eye with the machete and then using it to castrate the poor fellow. The guy was more cultivated than the others and considered himself an actor, complaining about the fact that I was hurting him during the fight in the river, where I had to push his head underwater. I was no Venantino Venantini and tried to be as gentle as possible, but his stupid cannibal wig, too large for him, kept moving and Lenzi was for a change screaming from the shore, so I had to grab him by his neck, which he found insulting. Well, in due time his fellows were to avenge him as I had done with the pig …

In the meantime, while I was snorting flour in the scenes pretending it was coke, not a single ounce of the real stuff was to be found, to the utter frustration of Danilo and myself, as different as black and white in every regard, but similar in our common search for our beloved drug. The problem was that if coca leaves were to be found at every corner, the locals didn't have the machinery to refine it and were just sending the stuff to big towns. It was usual, in the middle of the jungle, to see a little plane taking off from nowhere and quickly disappear. Once, in one of our never ending boat trips, I asked the owner what it was and he matter of factly said: "It's a plane loaded with coca leaves going to Bogota," as if it had been his grandmother going to church. For all our efforts we had to resign ourselves to smoke the leaves, whose effects were entirely different from the refined coke and not very exciting. Masini needn't worry, because smoking the leaves was an established local practice and no one would have arrested us for that.

As the shooting proceeded, more and more wild forms of life participated in the movie, both on and off camera. In the script Danilo's character was dying eaten alive by the piranhas, and when the day came all the local fishermen kept arriving with crates full of the little monsters that had probably been conceived in a brainstorming session between the Almighty and Carlo Rambaldi or Sergio Stivaletti. They were round and flat, the shape of a tennis ball that could fully open up and become just a mouth, with as many teeth as one could imagine. There was no problem in shooting them in the water, but Lenzi wanted a close-up detailing at least one of them biting a chunk out of Danilo's leg, and to achieve this momentous effect in cinema history, he asked the dresser to sew the fish to Danilo's pants. She was an old woman who had worked in the movies all her life, and she worked with everything from zombies to dinosaurs, so she tried her best here. But she kept yelling, "It bites!" and worked as fast as she could as to complete the work before the piranha died from lack of water oxygen. After 10 or more dead piranhas, even Lenzi's stubbornness had to surrender to the laws of nature.

For another occasion, I was having lunch on a pirogue with Zora in the middle of the Amazon River and, suddenly, she got all excited and pointed

The character of Mike Logan is about to lose his head.

at my back shouting: "Look, look!" I did and saw a big fish, very much like a dolphin but intensely red, jumping in and out of the water. "Please, let's get closer!" Zora asked me, so I started rowing in that direction and got quite close when I noticed that local extras in another small boat were following us at full speed and making alarmed gestures. Thank God I stopped and it was explained that the fish was indeed the local river dolphin, but, to match everything else in the surroundings, it wasn't friendly and lovable as the sea ones, but a son of a bitch whose favorite sport was to capsize boats and attack people. If Lenzi had known about these cannibal dolphins he would surely have cast one in the movie, possibly quarreling with it because it wasn't going on the right mark.

Day-by-day, with a lot of shouting and far more grinning than recommended in acting schools, I had embodied Mike Logan's sadistic instincts and vicious behavior. I had tortured, castrated and killed the native guide, I had killed the pig, I had shot dead a native teenager after attempting rape on his little sister in a scene that added the necessary sexually perverse touch to the revolting script, I had let my friend Joe die without giving a shit and, instead of rescuing Gloria and Pat who were kept prisoner in a sort of giant mole nest, I had cut the rope that could let them free. But my doom day was coming and the Indio revenge was arriving in three steps: castration, amputation of an arm and final death by head cutting monkey-style, with me tied under a table with my skull protruding from a hole. This done, the Cannibals were to feed on my brain and, in my opinion, become more stupid because of it.

The castration wouldn't have been a very difficult scene if compared to my previous movie demises as the one in *Apocalypse*, but a Lenzi movie is a Lenzi movie, so, to start with, the tree I was tied to turned out to be an ant nest and the damn things were all over me in a flash. I tried complaining, but Lenzi was in a hurry, so I was just sprayed with repellent and left to my destiny, which was to fall into the hands of the make-up man, whose intellect matched the one of a disabled piranha. With Lenzi shouting "Hurry up, hurry up!," the man thought no better than gluing the prosthetic penis to my real one, without any kind of tissue or fabric to protect it, so, when he took it off at the end of the scene, my yell was far more effective than the one I had produced when castrated. Mike Logan then took control of me and I literally kicked the man in the ass until I was stopped by the crew.

The cutting of my arm went on with no problems, but not so with the head. I had to do just nothing but stay tied under the table with my prosthetic skull protruding from the hole, and then get my face covered in blood and die, while the cannibals were feasting on what was inside Mike's sick head. Great! The only problem was that the "brain" was made of an obnoxious mix of mashed bananas and stage blood and our extras, not having attended the Actors Studio, reacted to it with disgusted faces instead of ecstatic grins as if tasting pate de foie gras. It took 20 takes to get to an acceptable result and at the end of the scene I was covered with mud, dust and stage blood. The prospect of staying like that for the four-hour boat trip back to the hotel was not very appealing, so I asked for a bar of soap, got naked and went into the river, something I had seen the natives do many a time. I was getting clean when, suddenly, something of undefined nature skimmed over my dick. I had a flash image of the piranha's mouth going for the flesh and literally fled from the water looking like Mickey Mouse flying away from danger, when he appears to get airy wheels attached to his feet.

Risking castration by a piranha was the final act of my jungle adventure. The actors went back to Rome, this time with an acceptable layover at Leticia, Bogota, Caracas and Rome. Thee rest of the crew went to New York to film the opening sequences of the movie. When they returned I only had to do a few interior scenes at the Rome studio, one of them the sex scene with Zora.

But before that happened, Mino Loy, just back from New York, phoned me in a state of utter desperation, saying that he needed my help. What happened was that Lenzi's fury toward the sound assistant on the first day had made the guy say "Partido!" but without actually doing anything, so all the jungle scenes (more than two-thirds of the movie) had no sound. A script for dubbing had to be done and it couldn't be the original one because many things had changed in shooting. So Loy begged me to stay at the cutting table and lip-read the lines. It was an ordeal because the machinery wasn't the computerized type now in use but the old one that had to be moved manually from here to there, but I managed to do it even if cursing Lenzi for his stupidity.

This done, the cabin interior scenes didn't present problems and Zora proved to be much less a prude than Lorraine had been in *House*. The sex scene went on smoothly with us chatting and joking stark naked in between takes. It was also the only occasion I heard Lenzi saying something funny when stating that sexy movies were the most relaxing for a director, because he had only to say: "Camera rolling! Undies down!" and enjoy the show.

Chapter 16
More Opera and a New Side Career

Cannibal Ferox had been an ordeal and I wasn't even satisfied with what I had done as an actor, but it had paid well and for some time I needn't worry too much about working and could concentrate on some private matters that demanded my full attention.

While I was at the other side of the world, "L" had profited from my absence and invaded the apartment, which was a huge loft with two wide terraces that only had two bedrooms, mine and "C's." We weren't a married pair, so we slept together from time to time, not necessarily having sex, but we also enjoyed our privacy and some side relations performed in our bedrooms. The word "privacy" meant nothing to "L," who was invading all the spaces and not just "T's" room at night. She had to be fought back by all means. It wasn't difficult, because "T" was waiting for my return as the Alamo survivors were waiting for reinforcements. His behavior and feelings toward women were typical of 90 percent of the male sex; he liked fucking them but he didn't want to be hand-tied and strangled by possessiveness and have a woman attached to him as a mussel to a rock, which was exactly what "L" was doing. But, as is the case with many men, he wasn't able to defend himself effectively and his reaction tended to be just getting morose and fidgety, as she became a royal pain in the ass. As my male readers will know, one of the most fearsome sides of a woman's character is the "Florence Nightingale Syndrome": tending to a man, curing him of his bad habits and turning him into Prince Charming; thus creating the wonderful sado-masochistic short circuit so many marriages are built upon. Many a time "T" had used me as a bogeyman to keep too ardent females at a distance; after all I owned the apartment and had some rights in dictating house rules. Truthfully, I had used him in the same way, but less frequently, because some gay men can get clingy at times, but not as much as women; they generally understand and value the "Bim Bam Thank You Sam" way of life, while the original formula "Bim Bam Thank You Ma'am" is just wishful male imagination.

So "L" had to retreat behind the "pre-Amazon" boarders and life went on as usual, but deep in my heart I knew that it was just a truce and that she was working on some secret weapon to be used in due time.

But, "L" apart, there was something strange in "T's" behavior. As much as I tried inquiring, I couldn't tell what it was and after a while I had to stop thinking about it because a new challenging job was offered me by Maestro Hans Werner Henze, a well-known German composer who lived in Italy and was the artistic director of a Music Festival in Montepulciano, a historic town in Tuscany. Henze, an open homosexual, had been courting me for a while and I always had politely escaped his passes, but this time he was talking business, offering me to direct *Cinderella* by Gioacchino Rossini, an opera I adored.

I had been an opera fan since the age of six, when my father took me to see Puccini's *Madame Butterfly*. A few years later I started to enjoy the box-seat offered me by my Jemolo-Morghen grandparents at the Rome Opera House and didn't miss a performance, with the privilege of watching some historic productions by Visconti. I collected opera records and, while boys my age were delighted by the Beatles and the Rolling Stones, I had been listening to Verdi, Bellini and Donizetti. Directing a real opera was a dream of mine, and *Opera*, by Luciano Berio, hadn't accomplished my artistic desires. It was a modern score and not very much to my liking. So I of course accepted, even if I was doing it almost for free, but I did it as a guest of the Festival, which covered lodging and expenses.

Hans Werner Henze, a well-known German composer who lived in Italy, offered Johnny a job directing an opera.

It was fun on one hand because I was sharing a house with Aldo Buti (who had always been my set and costume designer), his assistant and lover Maurizio, a debonair dandy and Patrizia Terreno, my former Lady Macbeth, who was trained in music and was my assistant on this occasion. I brought coke from Rome and we were feasting on it, but it stopped being pleasurable and became a neurotic obsession when I was faced with the problems Henze had created for me. *Cinderella* is a very difficult opera and requires not only good singers but also extremely good actors that could play-sing the comic and sophisticated roles and be fluent with the difficult words of the libretto. What I had was a 40-year-old Greek contralto in the title role (so short that when she was in front of her partner, an Australian tenor six feet tall, it looked like she could blowjob him standing), an English baritone who didn't speak one word of Italian and some other German and Dutch singers in minor roles. My Cinderella could sing in quite good Italian, but she was so bored after years of a mediocre career that she often mixed the words of an opera with others and sang some Verdi words for Rossini or the other way round. The tenor was as good an actor as a telephone pole and the others were just acceptable, but the real tragedy was the English baritone, who had the very important role of Cinderella's stepfather (instead of a stepmother as in the fairy tale) and tongue twisters in his part to drive mad an Italian. Patrizia was working with him alone every morning, but nevertheless, on opening night, he panicked, and instead of singing his first words, he just went "la-la-la-la-la." Rehearsals were nightmarish and I sought refuge in some sex adventures, in this case with a cello player in the orchestra or a Japanese painter who one night took me for a walk in the country and tried seducing me in a meadow while talking oriental nonsense such as, "Look—cloud in the sky—looks like dragon." I was snorting coke like mad and I was often sick. I knew I had to stop, but circumstances seemed never to be favorable.

When *Cinderella* was over, with some bad reviews and with Henze still waiting to be sexually rewarded for his nice offer, I got back to Rome and started working on another project that this time proved very satisfactory. Saverio Marconi, after the Cannes award recognized his *Father and Master*, was having a successful movie career and had become quite famous. He cleverly used this power to pursue his wish to stage musicals, and he got some money from the municipality of Tolentino, in central Italy, his mother's hometown, where they cherished him as a distinguished citizen and allowed him to produce a camera musical with just two performers, Marina Garroni and himself. The title was *Happy End*. I wrote the play and lyrics to the songs with Marina and had a lot of fun in portraying two young actors sharing a house and experiencing the many difficulties of money and career. It was a light comedy, but quite witty, and after the opening in Tolentino we brought it to Rome, in the same "Teatro delle Muse" that had witnessed my first meeting with Annamaria Spasiano. It was a lucky place for me, because *Happy End* had an immense success, with some fans coming back to see it more than one time and stage royalties coming out of curiosity for this new and unexpected hit. *Happy End* also made me meet new people who were going to be important in my future life.

Johnny signed on for Saverio Marconi's (pictured) *Happy End*, signing both as actor in the play and co-writing the songs.

My brother Marco came to see the show with a friend, a young journalist by the name of Giovanni Forti. He was bewitched by my charms and started courting me like mad. I didn't find him attractive but I finally gave in because he was very funny, witty and he proved to be the most phenomenal sex machine I ever played around with. At times it's true that you shouldn't judge a book by its cover. We became sex buddies, but we weren't in love and it was Giovanni who introduced me to his friend Fabrizio, a boy two years younger than me. With him I started a relationship that lasted more than one year. Fabrizio was very upper class and introduced me to his friends, who were young members of the aristocracy or the industrial bourgeoisie. In this group was a clever girl, Countess Carolina di Valmarana, who had been educated in England by her aunt who was married to an English lord. I was very attracted by her from an intellectual point of view and loved her company, but unfortunately she didn't arouse my sexual instincts, so we stayed merely friends. And it was Carolina who brought her father to see *Happy End*.

Count Paolo di Valmarana was the heir of one of the noblest Venetian families, the owners of the wonderful Villa Valmarana ai Nani in Vicenza (Nani meaning dwarfs in Italian), designed by Palladio and adorned with Tiepolo frescoes. The name of the villa came from an old legend, which said that a young Countess was a dwarf herself and wasn't allowed out so as not to realize that other people were different physically. But one day she climbed on the wall surrounding the villa, learned the truth and committed suicide by jumping to her doom. All her dwarf servants were petrified by sorrow and transformed into the grotesque statues that are on top of the wall. With a sense of humor, Count Paolo used to say that they hadn't improved much since. He was a movie critic and an important manager of Channel One of the Italian State Television (Rai). The revolution that opened the Italian T.V. market to private networks was about to come, but in 1981 it consisted of just the three state channels of Rai, Channel One being the most important. When he came to see *Happy End*, Paolo Valmarana was trying to produce the first T.V. serial in Italian history, based on the Rome Airport of Fiumicino and thus named *International Airport*. He liked the wit and humor that Marina and myself had put in the play and called us to be part of the group of screenwriters. The director was Enzo Tarquini, whom I had worked with in *Crude Oil Is Dangerous*. *International Airport* lasted for three seasons and later on Tarquini stopped directing and became an important executive for Channel Two. He loved the way Marina and I wrote and our ability to craft dialogue, which came from our acting careers, and he kept calling us to write miniseries and T.V.

Marina Garroni and Giovanni Lombardo Radice wrote the screenplay for Umberto Lenzi's *Daughter of the Jungle*.

Sabrina Siani (right) and Renato Miracco

movies. A new side career had started and I would keep writing for 25 years, only to be stopped by politics, as I will relate later.

Another fan of *Happy End* was Mino Loy and he too asked Marina and myself to write the screenplay for a movie directed by ... Umberto Lenzi! The title was *Daughter of the Jungle* and it was a light comedy based on the good graces of half-naked starlet Sabrina Siani as a female Tarzan featuring a farcical plot very much in the line of the comic-adventurous movies with Bud Spencer and Terence Hill. It was a producer's movie and I dealt directly with Loy; I got to see Lenzi only once or twice. I wrote the subject in Loy's office and I worked with the production budget limits: "They meet 10 soldiers ..." I would say, "three soldiers." Loy corrected, "In the fight on the yacht ..." was changed to "boat." "Two elephants arrive ..." became "No elephants." And so on. But Loy was a sport and it was fun.

Another important event in my life took place that year: the death of my grandfather Arturo Carlo Jemolo from a sudden stroke at the age of 91.

In the last years he and my grandmother had mellowed in their criticism about my professional trade and had been grateful to me, because I was the member of the family most concerned with their problems in old age, visiting them often and helping them with house necessities, such as selecting domestic helpers. The final part of their life had been burdened with great losses, because one year after my mother's passing, her older brother Guglielmo, nicknamed Titi, had died (also of a heart attack), leaving them with just their youngest daughter, my aunt Viviana. Viv was only 14 years my senior and I adored her because she was the person in the family most similar to me in many regards. She was living by herself, unmarried and determined to be free to do whatever she wanted, which was mainly traveling the world in quite an obsessive way that reminded me of the incessant trips of Empress Elizabeth of Austria. She was anorexic (a distinctive mark of the family), whimsical and possessed a bitter sense of humor that could be at times offensive. A fantastic person in my opinion, but not the devoted homebody daughter my grandparents had hoped for. They were constantly anxious about her whereabouts and she had unwillingly agreed to send a telegram every two days from wherever she was. She once went to

Iceland and the much-awaited telegram did not arrive. My grandfather, who was renowned for his pessimism, immediately thought the worst and, not knowing where she was staying, summoned a journalist friend, who was in Reykjavik for the Spassky-Fischer final match in the world chess tournament, to find her by all means. He succeeded, but Viv's fury was even bigger than her parents' worries and they cried for days after suffering all her insults on the phone.

To overcome the sorrow for the loss of his two children, my grandfather kept working at his lawyer firm and cemented his status as the national moral authority by writing a weekly article at one of the most influential Italian newspapers, complaining about the loss of values in the country, the increasing political corruption and the lack of morality. On the other side, my grandmother was always home, reading, praying and knitting, and the family used to reunite around her before dinner, sharing with her a glass of Scotch, a habit that had been suggested to her by her doctor as a heart support, but that she had stretched to the form of becoming a light alcoholic, even if in a very ladylike way. "Just a little bit more for my arteries," she said already tipsy, and we used to comment that her arteries should be indeed by then the size of the Mont Blanc tunnel. After two or three Scotches she could start singing risqué French couplets without imagining the subtext of the lyrics and her favorite was, "What did the bride have for dinner on the first night? A quarter salami and half a pigeon." If we tried to explain to her that there was a double meaning, she dismissed the idea by saying that we had "l'esprit mal tourné" (a dirty mind). Once I was alone with her, both quite drunk, she confronted me about my sex life with men (she had known about this from friends gossiping). "Doesn't it disgust you?" she asked. "I mean we women must do it to have children, but you are a man, why do you do it?" The idea that a penis could be something enjoyable was preposterous to her and I could only imagine what my grandfather's sex life had been like.

Considering the personality he was, my grandfather's death was a state affair and I was considered the most apt to receive the mourners that counted political personalities, Prime Ministers, Cardinals and even the President of the Republic, whose visit created a turmoil with security on every roof overlooking the house. For two days I smiled, shook hands and tried preventing my grandmother making blunders and not always succeeding. The last evening everybody had left when the doorbell rang. It was the Minister of Foreign affairs, one of my grandfather's students in the Law Faculty. His name was Colombo and I tried to make my grandmother understand who he was by underlining the "His Excellency" title, but she didn't hear me and went on like, "Colombo …we had a maid whose name was Colombo … are you a relation?"

When the funeral was over, I was faced with the fact that I was inheriting quite a lot of money. If my grandfather had been as unscrupulous and greedy as other reputed lawyers, he would have been a multi-millionaire, but he had always acted on strict ethical rules, helping those in need for free and limiting his bills to the point that once he sent such a small fee to Fiat (the car industry owned by the Agnelli family) that their accountants thought he had forgotten to include a zero and added it to the sum. When he received the money he immediately sent back what he hadn't asked for.

Nevertheless he left some good money to be added to paintings, furniture, silver and jewels, because my grandmother had decided to retire into a care facility for the elderly and was closing the house, which already belonged to Viv and that she was anxious to sell, thus closing the doors on a family life she had always abhorred.

My share was a third of the third that included my brothers and me (the other two going to Viv and to my cousin Andrew, Titi's son), but it was enough to buy from them the sole property of my huge loft and to save some money for the black moments I might face with my work, with long stretches between jobs.

I was running the high risk of spending a great part of my inheritance on cocaine, but a sudden revelation made me abruptly curtail my drug abuse. I found out what was bothering "T," making him sleepy and not quite himself. He had switched from cocaine to heroin. He was just sniffing it, but I had known many people that had started out so but then went into injecting it, with the everyday risk of an overdose. For the first time I took the fatherly role. I grabbed him by his shirt and hissed into his face that either he quit immediately and started seeing a psychologist or he could leave the house that moment. He was too clever not to see my point and did as suggested. I stated that cocaine too was out and that we had to stop selling marijuana and start a new life, clean of addictions. I sold what was left of the grass and have never touched coke since. Detoxifying was very hard, but I kept my promise and was greatly helped by Marina and her companion, Massimo Melloni, who had been my closest friend since teenage time. The year before their first child was born and during that summer I rented a little house by the sea with them. Sitting on the porch I felt like a 100 year old and didn't even have the force to stretch my arms for the baby who was taking his first steps. I fully realized how destructive my behavior had been and more so when I started having serious problems with my teeth, ruined by the stupid habit, so frequent among coke users, to rub one's gums with what was left after snorting. If not for cocaine a lot of my grandfather's money went to the dentist, preventing me from wearing dentures at the age of 27. As I have been honest in relating my addictions, I am still being honest when I say that from that moment on my only drug of choice was tobacco. I slowly stopped drinking as well and I am now almost a teetotaler. If you survive your youth, you have a chance of becoming wise.

Chapter 17
The Greatest Loss

The first part of 1982 went by quite eventless. I kept writing the *International Airport* scripts and got two small movie roles, one with Jerry London and the other with Sergio Martino.

London was directing a T.V. miniseries called *The Scarlet and the Black* about the story of Monsignor Hugh O'Flaherty, a real-life Irish Catholic priest who saved thousands of Jews and Allied refugee POWs in Nazi-occupied Rome. I auditioned for the role of Colonel Kappler, but I was too young and only got the diminutive role of a German soldier. But I had the privilege to shake hands with Gregory Peck, who was starring as Monsignor O'Flaherty, and I had a quick glimpse of Ava Gardner, aged and fattened, but her eyes still shining as stars.

The Martino work was also for T.V., as a mini-series in its longer version, but it was edited for a shorter version for movie theaters and the theatrical title was *Murder in an Etruscan Cemetery* [aka *The Scorpion with Two Tails*]. Martino was a rocky man of few words. He had seen *City of the Living Dead* and just told me, "I want you to do exactly the same thing you did for Lucio." So I twisted my shoulder and gave birth to a sort of Bob 2, a character whose name I don't recall as I don't remember anything about the plot, only that I was a demented servant and in love with the girl played by French actress Elvire Audray. My role appeared in the miniseries, but it was completely cut from the movie version, including my death, which took place in a fire, provided by pipes installed on the entire floor of some sort of crypt or dungeon. The pipes had holes where the flames erupted and spread, and during rehearsals they were acceptably low. But as soon as Martino called action the special effect guy pumped gas at full speed and I found myself in a flaming Hell, feeling quite like Scarlett O'Hara in the Atlanta burning, but with no Rhett Butler to rescue me. I wasn't wearing any kind of protection and so prayed to God, and I died by crouching on myself like a hedgehog. If anyone tells you acting is a no-risk business, don't believe it.

Strange as it might seem, I didn't have a T.V. set in

my house. My parents had considered it the worst capitalistic invention ever and never bought one, and "T" couldn't care less all the same. So, on June 25, 1982 I went to a friend's place early in the morning to watch the whole wedding ceremony of Charles, Prince of Wales, and Diana Spencer's marriage.

An English governess had educated my mother and she had passed to me a deep respect for the British monarchy, with accounts of the brave behavior of King George VI and the Queen during the war. I personally cherished Queen Elizabeth and had applauded when she refused to sign a diplomatic agreement with South Africa, still aware of the shame of apartheid. Deep in my heart, I am convinced that if Italy had had a decent Royal Family instead of the treacherous and coward Savoia the country would have had a much better destiny, probably avoiding some shameful Presidents and a clown such as Berlusconi as Prime Minister.

In this spirit I watched the marriage of the century and wished them all the best from all my heart, a wish that wasn't going to come true. Having witnessed her marriage, along with millions of other people in the world, I felt it was my duty to watch her funeral on September 6, 1997.

As it often happens in an actor's career, I went in the space of a few weeks from having no job to being fully busy. In the last part of the year I was offered three different roles, all of them quite intriguing: a phony rock star in *Flipper*, the first movie by my friend Andrea Barzini; a Russian spy in *The Atlantis Project* [*Progetto Atlantide*], a two-part T.V. movie by Gianni Serra and Count Morello Agonigi in the Tessari rendition of *Born of Love* [*Nata d'amore*] by Liala, the Italian equivalent to Barbara Cartland.

It was quite difficult to sort out how to divide myself into three parts for projects that were to be realized simultaneously, starting at the end of the year and going through the beginning of 1983. But fortunately Rai Channel Two was doing both *The Atlantis Project* and *Born of Love* and they managed to schedule me, considering that the Tessari mini-series was going on for more than six months and consisted of six episodes with me only being in four of them.

Tessari had requested one week of reading rehearsals, customary for plays, because he wanted the actors to get familiar with one another and with the very complicated plot based on the character of Lalla Acquaviva and her "reincarnation." The first Lalla was a girl populating the 1920s who lived a fantastic story of life and death involving many men; the second Lalla was her niece, living in the 1930s, who was similarly undergoing many changes in her life and ended up marrying the son of her aunt's impossible lover, my part.

I had tried reading the three books of the saga, but I had found them impossibly sugary and boring, which wasn't surprising because

Flipper, where Johnny plays the phony rock star

Liala, still alive and in her 90s, had been the best-selling author most cherished by maids and housewives. In her world everything was shining and luxurious, men were strong, athletic and domineering and women were incredibly beautiful and whimsical, their dresses and jewelry described in every detail. Lalla Acquaviva was, of course, the most beautiful of them all, almost a goddess. So I was quite surprised when in Milan, where we were rehearsing, I met the girl who was to portray this miracle of nature. Barbara Nascimben was a very tall girl with broad shoulders molded by constant swimming and a way of walking that reminded me more of Walt Disney's Goofy than Venus. She wasn't plain, but I wouldn't have turned to look at her in the street, as most everybody was doing with Lalla in the movie. The same lack of special physical charm possessed the rest of the cast, including me. My hairline had started to recede, and if still handsome, I wasn't the Prince Charming Lalla had depicted. The only exception was Urbano Barberini, a real Roman prince with a Pope in his family, who was 10 years younger than me, but he played my father in the first part of the story. He was simply and positively gorgeous and girls on the street did scream like idiots when he was passing by. But beauty apart, my fellow actors were all skilled and nice people and I highly respected Tessari for refusing to cast the mistress of Prime Minister Bettino Craxi as Lalla, as the Prime Minister was

Lalla (Barbara Nascimben) and Count Morello Agonigi (Johnny) from the Italian T.V. series, *Born of Love*

renowned for his love of women as well as for his corruptness.

As soon as I was back from Milan, Gianni Serra requested me and I began shooting *The Atlantis Project* in late September 1982, celebrating my 28th birthday on set September 23.

It was a co-production with France and Germany and the story was about a French journalist (played by Daniel Gelin) investigating the revolutionary movement in Morocco and its exploitations attempted by secret services of both the U.S.A. and the U.S.S.R. I was the Russian spy Duimich, cold, sarcastic and cruel, fighting with my American counterpart (German-American actor Peter Berling) and politically seducing the young Moroccan activist played by Michael Beattie, a black American model in his movie debut. Off set I moved from political to sexual, because Michael was a striking handsome boy and I knew he was gay or bi-sexual because I had noticed him some time before on the gay beach in Rome. As a matter of fact he was in a relationship with a rich Italian much older than he was, but it didn't stop him from starting an affair with me, the first I ever had with a fellow actor in a movie. It wasn't the love story to change one's life, but I was quite taken and, for the first time, I could detect a hint of jealousy in "T's" reactions when this black semi-God was wandering through the house in his underwear.

The first scenes filmed included some exteriors on the beach, where I had to blow up a hut by flying a remote-controlled model plane, filled with dynamite. Big Bomber was once again in charge of special effects and, as his name proved, fires and explosions were his cup of tea, but this time something went wrong. Because of the hut exploding, the scene could be shot just once and Serra, a little nervous man tending toward temperamental, had placed four different cameras to get the best possible result. Everything had to be timed perfectly: me playing with the prop remote control, the guy in charge of the actual remote and the hut exploding. We rehearsed everything carefully and the police and some firemen were present on set because the explosion was to be phenomenal. When action was finally called, I pretended to play with the remote, the model plane nose-dived on the hut ... and it just collapsed on itself with a melancholic "puff" and the saddest wisp of smoke in movie history. Rolling with laughter I watched Gianni Serra chasing Big Bomber on the beach and kicking him in the ass. I thought that maybe the pig from *Cannibal Ferox* hadn't fulfilled its vengeance on its killer the first time round.

It took some time to rebuild the hut and I spent it with Michael, making love and trying to teach him at least a few words of Italian. As is true of many Americans, he had been living in the country for quite a long time without learning a single word of the language.

And I was in bed with Michael one late October dawn when the telephone rang, bringing the saddest news I could expect. My uncle Pietro Ingrao was phoning me to tell that my father had died of a heart attack in Brussels, where he was attending a meeting of the European Peace Committee.

His death wasn't totally unexpected because he had always suffered from a bad heart and his first attack dated back to 1964. Others had followed and he had refused to lead the calm and stress free life his doctors had recommended. He wanted to be an active part of society; he was engaged on many fronts both in politics and civil rights fights and he loved life in all forms, including food and women. He knew what he was risking and had decided that living one day as a lion was better than a hundred days as a sheep. But all the same I felt destroyed because I had loved him much more than usual in a father-son relationship.

After my mother's death, my father and I were left alone in the house, because my older brothers were already independent and, without even noticing, my father had lavished on me all the love and devotion he had for my mother, to whom I was so similar both in looks and personality. Every morning he served me coffee in bed as he had done with her; even if only 15 years old, I was in charge of everything in the house; and he was giving me more than half his salary for house expenses, which included dinner parties I was giving to cheer him up. I accompanied him everywhere in his travels or mundane occasions and watched that he had everything he deserved, from new clothes to a spotless house. Sex apart, it was in all regards a relationship akin to a married couple, not in the least morbid, but nevertheless probably not too healthy for both of us. Feeling like King Lear, he called me "my Cordelia" and as a matter of fact I was devoted to him as Lear's daughter or Antigone to Oedipus.

My father had accepted my bisexuality quite well even if, of course, he was much happier when he saw me with a girl. He supported these male-female relationships as much as he was supporting Juventus, the soccer team he was devoted to. The girl in question was pampered, complimented, invited to restaurants and received the best of his wit and cultivated conversation and he had hoped, with all his heart, that I would marry Carolina di Valmarana, whom he specially cherished. But he was polite with my boyfriends too and gave me all the freedom and privacy I needed, too much maybe, because he didn't notice, or didn't want to notice, my alcohol abuse or some other excesses. I knew that I had the right for a life of my own, but I would have never left him alone, not even if "T" had asked me to marry in Sweden. The solution arrived in the person of Fabiola, a lady who had been a friend of his before marrying. She was divorced and they started a relationship that I encouraged and that led to marriage. Fabiola was a blessing for both our lives; she gave him everything I did plus what I couldn't give and she watched his diet and habits with a firmer hand than mine. She gave me back a family life that included her three children: Susanna and Francesca, both already married, and Francesco who was about my age. My brothers and I had birthday parties and Christmas dinners at her place, where my father had moved, and I spent many a holiday in her seaside house in Tuscany, spending time with Francesco as if he were my real brother and babysitting Susanna's daughters. Unfortunately, as I am correcting the galley proofs of this book, Francesco died prematurely, at age 60, and my heart is broken.

Fabiola had a big heart and a love for life not different from my father's, and she accepted all the new family members, both steady and passers-by, with affection. She became a close friend of my aunt Viv, and when my brother Marco adopted a little Eritrean boy, she acted like a real grandmother, even when people on the beach were staring when the little boy, as black as a charcoal, was calling her granny, wondering what bizarre genetics had produced the relationship. Her good nature got to the point of regularly visiting my grandmother at her nursing home, a sad if luxurious place, run by Mother Pascalina Lehnert, the iron German nun who had attended Pope Pius the 12th. My grandmother had never liked my father, considering him a bad match for her daughter, and she was secretly offended by his remarrying, but Fabiola's good heart and amusing chats finally won her over and she looked forward to her visits.

And Fabiola and my grandmother were the first persons Marco and I went to visit on that sad October morning of 1982. We didn't want my grandmother to learn about my father's death by hearing about it on television, and we had to decide with Fabiola about leaving for Brussels promptly, which we did with the great help of all the staff of the Communist Party. The need for action anesthetized my sorrow for a while and in Brussels I had to deal alone with all the unpleasant arrangements, as when a Belgian undertaker out of a stereotyped creepy movie chased me down to know what socks and underwear to dress my father with. My brother Marco had gone into a sort of trance and, even if he mastered French as well as I did, had begged me, almost in tears, to do whatever needed to be done without having him speak, including buying his cigars.

We came back from Brussels with my father's coffin and brought it to the funeral, which took place in front of the mathematics faculty and was attended by a thick crowd, including many political personalities standing by the coffin to pay homage and speaking afterwards. At the funeral I cracked suddenly and cried for hours and hours to the point that Marco had almost to slap me when we finally left him at the cemetery, where we had to wait for him to be cremated.

Director Duccio Tessari and his wife Lorella De Luca

When it was over we put his ashes to rest in Fabiola's family grave, a wonderful place facing Tuscany sea, the tomb having being sculpted by Fabiola's father, a reputed painter.

My sorrow was immense in those days and I only smiled once, when I read, among the thousand letters and telegrams of condolence, a message from the municipality of a little town near Bologna saying: "We will always remember his personality and high culture that he kindly showed us when participating at our annual lasagna feast." My father had been almost food addicted and I could very well picture him stuffing himself and being charming at the same time.

I would have stayed home crying for months, but work saved me, because only two weeks later Duccio Tessari called me to the set on Lake Maggiore, near Milan, where many of the extravagant houses depicted in the script had been discovered by the set designer. Working was a good cure in itself, but I will never forget the love and care I received during that sad occasion by Duccio Tessari and his wife Lorella De Luca, who was there to be with her husband but also had a role as my mother. And they proved to be a real mother and a real father to me, never becoming overwhelming but always ready to console and distract. Duccio left us many years ago, and after the manuscript of this book was completed, Lorella also died after being sick in the hospital for a long time. Visiting her and holding her hand was just a faint way of giving back at least a little of what they gave to me.

Chapter 18
Comedy, Drama and Romance

After a few days on the *Born of Love* set, I switched to the Barzini movie and left the formal clothes of Count Morello Agorigi to wear the leathers of the rock star Viscius.

Andrea Barzini and his wife Stefania were in the circle of my closest friends; I loved them dearly and was considered a part of the family that included their children, Chiara and Matteo, to whom I had been godfather. Andrea was the son of Senator Luigi Barzini, Jr., a very well known journalist who had achieved fame in the U.S.A. as well as in Italy for his book *The Italians*. He was a wealthy and influential man and Andrea had struggled in the movie world, not wanting to be considered a spoiled upper class brat. *Flipper* was his first movie and it was set in the musical provincial underworld of Northern Italy. The hero was a real country music singer, Andrea Mingardi, who was fighting for success against the phony fashionable music imitating the Anglo-American rock scene and I embodied it as Viscius, a tacky replica of David Bowie or Lou Reed with heavy and ambiguous make-up, leather jackets and a ridiculous chorus line of gay S&M dancers. During a performance similar to the one in *Singing in the Rain*, a technical problem with the play-back revealed that Viscius couldn't sing a note and Andrea Mingardi sang live in his place, while Viscius left the stage under a storm of insults and vegetables thrown his way.

It was a very funny over-the-top role. Considering himself a great star, Viscius, who was outrageously gay, was having continuous tantrums, screamed against journalists and photographers and he made demanding requests to his secretary, played by Andrea Barzini's wife Stefania. The cast included Christian De Sica (who was the son of the Academy Award winner Vittorio and would become a money-making machine in many screen comedies to come) and Margherita Buy, a young girl in her debut, so nervous and shy that it was difficult to foretell she would become the great star she now is in Italy.

A more recent photo of music star, Andrea Mingardi, who starred in *Flipper* (1982)

From comedy to drama, I left Andrea and his crew to join the *Atlantis Project* people who had started shooting in Marrakesh. Morocco fascinated me at first sight and I would have loved to walk around and play tourist, but I was faced with a problem I hadn't considered. In that country I was a coveted sexual prey. I was lean, pale and blue eyed and my blond hair, even if thinning, was still there. To the Moroccan bisexual males I was an irresistible temptation, and walking alone meant being surrounded by men of every age, build and height trying to get my attention by calling, "Monsieur! Monsieur!" The fear existed of them even physically molesting me. For the first time in my life I understood the discomfort of foreign female tourists who were dealing with heavy male attention on the streets of Rome. I "hired" two strong grips in the crew to come and visit the Medina with me so I could savor the incredible light and the unique atmosphere of the big Market Square, full of acrobats and merchandise resembling an Ali Baba movie, but for real. But, with my great ennui, when we got to the "sacred" part of the city, they were allowed in … because with their dark skin and black moustaches they were easily mistakable for Arabs. But I was left out.

A portrait of Christian De Sica, who also starred in *Flipper*

Not even the hotel was entirely safe and once a wealthy middle-aged man dressed as a Sheik offered me a drink. When I told him that I was there with a movie company, he went to the production manager and, as in the worst clichéd joke, asked how many camels I was worth.

After a while Michael Beattie joined us and, with his escort, I attempted visiting a local Turkish bath, something I always had wished to see, being very much in love with hot waters and spa of all kinds. An old skinny man scrubbed me to my bones and only with a swift movement was I able to prevent him from scrubbing my face, something the make-up man wouldn't have appreciated. I then asked for a massage and went through an incredible experience. As I have already mentioned I had achieved a diploma in sports physical therapy right after quitting my dream of dancing professionally. I was always interested in learning new techniques by getting a massage in different countries, but I wasn't prepared for the larger than life masseur, weighing at least 250 pounds, who briskly put me on a marble bench and started beating me with all his strength. I thought

Francesca De Sapio, who appeared in *Born of Love*, as she appeared in *Godfather II*

it was some kind of protest against Western colonization, but the Arabian man on the next bench was receiving the same treatment, so I patiently bore being hit, but I thought I would soon be on my deathbed when the giant climbed on the bench with the clear intention of walking on my back. He did, but I hadn't noticed that there was a bar on the ceiling over the bench and he was clinging at it, thus being able to calibrate his weight. With my utter surprise, when I got up from that rough abuse of my body I felt as light as a bird and with each muscle and bone perfectly relaxed. From there on I was to get an Arab massage any time it was available in every country I visited.

I was always with Michael and our relationship was evident to everybody, but I had also good moments with the others. Francesca De Sapio, who was also in the *Born of Love* cast, was there too as Daniel Gelin's wife, and we shared the cruel destiny of being denied from sunbathing, an iron commandment from the Tessari set where everybody had to be diaphanous as convenient to the 1930s upper class. But sitting by the pool with a large straw hat on, I had funny conversations with Daniel, who was bemused by my "old style" French and stated that talking with me was like being in a Moliere play. He told me about his difficult relationship with his daughter Maria Schneider, who had become a star after being anally penetrated by Marlon Brando in *Last Tango in Paris*. He was familiar with Marrakesh because it had been the location of Hitchcock's second version of *The Man Who Knew Too Much* and he took us to a wonderful restaurant owned by an old French woman who could have been either a spy or a madam and was probably both. I ate "pastilla" for the first time and was fascinated by the mix of sweet pastry and savory pigeon meat in this complicated dish that requires a two-day preparation.

Daniel didn't like our director a bit and got to the point of throwing a telephone at him, when asked to reach for it in the weirdest possible way because "it was good for the camera." Personally I liked Gianni Serra and got along well with him, but I could see Daniel's point, because Serra was indeed very "Italian" in his movie-making, all concentrated on images and not so much on the actors, to the point that he didn't care about not understanding a word we were saying, considering we were shooting in English and he didn't know it.

There wasn't even a real dialogue coach on set and once, in a café terrace in the Market Square, Michael and I got so bored of waiting and rehearsing for the lights that at the first take we said nursery rhymes instead of our lines. Nobody noticed. Serra's care for every detail was second only to the meticulousness of the director of photography, who was moving on set as if in a Zen Buddhist religious ceremony and always wanted actors to be there. I agreed on that because it was a chance to rehearse, something not very much in use on Italian sets, and I liked knowing what kind of light I was getting, but standing for hours in the North African heat wasn't fun. I protested once and the answer to my protest was, "The shot is like a diamond, it lasts forever." This was enough to silence even Sir Laurence Olivier.

But the long waits had their advantages because they were slowing down the schedule, and my contract stated I was to be paid a certain sum for a specified number of days; each extra day meant more money and I ended up earning almost double my original fee.

Suddenly a small revolution happened in town and risked compromising the movie. A local guy who had been hired to help with the production one night called a young woman who was working as an extra, telling her she was needed on set and by this lie tried to rape her. The next day a crowd of relatives and friends arrived on location shouting, protesting and demanding the man's head, who came to work as if nothing happened. He clung to me terrorized screaming for help and I panicked because people armed with clubs and knives surrounded us. At last the police arrived and settled the matter by arresting the inventive rapist. The seclusion of women and the impossibility for the opposite sexes to endulge in sex before marriage was indeed the cause for Morocco to be a real gay paradise, but it had its shortcomings as well.

From Marrakesh we next moved to the remote town of Ouarzazate, which was the last outpost of civilization before miles of wilderness, in this case the Sahara desert. There was no airport there and I traveled by night with Michael and a chauffeur, who was driving like a madman on the narrow road that climbed the Atlas mountains and roaring on the steep slopes as if at any moment we would collide with the huge trucks coming from the opposite direction, with horns ringing and curses in Arab thrown from both parties. God or Allah watched us and we arrived safe and sound to a place entirely different from Marrakesh.

Ouarzazate was a small town with just an old Medina (ancient downtown) and a bunch of more modern buildings, including just one spartan hotel for the few travelers who wished to visit the desert. Tourists were not really welcome and I could tell from the severe glances of the locals when I went visiting the old city. They weren't rude, but it was clear that they preferred Westerners and Christians to stay as far as possible; fortunately sexual harassment was absent and I could do some serious shopping with Michael in little stores that weren't selling tourist crap, just nice old blue pottery. I bought a few items for presents and a couple other items for myself that have been with me ever since.

Unfortunately Michael had just a couple of scenes to shoot there and soon flew back to Italy, where he got back to his official lover who was eager to pardon his casual affair with me.

I hadn't much time to feel deserted, because work was quite absorbing and it started at four in the morning, when I had to be ready for the Jeep which was taking us deep into the desert, where a real Tuareg nomad tribe had been hired to participate to the movie. To my shame I must admit that I am a real town person and that nature's beauties have never been first in my priorities, but the colors of the desert changing from dawn to daylight were an amazing sight that I looked forward to every morning. The Tuareg are notoriously beautiful people and, if the women were separate and unseen, all busy cooking our lunch of couscous, the men were participating in the movie with energy and kindness, being fierce and hospitable at the same time. I learned that you must eat your couscous from the central plate with your right hand, resting your left under your back, because it is the hand used five times a day for cleaning oneself before the prayers called by the Muezzin, a ritual cleansing that involves face, feet and genitals where you must sit as not to show the soles of your shoes, because someone else might have ruined theirs, with perhaps even a hole visible in their sole. It would be impolite to demonstrate that your shoes are in better shape than theirs.

The heat was excruciating but dry and so much more bearable than the Amazon humidity. My concern was to be in the sun as little as possible because of the Tessari movie, but at times I couldn't avoid it and when we returned to the hotel I was using milk on my skin as the ladies did in the 19th century. After one week of going back and forth from Ouarzazate to our shooting location, I was very tired and the Tuareg Chief, who could speak good French, heard me stating so. He was one of the handsomest men I had seen in my life, so when he seductively smiled and asked me why I wasn't spending the night with them, considering I had to be there next morning, I was highly tempted, but I then thought that if the prospect of making love with him was indeed attractive I risked being involved with some other 20 relatives and I didn't find that idea appealing. So I politely refused and went back into the Jeep for the long journey back.

On a Sunday I rented a car and a chauffeur and went visiting the old town that locals consider to be ancient Sodom, a sightseeing tour that I owed to my bisexuality. It was a fascinating place, all built in sand and it would have been long gone if it hadn't been restored in the early 1960s for Robert Aldrich's *Sodom and Gomorrah* and used for other movies ever since. When the old local guide learned I was Italian he asked me about Anna Maria Pierangeli, who had been Lot's wife in that movie and, to my great surprise, he cried when I told him she had died. Judging from his looks he had been quite handsome in his youth and I dare say that he must have had a love affair with the unlucky and unhappy Italian actress who had been James Dean's impossible love.

My Moroccan days were over and I bid farewell to a land that I had immensely liked and where I was to come back 20 years later. My last remembrance of the desert scene is a cherished one and it involved Gianni Serra's stubbornness punished by a camel. He wanted the animal to turn its head in a certain way and briskly tried manipulating it, but for his trouble he received a severe bite from the animal's huge yellowish teeth. On that occasion I learned that camels are real villains, very clever and with a lasting memory. If the owner beats one it can wait years, but at night, if given the occasion, the camel will kill the man by sitting on him. Brutal directors shooting with camels be warned!

In these months I had very little time for domestic matters, barely home, back from Morocco, I spent one week in Rome where I got the news that "L" had finally produced her secret weapon: She was pregnant.

Of course "T" was sure that she was taking the pill, but she had thought otherwise and was adamant about keeping the baby. "T" was confused and uncertain; on one side he was happy about the prospect of fatherhood because he was already 35 years old and liked children, but on the other hand he didn't want to get chained by "L" in any sort of marriage or life in common. He sought my advice and I told him to try at least once in his life to be very clear with her and nevertheless be very careful not to draw his defenses, because her obvious intent was nailing him, and the baby had been conceived for that reason. He spoke to "L" and stated that he intended fathering the baby but wanted to keep living his current life, as to stay at my place. She was surprisingly understanding and accepted the situation, but I was sure it was just a façade and that deep in her heart she was preparing for the final assault.

Director Duccio Tessari

Shaken by the news, but somehow moved at the idea of nurturing a baby "T," I went back to my Morello role that was now filming in Milan and on the Lake Maggiore.

In the final part of the story, where my role was predominant, the second Lalla got engaged with Morello, the son of her aunt's lost love, but she was jealous of his attachment to his work as a radiologist and more so when he started dedicating his time to a very sick girl with the exotic name of Onda Albar. Misunderstandings and quarrels followed with the result of a separation and Morello, out of compassion, married Onda to lighten up her last days doomed with tuberculosis. TB was the greatest ally of tearful writers and musicians for at least the past two centuries, to such an extent that they indeed mourned the day a cure was found and cursed Alexander Fleming's name for eternity. With Onda on her deathbed, Lalla realized her superficiality and begged my pardon. Of course at the end we were getting married.

It was my first time in the young lover role and it took some time to adjust to it, with Tessari always telling me, at times yelling, to smile. "You are not in a Fulci movie! Relax for God sake!" he kept saying, while fighting back my attempts to exclude as much as possible the letter "r" from my dialogue. The problem was, and still is, that my learning of French in childhood had left me with my "r" rolled as in that language, a way of speaking that in Italy is connected to the upper class and to gay people and that caused me more than one problem with getting roles or dubbing myself from English, a language that, thank God, pronounces an Italian or Spanish "r" only in Scotland. If Tessari had allowed me I would have transformed "Madrid" into "the capital of Spain," but he patiently convinced me that it was a stupid issue and that my "r" was anyway perfect for Count Morello Agorigi di Montalbano, an aristocrat and a Northerner, the part of Italy where the rolled "r" is more frequent.

Tessari was a splendid director and a wonderful human being and reminded me a lot of Margheriti. As Antonio he was always perfectly shaven and well dressed, with a tie and a fresh red carnation at his buttonhole. He was nice with the crew, who adored him, and had performed the miracle of turning a bunch of people on a monthly salary for life from Rai (and thus tending to be lazy and uncaring) into a movie crew that would have climbed mountains to set a dolly the way he wanted and were constantly on walls and trees to work with lights, unaware of risks and just happy with a "well done" from their beloved director. Duccio had a nice word for everybody, remembered who was married and who was not and how many children they had, and he never let a birthday go by without a cake and champagne. He was generous with money as he was with his affections, and I think he would have gone bankrupt many a time over if it hadn't been for his wife Lorella, also nice and generous, but with a more practical sense. Being always concerned with money and debts, Duccio's attitude toward life puzzled me and I really would have liked to be more like him and say, as he did, "If you owe a million to your shirt maker, just order a dozen more."

He understood actors and always liked to have a little role in his movies, in this case the faithful Fiorello, the butler of the Acquaviva family. Working with him would have been just Paradise if he hadn't had an incoercible penchant for jokes to be played on set. His humor was pervading the whole series and finally, in my opinion, mined its success, because a fake and weak world such as the one of Liala, all appearance and no substance, had to be taken seriously. But the tricks he played on set, and they were of course cut out from the final result, would have ruined the work of a De Niro or a Brando and thus were more dangerous for me, because my role was quite dramatic and I was used to concentration, a hard task to accomplish when, bearing my wife's coffin, I heard a choir humming "Jingle Bells." He had the wonderful habit of using music on set to create the right atmosphere and I will always remember the day when, shooting Onda's funeral on the lake with gondolas, he surprised us with huge speakers playing the melancholic notes of Offenbach's *Barcarole* that was going to give the right rhythm to the oarsmen. But music could be also part of his jokes, as when I was holding Onda's dying hand and "Cheek to Cheek" exploded or when, during a great grand ball scene with everybody waltzing, he placed the camera in a corner and said that whoever danced there would have a close-up, rolling with laughter to the unromantic and wild pushing that followed.

But once I managed to trick him and it happened in a love scene that was supposed to end with me kissing Barbara/Lalla; after a few seconds of passionate kissing his "cut" wasn't arriving and I understood that he was testing my reactions, so I started stripping of my clothes with my lips strongly tied to hers and went on until I was in my underwear and ready to take them off too. Only then he finally called cut, with the whole crew in tears and Barbara almost suffocating.

Poor Barbara was the only one who was having problems, because she was totally inexperienced and at times Duccio was forced to scream at her to get the right reactions. She was a nice girl in personal life, a good sport, unspoiled and with a very modern beauty of her own, but, as I had foreseen, the fashion of the period didn't become her a bit and, with the elaborated evening dresses with plunging necklines with stripes of fabric circling the neck, her broad muscular shoulders were fully revealed and she looked more a wrestler or Mandrake's servant Lothar than a high society belle. But while shooting *Born of Love* she met the famous singer-actor Massimo Ranieri, who was playing the villain, and they started a relationship that lasted for many years and consoled her of an early and unsuccessful marriage that had produced two daughters. Her acting career was short and she is now an executive manager.

The long months on the Tessari set, with intervals for *Atlantis Project* and *Flipper*, had created scheduling problems with my psychoanalysis sessions and my shrink, who was already worried because, in his opinion, my father's death had somehow stopped my progress. He agreed to see me on Saturdays and Sundays, which meant getting on a sleeping car in Milan on Friday night and being on another one on Sunday to be on set by Monday morning. The sleeping car from Rome to Milan was passing just at the back of our hotel, the super luxury Hotel Des Iles Borromèes, and after a while I got friendly with the guard and, by graciously tipping him, convinced him to slow the train enough to allow me to jump down and get to my room by just climbing over a fence instead of journeying to Milan and then back again to the lake with a local train stopping at every station.

But I also had days off during the week and got into the habit of going to Milan where my friend Livia had moved to from New York. She introduced me to her friends, who belonged to the business world or to the intellectual and blood aristocracy, and I became part of the "Milan Spring" that had blossomed with the election to Prime Minister of Bettino Craxi, who was legally and illegally financing this and that, thus creating a sparkling world of parties and galas that would be abruptly stopped in the early 1990s by the magistracy in the historic inquiry that the press called "Clean Hands" and that swept away, in only a few months, the entire ruling political class of the country.

I found a new and special friend in E.B. (privacy once again …), whom I nicknamed Mephisto from the Istvan Szabò movie that had made a star of German actor Klaus Maria Brandauer and who, after a while, offered me the opportunity to be his guest in his little but central apartment. Mephisto was a very serious and almost severe economic scholar from a wealthy Jewish family and was a prominent lawyer. He got up early in the morning and went to the university dressed as a gentleman and a professor should be dressed, to be revered and feared by his students for his deep culture and his sharp wit, but when he got back home he changed into leather and took me to the worst gay dungeons in town, modeled on the New York scene but not yet allowed in Rome because of the Pope's presence. We were of course fucking and he was attached to me more than I wished to notice, but he was too sarcastic and thorny to play the romantic and contented himself in sharing with me wild nights, at times leading to threesomes, and ironic commentaries on the gay scene. He was bisexual as I was, but in a more contrasted way related to his Jewish tradition (notoriously abhorring homosexuality) and quite surprisingly he married after a few years from our gay adventures and seemed to forget our sordid past, as I observed when I visited the freshly married pair. His wife, the elegant and frail heiress to a financial empire, very tactfully went shopping, leaving two old friends to their private conversation, and when I tried inquiring on his sudden change, Mephisto pretended not to know what I was talking about, even if sitting on the same sofa where complicated gay *Kama Sutra* positions had been performed. It was a hard lesson on how strangely the human mind can work, but I was anyway too embarrassed to keep seeing him.

But his marriage was yet to happen and I kept visiting him since he left me the home keys when he went to the U.S.A. for one sabbatical year. It was a thoughtful idea and I used his apartment a lot because new work brought me to Milan in 1984.

For the time being, when *Born of Love* was over, I went back to Rome in time for the birth of "T'"s daughter. The baby girl was the most beautiful infant one could imagine, almost looking like the winner of an extra-terrestrial beauty contest, with a perfectly shaped bald head, immense blue eyes and perfect rosy lips. Walking her in her stroller, as I was often doing, was like parading with Grace Kelly or Elizabeth Taylor and people were continuously giving out delighted screams and making stupid noises at her. Remembering from my infancy how the experience was unfit for a baby, I tried cutting the compliments short, but when "T" put her on my bed in the morning to get dressed, I contemplated her as if I had been in front of a masterpiece by Titian or Raphael. "L" seemed subdued and wasn't often at our place, looking quite happy if I babysit, but I knew that she was scheming some plot, and time proved me right.

The three movie engagements ended with my last interior scenes in *Atlantis Project*. Duimich, my character, had kidnapped the American spy and was watching him while lying on a bed and reading a book, with some sarcastic comment emitted here and there. I caught the occasion to have a real book to read and I selected one that contained three plays by English playwright Alan Ayckbourn. It had been a gift from the D'Amico siblings, Masolino, Silvia and Caterina, who were the one son and two daughters of Suso Cecchi D'Amico, the most important screenwriter in Italian cinema history. Masolino, who was a theater critic and loved my work as a director, had recommended Ayckbourn

Costume designer and Academy Award-winner Gabriella Pescucci, working on the recent Showtime series, *Penny Dreadful*

to me saying that, in his opinion, I was the only one with enough of a British sense of humor to stage his works in Italy. I didn't have a company of my own and distanced myself from the theater a bit in favor of movies, but reading Ayckbourn's plays proved to be the funniest experience I could imagine and I was laughing so much that I had to stop reading to get into the mindset of the cruel Russian spy I was. I couldn't foretell that in years to come Ayckbourn was to become my winning card on the Italian stage poker table.

I could have been satisfied with my achievements in 1983, but I completed the super busy year with an exceptional goal: participating in a movie that was to be recorded in cinema history, but without being seen in a *single* frame.

In full summer, the dance school I was attending called me saying that Sergio Leone was looking for American-looking dancers for a scene in his *Once Upon A Time in America*. I had been in movies with big roles before and so played hard to get, but as soon as I was told what the fee was, I got into a taxi and raced to the studios in Cinecittà.

The scene in question was the party for the end of prohibition where some people were dancing the One Step. Leone was shooting everything from every possible angle and point of view, including one of a champagne bottle, thus arriving at editing with miles and miles of footage and only then deciding what he really needed. This expensive and quite unusual way of directing was a blessing for me, because the scene took 10 days to be completed at the amazing payroll rate dancers were getting. As a matter of fact nobody in our group knew a shit about the One Step, a very special dance popular in the 1930s and only faintly similar to The Charleston, and we had to be trained by the choreographer who was as old as Methuselah and as gay as gay can be. The dance was based on hitting the floor with alternate feet on a two-thirds rhythm, and it was quite noisy, so we were amazed when the assistant director asked us to dance it silently because we were just in the background and we were disturbing the close-up scene of Mr. De Niro and Miss Darlanne Fluegel. We tried to accomplish this request and I succeeded in what I had done up to then, hiding behind a column, because I loved the money but I didn't want to be spotted there working as an extra. The column in question was very close to Mr. De Niro and I can testify with certainty that he wasn't uttering a sound that could be audible during a party sequence, but that he was just thinking his lines out loud with the faintest murmur. It wasn't the only peculiarity of his Actors Studio behavior and the whole of Rome was laughing at some of his tantrums like the one connected to a furry collared coat.

By contract he was to approve every single sketch of his costumes, sign off for the costume designer and future Academy Award-winner Gabriella Pescucci. One morning she arrived with a furry collared coat and De Niro looked puzzled and said he didn't know about it. Miss Pescucci showed him the sketch with his signature and he apologized, but he stated that he needed to postpone the scene for at least three days because if he was to wear a fur collar, he needed to re-think his whole acting strategy. Needless to say the fur collar disappeared in a flash, but the story spread around and was told to Flora Mastroianni, Marcello's greatly betrayed but never divorced wife. Marcello was shooting in Brazil with Sonia Braga and called Flora on the phone as he usually did. She asked him what he had worn that day on set and he said he didn't remember. She insisted asking again and he said: "Flora, have you gone mad? What the fuck does it matter? Some pants and a shirt!"

Flora yelled back: "You idiot! If you knew what you are wearing you would win an Academy Award too!"

From column to column I managed not to be seen in the movie, not even if one plays the scene in slow motion. I enjoyed the money for a well-deserved holiday.

Chapter 19
A Deadly Impact and a Theater Comeback

From the fireworks of shooting three films simultaneously I went into the silence of "no job in sight." I had enough money to keep me going with the *International Airport* scripts to write, but I missed action and the set life. So, when I saw a newspaper ad looking for an actor to play Russian poet Vladimir Mayakovski, I sent some photos and a resume. It was a weird and unusual way to cast people and I doubted whether it was serious, but director Gianni Toti got back to me and it turned out that the production was by the same Milan Rai office that had been in charge of *Born of Love*. They had a section called "Experimental," with the aim of helping unusual projects with a cultural value, and *Mayakovski* was one of them. The Russian poet had been a tall, imposing and dark-skinned man and I resembled him only in my strong cheekbones, but Toti was enthusiastic about having me and so I found myself back in Milan and in Mephisto house. But the atmosphere on set, with the same crew that had worked on *Born of Love* was indeed very different. Toti was a lunatic and intellectual deep into avant-garde philosophical puzzles and the founder and Maestro of "poetronic" (whatever it meant) and he would address the crew by saying things such as, "We must get into the frame ..." ... dramatic pause ... "...and into the frame's timing!" What followed wasn't exactly cheers and applause but laughing and some suffocated raspberries, which made him retire into himself, feeling very much the persecuted hero. I hadn't a clue about what I was saying and why and wandered around on set with my hair dyed black, invoking the Tessari spirit to rescue me and I was pissed with my partner, an American-Italian actress, Amy Werba, who pretended to listen carefully to the gibberish Toti was instructing us with.

Many scenes would be completed later on with the use of projections featuring original films with Mayakovski and his companion and lover Lili Brik, so we were mostly doing nonsense in front of some black or green screens and I felt like a perfect idiot. When Toti once told me that he couldn't see video-poetry in my eyes, I thought about strangling him, but I decided to silence him instead by telling him to show me what I should do, which of course he could not do.

Thank God it was short and, after a couple of weeks, I was back in Rome and welcoming 1984 even if it didn't bring any progression in my career.

I was a guest star in one of the *International Airport* episodes as a scientist escaping from the Russian secret service (the Cold War was still on, at least in fiction) and I had a role in another miniseries directed by Sergio Martino. It was called *To Catch an Art Thief* and it starred Giuliano Gemma as a policeman dealing with different thefts of art manufactures. In one episode I was a young aristocratic scoundrel, the grandson of Caterina Boratto, a great beauty of the 1930s, and in love with a girl played by Patrizia Pellegrino, a young Neapolitan starlet who wasn't Bette Davis, but who I found very sexy. We had a love-sex scene in an open car, and when I suggested rehearsing it, she heartily agreed

A publicity pose of Patrizia Pellegrino

and reacted to my heavy petting with some delighted laughing. But, raising my head from her bosom, I saw Martino towering over us with flaming eyes and immediately understood that I had made a blunder—*he* was bedding her. The incident went without consequence and he proved to be the brisk, effective director he had been in *Murder in an Etruscan Cemetery*, getting from me a nice and witty performance. On her side, Patrizia was of great help when I had to drive the car with her by my side. I couldn't drive and a short lesson from a grip hadn't been of much help, but with great ability she succeeded in using her feet on the pedals instead of me, leaving me just the simple task of turning the wheel. She had a bit of a career in T.V. and movies and then married into big money, but she insisted on being an actress and went on stage in light comedies. Quite recently I went to see a play she was in and could admire the work of her cosmetic surgeon. She hadn't a wrinkle and, if she was turning swiftly, her plastic-marble tits stayed in place for a second before following her, but she had decided to wear an evening dress with a back neckline down to her ass and either she never looked at her back or she was demented, because it was literally falling apart in wrinkles and folds. Women are crazy and every day I see on magazines or T.V. a former beauty turned into a hard-boiled egg or the model of some Picasso painting, with eyes at the sides of the head and lips looking like overfed goldfishes. And, as Patrizia, they are not even as clever as to hide what couldn't be manipulated. Quite often I see an octogenarian with face skin as smooth as a frozen rose and an entire dead turkey falling from her neck; I mean, dolly, don't you have a mirror? Aren't you smart enough to wear turtlenecks or a scarf? Valentina Cortese went under surgery in her 50s, but, apart from her oval, no one ever saw an inch of her skin ever since and wonderful Virna Lisi recently died at almost 80, but beautiful as ever ...

Producer/director Fabrizio De Angelis

If 1984 was quite eventless as far as movies and theater go, it brought a great change in my private life. "T" had grown mad about his daughter and, at this point, couldn't live without constantly seeing her and that was exactly what "L" was waiting for. She had cooked him on a low fire and when he was ready to be eaten she suddenly started either being overwhelmingly present at our place or refusing to let him have the baby by himself. It was an unbearable situation and she had counted on the fact that even my patience had limits. I was forced to ask "T" to do something and he unwillingly decided to go to live with her. On that occasion I confronted "L" and told her she was making the mistake of her life by blackmailing a man who didn't love her and was accepting her demands to live together only because of their daughter. But she felt victorious and was almost exploding with pride and so dismissed me by saying that I was just jealous.

I had started my love affair with "T" at 13 and I was now turning 30 and we had shared a house for five years, so the new situation was quite difficult and sad. We didn't break up or quarrel but our relationship slowed down a lot; we kept seeing each other more and more rarely and almost stopped having sex.

The only one to mask his obvious satisfaction under the usual emotionless mummy mask was my shrink, who had always considered "T" a big hindrance on my way to maturity and self-determination.

Work came once more to my rescue and at the end of the year I willingly accepted the villain role offered to me by Fabrizio De Angelis, a producer and director I had met at the Tessari evening gatherings and who was known for his action movies under the stage name of Larry Ludman.

An Italian lobby card for *Deadly Impact*

The title of the movie was *Deadly Impact* and it revolved around two gangsters kidnapping a guy and his girlfriend because he was a computer genius and had found a way to bankrupt the Las Vegas slot machines. Two policemen, played by the notorious pair of Bo Svenson and Fred Williamson, were chasing us and the very weak plot was just an excuse for shootings, helicopter scenes and car accidents.

Experience had taught me to understand from the characters in the script if I were to have good company off the set or not, and in this case my only hope relied on the Italian guy playing my fellow gangster. So, when at the Rome airport I met Renato Zamarion, I was stunned by how good looking he was, but I could have committed suicide on the spot when he introduced himself with a thick Roman accent saying: "Hi, I am Renato. I love pussy and I am a hot supporter of Roma soccer team." He spoke just a few words of English and he was on his first flight abroad, so I escorted him through the airport with loudspeakers mumbling information about connections from Rome to New York, from New York to Chicago and from Chicago to Phoenix, where we were going to shoot the movie. He admitted that without me he would have probably ended up in Hong Kong and, getting to know him better, he turned out to be a nice fellow and not totally inexperienced, because he had graduated from the National Drama School. As a matter of fact, his company was to be the only pleasant thing about a movie entirely to be forgotten.

Fabrizio De Angelis seemed a polite and smart guy when sitting on the Tessari couch and playing parlor games, but on set he was aggressive, brisk and with the advantage of being both producer and director, so there was no one to complain to about the way Renato and I were treated. The movie was entirely filmed on location. During the Phoenix scenes Svenson and Williamson had large air-conditioned vans to stay in between takes and get changed, while Renato and I were getting make-up on a chair in the street and changed behind cars, as not to show our underwear to the entire Phoenix population. In the long car sequences, if there was anything to do more complicated than give gas and slowly drive away, the American actors had stuntmen and dummies with their features, but not so with the Italian garbage (Renato and I). Renato was luckier than me because he was driving the car, so in difficult chase sequences he had to be substituted by a famous stuntman, a French guy by the name of Alain Petit, who didn't speak a word of English or Italian and relied on me to translate all the instructions. I was the passenger and there was no dummy dressed with my clothes to undergo dangerous speeding, taking dangerous turns or spinning right around

An Italian locandina for *Deadly Impact*

and I wasn't even allowed to wear a security belt, because it wasn't gangster-like. To make things scarier, Alain liked talking with me about his dangerous work and expressed his philosophy by saying: "La vie, la mort … qu'est ce que ça fait?" ("Life, death…what's the difference?"). I tried telling him that it did make a difference to me and I also tried asking De Angelis why on Earth I hadn't a dummy, considering I was involved in the most difficult stunt scenes. His disdainful macho answer was: "What are we doing here? A dummy movie?" So I crossed myself and went into the seemingly never-ending chase sequence in the streets of Phoenix, a town most similar to Los Angeles, where if by chance, on your free day, you wanted to go to see a certain film listed in the newspaper, you were to discover that the cinema was 60 miles away and only occasionally

Anglo export trade ad for *Deadly Impact*, here titled *Giant Killer*

could Renato and I induce the production to give us a car to use off set. In this movie "risk was my profession" and, not being on cocaine anymore, I had lost the audacity of my Atlanta days and was positively shitting in my pants, as when the car chase abruptly stopped in a no exit narrow alley. Renato was to get out of the car and run away through a fire escape, but I had to jump on top of our car, take out my gun, wait for the cops' car to arrive at full speed, shoot at them and only at the last possible moment I jumped off and flew through the air, with the other car crashing into ours a second later. If in that second my pants were to get caught, I could die and that was a fact. With both cars getting destroyed, the scene could be shot just once and I was positively shaking with terror. All went well and I got the crew's applause, but De Angelis complained saying that I should have waited longer. When watching the movie on-screen later, I couldn't help noticing that the camera was so wrongly angled that my bravery was almost entirely lost: props to Mr. Ludman!

Of course the scene was nothing when compared to what Alain was doing when driving in the many car crashes generated by the police chases and I was astonished when I saw him jump a bus, crash on the back of the car and come out of it without a scratch. He had protections and the cars had special reinforcements not to splash like squished oranges, but the real secret, as he explained to me, was being able to live the crash moment as in slow motion and see in what way the car was curling up on itself, thus doing the same with your body, but moving in the opposite direction. It looked to me like a very rare God's gift and I wasn't surprised he got paid for the bus jumping almost what I was paid for the entire movie. But I surely would have asked for much more money if I had known the risks I was running myself, not only with cars, but getting worse when we got to shoot another chase scene, this time with helicopters.

I had never been on one and immediately realized that it made me queasy. It would have been bad enough if I just had to sit there and say some lines, but I had to lean out of the window as much as possible and shoot at the police helicopter chasing us. The very idea made me even queasier and I could do it only because Marcellino, the diminutive electric grip I knew since my first movie, noticed my terror and volunteered to curl his little body on the helicopter floor and cling to my feet, God bless him wherever he is.

Johnny (right) with buddy co-actor Renato Zamarion

I was shooting with quite a big automatic weapon, which of course was charged with blanks, but the wrappings were nevertheless going to fall from the sky on the town below and it seemed to me somehow risky for people, but when I inquired about it, the polite response I got from De Angelis was: "Is it your fucking business?" So I stopped worrying and concentrated on what I had to do, trying not to vomit on the Phoenix population plus translating to the helicopter pilot the instructions I received from the ground via radio in Italian. I was listening to them with earphones that I had then to hide before shooting, but the connection was disturbed and the helicopter was making a hell of a noise, so it was hard to understand what they said and even harder to communicate with the pilot, who had headphones on to hear me and had the most impossible accent from God knows where. With a lot of shouting and cursing we completed the sequence, and I hoped never to get on such a flying monstrosity for the rest of my life.

In our free time, Renato and I were wandering about in malls and restaurants and I got to love him very much, because under the macho appearance he was really a sweet, sensitive guy. We stayed by ourselves until the day I was, surprisingly, picked up in a record store by the shop assistant, a little blonde girl who complimented me on my choice of pants and t-shirt, which fulfilled the not impossible task of being classier than what generally was worn in town, and we openly flirted.

She said she had a college degree and so I was thunderstruck when, having heard I was from Rome, Italy, she asked me with an impossible Texas drawl: "Itaaaly, it's in Euuurope, isn't it?" I answered that indeed it was and thought that old dear Europe might be facing its downfall, but if a university graduate from any European country had asked if New York were in the U.S.A., that person would find him or herself back in primary/elementary school. She seemed stupid and uninteresting, but I agreed to date her and a friend of hers because I thought that Renato would have enjoyed some feminine company. So we went on a date and she arrived with a friend who was from a Mexican family, much less attractive than her but one million times more intelligent and, not intending to have sex with either of them, I told Renato that the pretty one was "his" and the other one "mine." He indeed fucked her on a beach, while I was having a polite and interesting conversation with the less attractive one who was surprised I could speak Spanish and insisted on introducing me to her parents. So, on another night, Renato took Miss Stupid somewhere (God knows how he managed to communicate considering his English) and I had dinner with Miss Clever at her parents' place and found out with utter surprise that they had been living in the U.S.A. for more than 20 years but couldn't speak a word of English. They had a job that didn't require speaking, they needn't communicate to shop in American malls, they had friends only in the Hispanic community and they only watched Spanish channels on television. I had tried all my life to learn at least a few words of the local language wherever I was and that kind of attitude was incredible for me, but they were nice, down to earth working class people and I refreshed my Spanish talking about their daughter, who made them proud because she had graduated in an American university and had a much better job than they did.

On another night I made fun of Miss Stupid when she took us to a gay disco because apparently it was the "coooleeest" in town and with the best music; I pretended to be scandalized and Renato, who was fully aware of my bisexuality, hardly restrained laughter at her contrite apologies.

Besides Renato my relationship with the rest of the cast was non-existent and at times rather difficult. Alain Petit needed my attention for the short time he was with us because he didn't speak English and I was the only one around speaking French. He was a nice person, but I have never been at ease speaking three languages at a time as I was in Phoenix (Italian with Renato and the crew, French with Alain and English with everybody else), so I often got confused, as once in the hotel lobby where I was helping Alain to book his flight back. I was speaking fluently to both he and the lobby employee, when I realized they were looking at me in bewilderment: I was just talking in English to him and in French to her.

Translations were needed also by Rodolfo Ruzza, the handsome green-eyed prop guy I had often worked with, because he was trying hard to nail whatever American chick who fell for his Latin charm and an average conversation could go as follows:

Rodolfo: (In Italian) Is she going to give it to me or not?

Me: (Translating) He says he would like very much to date you.

Chick: He is lovely, but I am married and my husband is jealous.

Rodolfo: (In Italian, after translation) What the hell, I just want to screw her; she can keep her husband.

And so on.

Fred Williamson was a quiet man, always by himself, reading a newspaper and smoking his cigar, or chatting with Bo Svenson, who had been his buddy in many movies. But the real problem was Bo. He was gloomy, often half-drunk and he seemed to be somehow jealous of me. He was hurting me when we were fighting and his general attitude was borderline impolite. I was old enough and with enough movie experience to defend myself, but I detected that his behavior was due to some inner torment and I tried being patient.

Action star Bo Swenson

When confronting him on a roof in the scene that followed my almost suicidal escape from the car, my dance skills were once again quite useful, because De Angelis wanted me to hide in between two chimneys no larger than 20 inches and then suddenly jump out at Bo.

I could do it only assuming a perfect "second position," spreading my legs and bending my knees, molding myself as flat as an Egyptian bas-relief, but De Angelis took it for granted as he was doing with every effort on my part. I positively detested the man even more than I had detested Lenzi. Umberto was pompous and self-centered, but with a desire to be acknowledged that made him at least human, while De Angelis was cold blooded and petty, much more a real gangster than my character in the movie.

A few scenes had required more time than scheduled and filming was hurried up because Christmas was approaching. A huge neon sign on our hotel was making a daily count down with "15 days to Christmas, plan your party now! 14 days to Christmas …" And the crew was determined to spend the festivities with their families.

So, one day while De Angelis was shooting a scene with Fred and Bo, Renato and I got into our car with the camera mounted on the hood and were instructed to drive around and deliver our dialogue a few times, with me being in charge of the clapper-board, pushing the button for camera to roll and deciding when at least three good shots were in the can. In other words: "Do it yourself!"

Shooting in Arizona was also an occasion to clash with divergent sides of the American Way, something I tried to always avoid. Being in the streets all day, I noticed that Phoenix was quite a peculiar place, because of the massive presence of retired people from all over the country who came to live there as an alternative to Florida, enjoying the benefits of the dry desert heat. The town was packed with these wrinkled, tanned mummies who were in generally great shape and one of them was the chauffeur who was driving me on set when we moved to the desert scenes, on location about 50 miles out. It was a long straight road with no one in sight, but he carefully respected the incredibly low speed limits and the drive took some time. To be polite and make some conversation, I thought of talking about cars, even if I knew nothing about the topic, because my driver seemed to be very keen on them. I saw a commercial on T.V. and asked him, "Have you seen these new Toyota Corollas?" He looked at me with a stare of pure hate from his baby blues and coldly half mouthed, "I'd never buy one." I asked why and his answer was, "Because I have a lasting memory." I was puzzled for a moment and then realized that he was referring to the car being Japanese and he meant he didn't forget about Pearl Harbor. I never checked, but I guess Arizona was politically supportive in electing the Bush presidents.

Another incident connected to a local way of thinking occurred when, shooting downtown, a Native American stopped by to watch what was going on, out of sheer curiosity. I noticed that there were quite many wandering around and looking miserable and I was aware of how much they had been exploited, so, when a tall All-American policeman chased him off quite roughly, I took the man's defense saying he was doing nothing wrong, and I didn't surrender until the production manager dragged me away scolding me for not minding my own business. I guess if I retire I won't get mummified in Phoenix.

We finally completed the Arizona schedule and moved to Las Vegas only 10 days before Christmas, as the neon sign was recording "Only 10 days to Christmas, plan your party now!" Saying goodbye to the hotel, I wondered if on Christmas day the sign will say: "It's Christmas, fuck yourself!"

The road to Vegas on a bus presented me with a wonderful presentation of both sun and moon in a beautiful sunset sky over the desert, with the even more amazing glow that anticipated Las Vegas. The night sky grew brighter and brighter as if some nuclear incident had occurred, and then, when on top of a hill, there it was: Las Vegas and its millions of lights.

But if the town was amazing from a distance, staying in Las Vegas proved very difficult and I got to think that if Hell does exist mine would have been the Casino City. I was good at playing poker (the original game, not the many American variations), but apart from that, gambling of any sort never tempted me. All the people in the hotel lobbies mindlessly fed coin-after-coin into the slot machines representing a worse variation of brain-dead zombie than in any Fulci movie. The electricity in the air, coming from the millions of slot machines and other games, was so intense that I was getting an electric shock whenever touching metal, and I learned to always have some tissues in my pocket to deal with door knobs or keys to avoid static charge. The population there seemed to consist of only gamblers, casino staff and hookers and the buildings all appeared to be only hotels, casinos and quick marriage churches. I never got to observe where the real people lived.

Anyway, we hadn't time to wander about, because shooting became sheer madness, with two different crews alternating in 24 hours and we actors had to always be in the hotel, which was also our set, and were allowed to get sleep and food only when not needed on set. With people knocking at my door and calling me to work at any time, I completely lost track of time and couldn't tell if it were day or night.

When it was over we finally returned on our plane and arrived in Rome on December 23. I slept an entire day and went to Christmas dinner at my stepmother Fabiola's place. After my father's death she had reunited the family around her and was a loving mother to my brothers and me as she was to her own children. My brother Daniele, in the ups and downs of his mental illness, had managed to marry and have two children, one girl and a boy, and they loved their granny Fabiola very much and could enjoy, through her, the Christmas tradition of tree, presents and carols.

We completed the film in early January of 1985, with some interior scenes filmed at various Roman studios and in these last days I discovered a new and unexpected side of Bo Svenson. The man looked lost, maybe because of the language or because his buddy Fred wasn't there, and his attitude toward me changed completely, to the point that one morning he dragged me into his dressing room and talked to me about his life and the many problems with his wife. As I had suspected his aggressive behavior was due to a difficult moment in his life and we parted as friends. Meeting him once again in 2011 at a convention was a real blast, and we had a wonderful time. He aged wonderfully and, if not a teetotaler, he has severely cut back on his drinking. As a matter of fact he was the first one to suggest that I should write a book on my life, and so, thanks Bo, here it is.

I hated *Deadly Impact*, but when I saw it released I was quite pleased with my performance as an icy cold assassin who looked like he was coming out of some action comic strip, without a hint of humanity or compassion. I saw the movie in a theater in Rome and the guy sitting in front of me, quite clearly mentally deranged, was so enthusiastic about my villainous actions that he kept mumbling, "Son of a bitch … I'll kill you … you motherfucker …" I slowly slid down in my seat and tried hiding my face with my cap as much as possible, but I was quite pleased with the spontaneous reactions my character was getting from that weirdo because it meant I had done a good job.

With no other jobs in sight, I tried reorganizing my domestic life without "C." The apartment had been too large for two people and was positively excessive for just me, so I decided to rent "T's" former room, thus getting some additional economic help for my bills and the wages of Fernanda, my cleaning lady. She had been with me for some time, coming three times a week for three or four hours, and she was the most fantastic synthesis of the Roman way of thinking and behaving embodied in a working class lady who had just two years of formal education and had started working as a child. She had the Roman sarcastic sense of humor derived from having seen ages and ages of history and thus not taking anything too seriously. She had a brisk wit and often used foul language, such as when she nicknamed a very large and difficult to fold wool blanket I had knitted "the maid's cunt," because it was "going everywhere." In the same way she referred to her own married daughter as "that whore of a daughter of mine," not because the young girl was cheating on her husband, but as a term of endearment.

She had accepted my living with "T" without comment, but had sided with me in detesting "L" and I was now ready for my first roommate, an American dancer and teacher in Rome for the long term, whom I had found through the dancing school I was still attending. Ballet was something deeply rooted in my bones and muscles and at times I regretted not having taken it as a profession as when, studying with the famous American dancer Dennis Wayne in a class of 50 people, he came by me and asked how old I was. When I told him I was 28, my age at that time, he had sadly shook his head, whispering "too late," as to say that I had the perfect body but it was too late to get into the profession.

Richard Haisma, my roommate, was a bearded red-haired giant that no ballet company would have considered and was, as a matter of fact, only into a special form of modern dance following the teachings of Alwin Nikolais. We became lovers on the very first night and he felt guilty because he had a steady relation in America, but he overcame it and we had a fantastic time as sex buddies and I experienced some of the best sex ever. He wasn't really happy about me speaking English because he was one of the few Americans I met who wanted to learn Italian, and he tried so hard, continuing to study it when back in the U.S.A., that he is now fluent and almost accent free and can read complicated poetry such as Dante's *Divine Comedy*.

Some more T.V. work materialized with two guest appearances in miniseries: *Father Brown*, from the Chesterton books, directed by Vittorio De Sisti and starring Emrys James in the title role, and *The Judge* by Giulio Questi, starring Swiss actor Jean Luc Bideau as a former court judge who had switched to private investigation and was pretty much modeled on Philip Marlowe. Both De Sisti and Questi were esteemed professionals and everything went smoothly.

Italian T.V. seemed to cast me only in roles of debauched aristocrats and the two characters in *Father Brown* and *The Judge* were in that line, but a more creative challenge arrived, this time with me as a director, when my old pal Saverio Marconi asked me to stage *The Courtesan* by Pietro Aretino, a 16th-century play with more than 20 characters, written in old Italian.

After the success of *Happy End*, Saverio slowed down his movie career and settled in Tolentino, where the municipality financed an acting school he was directing. Marina Garroni had moved there too with her family and was teaching in the school. *The Courtesan* was intended as a big event for the re-opening after extensive rennovations of the local historical theater, named after the Tolentino-born composer Nicola Vaccaj. Saverio had selected the play because he starred in it as a boy and because of the vast number of characters. He wanted to have a mixed cast of professional actors (himself, Marina and our friend Michele Renzullo, who had also moved to Tolentino), people from the local amateur theater group and students from the acting school and the entire town would be

Emrys James played Father Brown in the series with Johnny

involved in preparing the costumes and building the sets by Aldo Buti, reproducing some old aqueduct arches where people had built houses and churches as it actually happened in Rome in both the Middle Ages and Renaissance. All in all there were more than 100 people involved, including the students of the art school who were patiently gluing the polystyrene bricks to the arches and painting them in the pink-brown tonality of a Piranese drawing.

Directing the play was almost like directing an opera, and as a matter of fact I asked for musicians on stage and included some songs and couplets in the production. The play had two different plots mixing and crossing. The first one told the story of Parabolano, a rich but vulgar man who wanted to act more gentlemanly and was making love to a noblewoman, only to be tricked by his servant Il Rosso (The Red) and an old pimp named Alvigia, who arranged a sexual rendezvous in a dark room with the wife of a baker. The second plot dealt with the misfortunes of a young, stupid man from Siena, Mr. Maco, who had come to Rome to become a courtesan in the Pope's court and was mocked by a bunch of false philosophers and teachers placing him in the most ridiculous situations. Saverio, Marina and Michele were starring as Il Rosso, Alvigia and Mr. Maco, but around them was an entire world swarming with priests, Jews, fishermen, soldiers, servants and artisans who were to be played by the students and the amateurs. Aretino's final aim had been depicting the corruption of Rome (The Courtesan of the title) and the underworld creeping around the Pope's throne. It was hard to avoid a gap in quality between professionals and amateurs, but the savory Old Italian allowed some dialectal inflections, and the eagerness of the local people to not be lessened by the actors gave some wonderful results.

I put all my strength into directing and as much strength into organizing the opening night. We invited actors and personalities from Rome and all the national drama critics, and with my utter joy my uncle Pietro Ingrao, who was President of Parliament, attended with his wife in the Royal box, pampered by the Major who was positively overwhelmed with pride.

To my surprise among the guests was Lisa, my former girlfriend from my school days, who had come with her aunt who was an important manager in the Rome National Theater.

After the triumphal opening night a spark rekindled between us, and that very night we ended up making passionate love in my hotel room.

Chapter 20
Falling in Love Again

Lisa was the girl I had found most attractive in my whole life, since the day she joined our second year high school class wearing a phenomenal mini-skirt that created a sensation and almost caused a fit to the bigoted and ugly female literature professor. She had a classical beautiful face with perfect fawn features and a sexy lean body, and when she bent down to drink at a street fountain a car crash was potentially bound to happen. Not only she was beautiful, but also very clever and with many interests which ranged from music (with a conservatory piano degree) to politics and from theater to medicine.

I fell in love with her and became her boyfriend, even if I was having affairs on the side with "T" and Dado. Apparently some teenagers can stretch the duration of a day to at least 36 hours, only a precious few dedicated to sleep.

She was in love with me too, but a variation of psychological impotence prevented me from making real love and, after a while, this caused our separation. But we stayed friends and had other moments of sexual passion and we were finally able to go "all the way," but we never resumed being a couple and just had some occasional sex, which once involved her then current boyfriend, who was bisexual as well.

As I had occasion to mention, she became a doctor and specialized in gynecology, both working in a hospital and in her private practice where she helped many poor women and educated young girls in sexuality. Politics was still a strong issue for her and she joined the Communist Party which then transformed into the present Democratic Party.

But all these activities didn't prevent her from playing the piano, singing in a choir and at times helping me in my theater activity. Her energy was as inexhaustible as her curiosity for all aspects of life.

When we met up again in Tolentino, we were both 30 years old and single. The lovemaking nights led to a steady relationship and after a while she moved in with me. Richard had gone back to the States and I hadn't yet found another roommate.

For the first time in my life I was perfectly happy, and the issue wasn't choosing between one sex or the other, but being with this special perfect person who was right for me. I liked every thought in her mind, every feeling of her heart and every inch of her body, and when I was inside her making love I felt as a Pilgrim who had finally found his Promised Land. Sex with her was an exciting pleasure but also served as nutrition for my soul. I guess that's the recipe for perfect love.

We had many friends in common and met with them often, and it was clear that everyone was very happy about our reunion. The only small shortcomings came from her side of the family. Her parents had divorced and her father, a radiologist, had married his secretary, a namby-pamby woman whom Lisa disliked but tried to befriend, because of her stepsister, a little girl she was very attached to and ever more so after her father's premature death. Her mother was a very peculiar character, never easy. Much older than her former husband, who had been her second, she was clever and cultivated but very mentally disturbed, with a form of bipolar disease that could take her from heavy depressions to exaggerated vivacity and both were to be feared. Lisa tried to take care of her, but she always lived dreading to become like her and visits always left her perturbed.

I had known Anna, her mother, since I was a teenager and I could cope with her in small doses, and I had no problems in being polite and sociable with the stepmother, but the baby sister was to provide me with quite a shock. She was lively but a bit boring, as girls often are when eight or nine years old, wanting the moon and acting like dolls, but I would never suspect that she would attack me sexually, as it happened once we were left alone.

We were in Lisa's father summer place by the sea and Lisa had to run back to Rome because one of her patients had an anticipated delivery. She was to come back in the evening and I was left with her stepsister, which was okay by me. But as soon as we were alone the young predator started climbing on my lap and putting her hands everywhere, including my pants, in what seemed rough playing, but all this had clear sexual undertones. I was transfixed with embarrassment and immediately decided to go for a walk, even if the weather was awful and going to the beach impossible. So I took her to a bar that had some electronic games and provided her with all the money I had to keep her busy, but after a few hours it was time to go home and eat. As soon as we were back she resumed her approaches and the nightmare of escaping and trying to induce her to play some quiet game went on until Lisa returned. Lisa didn't pay much attention to the episode, saying that the little girl was competing with her and her actions were quite normal, but I was shocked all the same. I had seduced "T" when very young, but I was 13 and sexually mature. But an eight-year-old girl? Thank God I never had the slightest pedophiliac instinct, but the episode led me to think that there's still quite a lot to investigate concerning children's sexuality.

On the work front, my months of unemployment were interrupted by a request to work with a small theater company known as Società Per Attori (The Actors Company).

One of their actors had seen and loved *Happy End* and had suggested my name when they decided to stage something different from the classical plays that had always been in their repertoire. I immediately thought of the Ayckbourn plays that had almost caused my death from laughter when reading them. After meeting with the manager, a good-looking bearded man named Franco Clavari, and the four steady actors in the company, I was uncertain and fluctuated between *bedroom Farce* and *Absurd Person Singular*. The latter had a smaller cast of six, but required very complicated scenery with three different sets for the three acts, so we decided to stage *bedroom Farce*, which had a cast of eight, but used the same set all through the play, consisting of three bedrooms in three different houses.

There was a lot of time to prepare everything because rehearsals weren't scheduled before the end of the year, but I started work on completing the cast with the four missing roles and Franco Clavari asked me to hire, if possible, someone with a little fame who did not require a high fee. I immediately thought of Alessandra Panelli, my long-time friend who had shared the Spoleto apartment with me and always tended to me when I was drunk. The public knew her name because of her parents, but she had also made a personal career on stage and, most important for popularity, in Saturday night T.V. shows. She was uncertain where to accept the job because of the little money offered, but Masolino D'Amico, who was to translate the play and was an authority on English theater, convinced her by saying that she needed to do something entirely different from her parents' career, so as not to be always considered as "the daughter of." She accepted the offer and suggested we cast her boyfriend as well, a young actor named Stefano Viali. A friend of Stefano's, Gianluca Favilla, completed the cast. Everything being settled, we said farewell until the time to start rehearsals.

Alessandra Panelli

I spent the whole summer in Rome with Lisa, who had to work in a hospital in Ostia, Rome, a seaside resort quite near a gay beach named "The Hole." The beach was named "The Hole" not because of some sexual context, but because it had been located on private property and nudists had started going there by sneaking through a hole in the wire. Lisa was fully aware of my bisexuality, but she wasn't in the least jealous or worried and often drove me to the beach, went to work and picked me up when her workday was over. I liked the gay beach because of nude sunbathing, but not once was I tempted by hanky-panky in the bushes, to the utter surprise of people who had known me for a long time.

We were having a wonderful time and were never bored with one another because she had always been interested in show business and I had a real passion for medicine. My mother and her brother had been doctors, and so was my brother Marco, and when he was a university student I helped him memorize the terribly difficult names of bones and muscles. This went to my advantage when I attended sports physical therapy classes that included many disciplines in the scientific area. I learned much more from Lisa, who never defended her

An Italian lobby card for *Big Deal on Madonna Street*

profession as a sacred sect. She thought that everyone should be able to cure himself or herself for minor diseases, which as a matter of fact I did all my life.

At the end of August I got a call from Silvia D'Amico, Masolino's sister, who was a producer and wanted me to have a role in her next movie, a sequel to Monicelli's *Big Deal on Madonna Street* that her mother Suso Cecchi D'Amico had written and was to be directed by Monicelli's long-time assistant, Amanzio Todini. The cast included actors from the original movie including Vittorio Gassman, Marcello Mastroianni and character actor Tiberio Murgia, who was Sardinian but after the success of the movie had spent his life portraying Sicilian characters similar to the one in *Big Deal*. Alessandra Panelli had a role too, but we hadn't scenes together. I was to play a dandy gangster to whom the Mastroianni character had to deliver drugs, and my scenes were going to be shot in Trieste, an Italian town that I had never visited but longed to see because of its proximity to Yugoslavia, the home country of my grandmother Harasim.

A few days before my departure, Lisa complained about the IUD she was using as a contraceptive, saying it was bothering her. I told her honestly that in my opinion she could skip it; we were both adults, working, and with the equity involved in owning a house, we could afford having a child.

I left for Trieste without foretelling the consequences of my words.

Silvia D'Amico was a good friend and had managed a 10-day stay, even if my scenes only required two or three days' work. I had time to visit Trieste and enjoy the special Austro-Hungarian atmosphere that inspired so many writers from Italo Svevo, who was born there, to James Joyce, who had worked in town for some years as a bank clerk while writing *Dubliners*. When visiting the Miramare castle my nostalgic thoughts went to Maximilian of Hapsburg, who had built it, and to his wife Charlotte, who had been segregated there after going insane after the disastrous Mexican adventure that had given her husband an imperial throne and a cruel death. I had read a lot about them and liked the movie with Bette Davis, Brian Aherne and Paul Muni as Benito Juarez. All considered, my grandmother Harasim was born as a loyal and faithful subject of His Imperial Majesty Franz Joseph, and something had stuck in my blood.

But more than sightseeing and playing tourist, what amazed me was meeting Marcello Mastroianni and finding out that he was not only the wonderful actor the whole world knew about, but also one of the best human beings I'd ever met.

I was nervous about working with him and, detecting it, he pretended to be insecure of his lines and asked me to rehearse just with him. He was so nice, simple and unaffected that I relaxed to the point of forgetting about my dancer feet, which unfortunately can be seen in all their awkward glory in the movie.

Marcello Mastroianni

But what was phenomenal about Marcello was his off-set attitude. He treated everybody with humor and affection and was so generous that if he were around it was impossible to pay for one's coffee. Once, in the hotel lobby, he was sitting with a newspaper with his back to the bar, so I tip-toed to the counter and whispered for a coffee, but when I tried paying, the barman told me, "It's on Mr. Mastroianni." The man had both a kind heart and a radar-detecting one that knew what cast members were doing if even at a great distance and with their backs turned. When Sunday arrived he surprised the whole cast and crew by renting a big yacht and took us on a cruise in the Trieste Gulf with a catered meal on board and with lots of wine and liquors, something he was too keen on and that ultimately affected his liver, contributing to his premature death. During the cruise he involved everybody in group sing-alongs and sang himself some risqué couplets of his own invention. He was funny, delicate, boyish and protective at the same time and it was no wonder that so many women had loved him madly and not just for his looks. A few years later I would have the honor and pleasure of seeing him quite often, because he was the best friend of my father-in-law to be.

I went back to Rome in high spirits, opened the door and fell right into a coup de theater plotted by some screen-player from *Beautiful*; Lisa had gone.

She had left a letter saying that she needed time to think about our relationship, but every grown up with some experience knows that this is just a bad cliché for "game over."

I was thunderstruck, and much more so than when we first met. I found her entirely changed; she was cold, embarrassed by our situation and without explanation other than that she didn't feel ready for any kind of marriage.

It was crap and we both knew it. When, later on, I had the necessary detachment to think clearly about it, I came to the conclusion that talking about children had led her to think that I wasn't the sort of man she could trust for a family life because of my complicated sexuality, the ups and downs in my work, my need for freedom and God knows what else.

Not for me to tell if she was right or wrong, but when she left me I was positively destroyed. My shrink, who had been openly in favor of the match, dropped his mummy mask for once and scolded me because I wasn't trying to get her back. But I felt deeply hurt and I doubted, with her brains and maturity, that serenades or dozens of roses a day could win her back. My theories about her need for more security were confirmed when, a couple of years later, she married a bank manager and had a daughter. But I knew about it from friends, because I couldn't face the idea of meeting her for many years to come.

Chapter 21
Theater Triumphs and
A Pain in the Ass (in Outer Space)

I stayed gloomy and remained depressed for some time, trying to find solace by savagely indulging in occasional gay sex, a form of revenge that didn't give me any sort of actual relief.

Luckily in the fall I started rehearsing *bedroom Farce* and the work helped me out of the impasse in my private life.

Alan Ayckbourn is famous in England and other countries but is totally unknown in Italy. There have been some attempts in staging one or two of his plays, but the approach leads to the heavy farcical one of the Italian tradition, which demonstrates that his wit and sharp sense of humor in depicting the middle class has collapsed under the weight of actors pulling faces and being painfully aware that what they are doing is "funny." On the contrary, the secret when staging Chekov, to whom Ayckbourn has often been compared, is to play it utterly serious and get into character as if playing drama; everything has to be absolutely realistic, thus giving the audience the impression of watching the comic misadventures of the characters as though watching from a keyhole. Ayckbourn's ability with dialogue is exceptional and his characters are absolutely believable, lively and perfectly motivated, even when getting into utter nonsense. This was real paradise for every actor who could manage to look beyond real life and the stage, a quality not so frequent in Italy. Another peculiarity that had clashed with Italian theater habits was that Ayckbourn mostly wrote for groups, modeling characters on the actors he had in his Scarborough Company before even thinking of the London stage, while 90 percent of Italian productions had a star (or two) in it if the play's budget allowed. But fortunately what I had was exactly a group of young players and surely Alessandra, who was the only one with some fame, wasn't the kind of actress attempting to prevail on others.

During the first day of rehearsals an incident occurred that was right out of an Ayckbourn play, but at the same time dramatic and ridiculous.

Alan Ayckbourn, playwright

Considering we were just going to read the script, Franco Clavari had asked us to meet at his place and had charged one of the actresses, Maria Luisa, with the task of preparing everything, because theater was for him just his side profession and he was busy with his pressing office work at a major oil company. Maria Luisa climbed on a chair to get something from a cupboard and fell, breaking a leg. When I arrived with the others, we found her moaning in pain and were deeply embarrassed because, aside from Alessandra and myself, we hardly knew one another and we surely couldn't rehearse over a wounded body. We called an ambulance and after she left we started work, but before it was over, Franco informed us that she was going to wear a plaster cast for a long time. Her role was the one of Kate, a childish woman who was constantly playing rough games with her husband and hopping on beds, and it was impossible for her to play that role with a restrictive cast. So I searched frantically for another actress and called my friend Doris Von Thury, an American-German girl who was an extremely good actress, but she was otherwise engaged and suggested to me a friend of hers who was living in Florence, Lucilla Salvini. She came from Florence and I auditioned her with good results. She was eager to do it and didn't care about the scarce payroll or being put up somewhere because there was no money to provide her a hotel stay. So Kate she was. All this could seem uninteresting and it would be if the events, starting with just climbing on a chair and breaking a leg, hadn't radically changed the destiny of entire families, as I will later explain. It was just as in Ayckbourn's play *Intimate Exchanges* where the actors, night by night, can make a different decision that will lead to a certain plot progression instead of another, starting with a cigarette that can or can't be lit, which gave the title of *Smoking No Smoking* to the film version by Alain Resnais. Maria Luisa falling from a chair proved to be such a powerful force.

Bedroom Farce is about the mad night of three married couples who are overwhelmed by a fourth, who imposes on everybody's fights and reconciliations.

One of the couples is a long-time one, but, even if both in their 30s, Giannina Salvetti as Delia and Gianluca Favilla as Ernest managed to be very believable and utterly funny.

Rehearsals went well and I gave my all in directing the actors, hopping up and down from stage to demonstrate what they should do. The many films and T.V. series I had been in proved very useful in knowing exactly what kind of realism should be used in acting, because even in the most extreme genre movies, I had tried with all my heart to be believable.

The only problem arose when we had to fit the scenery into the minimal stage of the Roman theater, where we were going to open. To give the actors some more space downstage, I decided not to use the curtain and that decision led to a very funny incident. The Nick character, played by Gianfranco Candia, is suffering from excruciating back pain and is in bed for the entire play. I thought it was amusing to have him in bed from the beginning, when the audience was entering and getting seated and to leave him there also during the intermission. He agreed, but on opening night, by the end of the second act, he was badly in need of peeing and finally couldn't restrain nature's calling and relieved himself in his pyjamas.

Apart from this toilet inconvenience, the play was a great success, with even more laughs than expected and huge applauses. We were overcome with joy, but feared it was all for nothing when, on the second day, an amazing snowfall overcame Rome and interrupted car traffic and public transports. Nevertheless people didn't stop coming because of the word of mouth proclaiming it was the comic hit of the year and not to be missed. The 120 seats of the little theater were always sold out.

I was very pleased with the company and I thought that with Franco Clavari I had finally found a money-providing partner for my creative skills. He was cautious as a general manager and administrator should be, but he loved and understood the stage work and was constantly coping personally with whatever problem arose. He was obsessed with cleaning and on opening night I had to drag him backstage not to have the audience arrive with him still vacuuming. We parted with plans for *Bedroom Farce* to be continued next season, mount a tour and add additional plays to enrich our collaboration.

Bedroom Farce rekindled my theater fervor and, to be honest, I didn't miss movies or T.V., so when Antonio Margheriti called me to play pirate Israel Hands in the six-episode T.V. space version of *Treasure Island*, I had a few doubts about committing to it. On one hand I adored Margheriti and I was keen to work with him, even if it meant reading the telephone book, but on the other it was a six-month engagement and Rai was offering a fee that was almost offensive.

Italian state television had been overwhelmed by the market opening to private networks and was responding in the worst possible way. They were trying to compete with the three channels owned by Silvio Berlusconi (not yet in politics) by lowering the quality level of their programs and filling them with vulgar comics, half-naked girls and quarrelsome talk shows, but they weren't eager to pay market fees to entertainers and show girls, and questionable so-called masters were migrating toward the rich land of five-year contracts with Channel 5, Berlus-

A Spanish poster for *Treasure Island in Outer Space*

coni's flagship. Actors were recruited for specific projects and, of course, if they had to choose, they preferred the generous payrolls of private networks that, by the way, accepted negotiations with agents, something the state T.V. found unbecoming, if not illegal.

My agent (Pino Pellegrini, who now ran his own firm) couldn't be of any help, and I alone had to deal with the sour, spinsterish lady from the legal office who only dangled the small chance of getting a slightly better fee.

At the end I decided to accept, because I hated the idea of saying no to Margheriti and because filming was entirely in Rome, allowing me to stay in touch with the *Bedroom Farce* company and quietly work on further projects. Another point in favor of accepting was that the rest of the cast included David Warbeck, Philippe Leroy, Ernest Borgnine and Anthony Quinn (who starred as Long John Silver).

As soon as I started working I realized that dealing with small payrolls wasn't the only shortcoming of the Rai production. The scenery and special effects of spaceships, planets and androids had been built by state T.V. Studio people and everything was childishly inadequate as though coming from a bad 1950s movie, fully showing the limitations made of wood and grossly designed adhesions. Furthermore the whole crew was made of steady employees and, not being on location, they were just thinking about getting back home, eating pasta and watching soccer games. Everything was sloppy, slowed down and borderline unprofessional, especially considering that the science fiction movie standard had been raised considerably by recent productions such as the *Star Wars* series. We had to cope regularly with strikes and other union problems. At times things became ridiculous as when we waited one hour because the clapperboard man wasn't there. I was getting into the shot later and volunteered to do it, arousing a choir of protests because I was suggesting breaking some sacred rule in defense of the working class. Movies are made of the blood, sweat and passions of people working in them who want to be at their best to be called for further jobs. So creative apathy can destroy even the best of projects.

Poor Margheriti was totally different from the man I had worked with in *Cannibal Apocalypse*; he was cornered from every side and couldn't show his talents because he had to deal with problems that had nothing to do with the story or the acting, the main challenge being Anthony Quinn's personality.

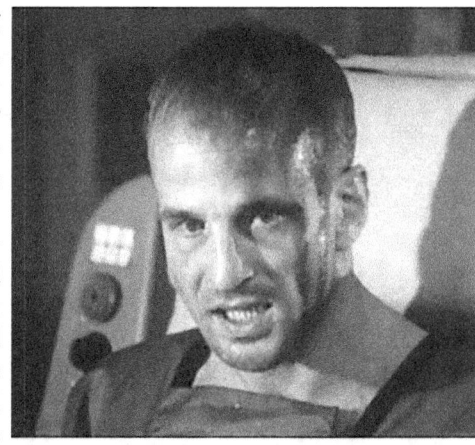

Johnny as Hands from *Treasure Island in Outer Space*

When I was introduced to him he barely nodded; I thought he was having a bad day, but I was to find out that "good morning" wasn't in his vocabulary and that it was just one minor inconvenience in working with him.

Sitting on a special leather throne he had built himself, His Majesty The Star was in charge of everything, from dialogue to positioning. He rewrote the script daily and would thrust it at you just muttering: "New lines for today." Thank God I had a surprising memory and could learn three or four pages in 20 minutes, but it wasn't the same for others who were cursing and sweating trying to learn the new pages, terrorized by incurring his royal disfavor. Mr. Quinn seemed pissed with anything Italian and once kicked Bruno Zanin, the boy who had been the protagonist of Fellini's *Amarcord*, in the ass because of his bad English. On this respect he wasn't totally wrong because there was more than one actor who wasn't at ease with the language, and that had been a major fault in casting, but Quinn's attitude was nevertheless inadmissible. But he was the "star" and nobody dared contradict him.

He wasn't openly aggressive with me, but in our scenes in the restricted corridors of the spaceship, he was constantly stepping on my feet or casting shadows on my face, with the result of me having to move right and left as though we were in a boxing match.

At times I looked Margheriti squarely in the eyes and those orbs were saying, "I am sorry, there's nothing I can do about it."

Quinn was jealous of fellow actors and in constant need of out-staging them as if he still was the poor Mexican boy struggling for success in Hollywood and not a worldwide known star and the winner of two Academy Awards. But if he was impolite with his colleagues, his behavior with the crew reminded me of slavery before the American Civil War. Our costumes had no space to hide collar microphones and the poor grip holding the boom was always lying down at our feet. If he wasn't quick enough in standing after "cut" was called, Mr. Star would walk on him without a second thought. His personal dresser was mistreated to

A montage of sequences from *Treasure Island in Outer Space*, featuring Ernest Borgnine (upper left) and Johnny (lower left, sitting at the console)

the point of crying every day, while his Italian wife Iolanda, a former dresser herself, came visiting on set wearing more jewelry than a Neapolitan statue of the Virgin Mary.

He was positively the real Mafia Don and playing Vito Corleone would have been for him as easy as drinking a glass of water. In support of this idea I once overheard a conversation with him talking about his son's acting career saying he needn't worry because, "Dad will take care of everything!"

What he had to complain about as for his costume was a thick mystery, because we were all wearing the same one-piece space suits, designed by Academy Award nominee and Emmy winner Enrico Sabbatini, and nothing could be wrong with them apart from the fact that they were made of very light material, half fabric and half plastic, which was so tight that if by misfortune there were a drop of pee dripping after going to the toilet it would spread all over your crotch in the most embarrassing way. I was as skinny as ever and not worried about the tight suit revealing a protruding stomach or a fat ass, but the pee problem was serious and I solved it at home by making a sort of sanitary towel with toilet paper and folding my penis in it.

Other actors posed no problems, but I had very little to do with them, just a few group scenes in the pilot cabin involving David Warbeck, who was always in a good mood, and Philippe Leroy, who seemed to be living in the remotest planet of the galaxy and often learned the wrong scene. "Hellooo! I am fully rrrready for 218!," he would say in his thick French accent when arriving in the morning. But then he was bewildered by the fact we were shooting 507. As a matter of fact we were shooting six episodes without any type of time continuity, and it was quite difficult to remember at what point of the story you were at, but Philippe didn't even bother to read the call sheet or was too vain to wear glasses.

The leading role of the boy Jim was played by 12-year-old Itaco Nardulli, a child actor constantly oppressed by his parents and by the professors in charge of having him study for school in between takes. He was remote and polite as an adult and with a touching hint of melancholy in whatever he was doing, as if already bored with life and his was unfortunately very short because he died at age 17 during an underwater fishing hunt.

Shooting went on little-by-little as the months were going by. Because of the crew being so lazy and slow, the usual time wasting was 10 times longer than usual and I spent hours boring myself to death; so I decided to resume knitting and got the surprised approval of German actor Klaus Loewitsch, with whom I was sharing my dressing room.

Israel Hands wasn't a difficult character for me and was very much in the line of others I had played, such as the part in *Deadly Impact*, a cold blooded and treacherous snake who wouldn't hesitate in killing a young boy, and that was the theme of my last long sequence. I was tricking Jim into believing I was on his side and then attempted to murder him. He escaped, I chased him all inside the spaceship and I finally threw a knife at him, but I only wounded his arm and he bravely took the knife out and threw it back at me, hitting my eye and making me fall out of a window and die.

With our crew's lack of energy it took days to complete the sequence and, at the end, I was stuck for two days with the bloody prop knife in my eye. Not seeing from one eye made me dizzy and unbalanced, and furthermore I couldn't get out of the studio to eat or go to the toilet, because the special effect was causing horrified screams from the girl chorus line next door. The dear and always caring Margheriti asked for a heap of sawdust to be put in a corner, and I peed there and spent the rest of the time sitting with both eyes closed. On the last day the production manager approached me and timidly asked if we could allow visiting school children into the studio. I hadn't the energy to say no and stayed there, like a wax statue in a museum, while a line of a 100 teenaged school boys passed in front of me and commented in every possible way from "Cool!" to "What the fuck!"

There was a section of the series that was going to be shot in Morocco, in the same Ouarzazate location I had visited with *Atlantis Project*, and the close-up of my death out of the spaceship was scheduled there. I didn't want to go by all means and begged Margheriti to find another way. He was his usual generous and friendly self and agreed by shooting the scene with a little pond recreated in the studio that could be seen from the spaceship window. I jumped from some 30 feet onto a mattress and then, in close-up, hit the pond, apparently dead, and bid farewell to *Treasure Island* with the energetic crew applause.

When the movie was finally released all my fears proved true, as the scenery and childish special effects were as bad as suspected, but I was anyway pleased with my role that, for once, I had dubbed in Italian, preventing with my presence a major mistake in the translation of an important Anthony Quinn line which meant exactly the opposite of what his dubber was saying. This was the sloppiest production I had ever been in.

Right after the end of my contract I had to deal with my grandmother's death. The decision of retiring in a home for old people had proved a big mistake, because even if it was a place provided with all comforts, it did not allow for family members to attend meals and that had been the best time for the family to visit her. So her last years were lonely and bitter and she lost any desire for living. I had tried to visit her as often as possible, and on one occasion I walked into the stormy fury of her brother, my great-uncle Raffaello Morghen, who had been informed of my use of the sacred family name in what he thought were unbecoming movies. He was a well-known scholar in Medieval history, but he had the same name of his famous ancestor the engraver and had inherited the role of head of the house of the Gherardini, which included the patronage of a beautiful church in Florence where he is now buried. It wasn't difficult to understand that zombies and cannibals weren't in his bloodline.

After my grandmother's burial, I spent the great part of late spring and summer in Tolentino, because Saverio and Marina had asked me to direct the school play for senior students getting their diploma at the local acting school, and then to join the company Saverio had created after *The Courtesan* for a summer tour with Achille Campanile, the most renowned satiric writer in modern Italy. As for the school play I selected *Yerma*, by Spanish author Garcia Lorca, because it had a cast with many women that fitted the girls' predominance in the class. To give each a moment of glory the title role was shared among more than one actress and a symbolic red shawl indicated who was Yerma in each scene. Working on it I got to adore the dramatic poetry of the play and I was to stage it two more times in the future. The summer tour was also very satisfactory and a lot of fun. I played a maniacal patient in a dentist waiting room in the first act, the father of a widow with Parkinson's disease in the second and a stupid pompous lawyer in the third.

After the Campanile show there was a 10-day tour of *The Courtesan* in Sicily, very well paid but terribly organized, with outdoor performances in squares that hosted, at the same time, fun-fairs and stalls selling ice cream. Marina was pregnant with her second son and didn't feel like exhausting herself in the Sicilian heat, so a girl from the school substituted for her and I was Parabolano, because the amateur actor in the role couldn't take time off from work. Even if in the worst possible conditions, I had great fun playing the silly, bombastic boor pretending to be a Romeo; I was famished for comic roles and the future was going to accomplish my wish, strangely enough, starting with a horror movie.

Chapter 22
The Airy Spirit of Horror

Since the Savannah days I saw a lot of Michele Soavi and our friendship had grown increasingly intense. We were always in touch and frequently together, spending weekends and holidays at seaside resorts in his roaring James Dean Porsche or sleeping at each other's place. Michele was living at his mother's wonderful villa in the Via Appia Antica, beside the ancient Roman road paved with stones 2,000 years old and surrounded by tombstones of patricians and noblewomen. It was the spot where a lot of celebrities had their mansions, everyone from Gina Lollobrigida to Franco Zeffirelli, and Lidia Olivetti's place was just as good, with a huge park and stables for her beloved horses. Michele's mother was a peculiar character, acting like a 15-year-old girl of her generation and suitably dressed like a doll in baby blue or pink, with white collars and lot of ribbons. Michele was treating her more like a little sister than a mother and patiently raised his eyebrows when she needed something from him, calling out "Micheeeeeleeeee!" with her high-pitched voice. He had friends in the area such as the sons of "Mr. Volare," singer-actor Domenico Modugno, and at times we saw them, but we generally preferred to be by ourselves, talking, smoking pot and creating projects for future works. Just passing through a hole in the net surrounding the villa, we could do all this watching the stars at late night while sitting on the monument of some long gone Roman senator. He wanted by all means to be a director and we wrote a few treatments together, ghost stories or thrillers, with him fantasizing and creating visions and me trying to infuse some logic into the story.

Needless to say, I was madly in love with him and he was taken too, but sex preferences separated us. Our friendship was nevertheless very physical with a lot of hugging and kissing and, with a sense of humor free from any desire to defend his ladies' man status, he stated in later years that I had been his only boyfriend. As much as I would have loved to have sex with him, what mesmerized me was his attitude toward life, both animalistic and poetic. He reminded me of French poet Rimbaud because he was an artist in the purest sense of the word and his only desire

Michele Soavi (left) and Dario Argento

The VHS cover art for *Stagefright*

was to embody his fantasies by painting (something he was pretty good at) or by filming/directing, as he finally succeeded in doing.

He was "light" personified, a burning flame or an airy celestial spirit, but his imageries were gloomy and tormented, mostly inspired by painters such as Hieronymus Bosch or Munch and writers like Lovecraft and Poe. Totally uninformed and uninterested about Freud or Jung, he was nevertheless acting out a very healthy auto-analysis process by projecting the dark side of his personality but being in private life one of the most generous, warm and open-minded individuals I ever met.

He had a strong professional attachment to Aristide Massaccesi, a controversial producer and director of genre and hard-core movies, and all our treatments ended up in his hands but weren't realized until he decided to sponsor his debut by producing his first movie, whose original title was *Aquarius* but is now known by many different titles such as *Deliria*, *Bloody Bird* or *Stagefright*.

I hadn't time to participate in the writing process, but I was constantly informed about the progress and knew about my character, a gay dancer in a company rehearsing a show. When Luigi Montefiori completed the script, Michele asked me to revise some dialogue and add some behind-the-scenes bitching typical of the stage world, which I happily did, fishing into my personal memories.

The plot had been cleverly arranged for a low-budget movie; the company rehearsing a show was attacked and killed, one-by-one, by a serial killer who escaped from jail, and 90 percent of the movie was located in the rehearsal theater, actually an abandoned studio some 20 miles out of Rome that could

The birdman takes a leap on stage.

be rented for almost nothing: no scenery, a few costumes, some special effects and the actors.

Fees were very low, but I didn't care: I wasn't in strong need of money and I would have paid myself to be in my buddy's first movie. Furthermore I liked the role immensely because Brett was a bitchy, gossipy, sharp-tongued gay dancer and my comic skills had space to blossom in full glory. Unfortunately I wasn't in professional shape for some bits of the choreography that had to be performed, and I had a double for complicated pirouettes and jumps. At least my feet were free to point one east and the other west as they pleased.

We started shooting in late summer of 1986 and, if the scarce payroll didn't bother me, it wasn't the same for the general lack of comfort and organization. There weren't chauffeurs to drive us on set and I was getting there in a car driven by Robert Gligorov, a model who had a role in the movie and had the problematic habit of listening to rock music (which I hate) at loud volume, thus making it impossible to concentrate or go through my lines. He was a self-centered pain in the ass and as stupid as could be, but fortunately I only had to cope with him in the car and I had almost no dialogue with him in the actual movie. Other members of the cast were similarly uninteresting and barely professional, such as Jo Anne Smith, a dancer used to the "tits and ass" performances in Saturday night T.V. shows. On the other hand they were balanced by nice people like Barbara Cupisti, who I knew well because she was Michele's girlfriend and had a hostess role in *International Airport*, or Mary Sellers, a very clever and witty American actress I became friends with and was my closest partner in the script. In the middle stood David Brandon in the leading role of the director of the troupe. I saw him on stage in his many roles in Lindsay Kemp's company and I thought he had a great presence, but I couldn't get to know him better because he was always by himself and looked grumpy, either for personal reasons or because he was snubbing the movie as a silly B-thing. He was a professional anyway and never caused trouble.

The fiend in the bird suit approaches with an axe.

Car rides with Gligorov weren't the only inconveniences of the low-budget production. The old studio was positively falling apart, dirty and dusty, which was fine for the general atmosphere of the movie but less so for taking a nap on some broken down and dusty sofa, without risking having lice all over you. I was and am a "horizontal" person, and if not for special reasons such as being in front of a camera, I tend to live on beds or couches and, if I don't have a dressing room or a van, my first goal on whatever set is to find a place to lay down, but a place not infested with 20-year-old dirt. Furthermore there was no air conditioning and the tin roof in full sun was reflecting all the heat inside with an unpleasant sauna effect and resulted in lots of make-up fixes. We were sweating profusely and costumes were never washed or changed, so after a while we were stinking like unwashed commuters on a train, not the best feeling to have on a crowded movie set.

But there is a famous Stanislavsky theory summed up as "use it," which states that an actor must turn whatever unexpected inconvenience to his favor by using it as in character and reacting as the character would. We weren't adopting it consciously, but it worked all the same because our edginess and discomfort about the above-mentioned shortcomings was just perfect for people locked up in a place where a murderer was hiding in the shadows and ready to jump out and kill.

But the real engine of everyday work and the reason for us to function as a group was the incredible energy that Michele was putting into his direction. Different from all other directors I had worked with, his passion for horror was real and tangible and not just a cynical submission to what was presently fashionable. He carefully sketched every scene in a storyboard and was constantly excited about inventing a new angle or a clever solution for a problem. Skilled in whatever craft from grip to electrician, he was always helping the crew in first person and his dedication was contagious. We all wanted to give our best and participate in his dreams coming true.

The movie was studded with symbolic references to atavistic fears, the main one being the owl mask that we were using in our show-within-the-show and that the killer stole to perform his murders, which reminded me of Agatha Christie's *Ten Little Indians*, because we were killed one-by-one, with suspects and tensions spreading in the group. Our deaths paid a visible homage to other famous movies and the mirror game of quotations and references was a definite plus.

Mayhem or art on stage?

Mary Sellers was killed in a shower as in *Psycho*, Martin Philips, who played the assistant director, was drilled like I had been in *City of the Living Dead*, but the main homage was to *Texas Chain Saw Massacre*, with Jo Anne Smith severed in two and Gligorov and David Brandon similarly dispatched, with the addition of a hatchet to cut off David's head. But there wasn't unnecessary insistence on blood and gore and the rhythm of the cinematography was frantic and involving. I was killed with a hatchet too, but not by the killer who had gagged me, tied my hands and put the owl mask on me, so that I would be mistaken for him. My friends killed me and it was David Brandon who ripped the hatchet into me.

Because of his imposing stance, six-foot-tall screenwriter Luigi Montefiori played the killer under the mask; he had had a solid acting career in Westerns, spy stories and horror movies under the stage name of George Eastman, but he was slowly switching to just being a screenwriter. In later years I was to meet him a lot because we were active participants in the same guild. Michele provided another guest appearance in the role of a stupid policeman, who sat in a car eating all the time while the violent butchery inside the theater was performed.

When we were halfway through shooting, the production was shut down because of lack of funds, and for the first time I detected tension between Soavi and Massaccesi, who had otherwise been present on set but never interfered much in the creative process.

There was a 10-day stop and I concentrated on finding a new housemate. My long-time friend Melania Molfesi, a dancer who had been my Titania in *A Midsummer Night's Dream*, was a steady presence in *Fantastico*, the Saturday night show combined with the National Lottery, and she provided me with a list of

A French poster for *Stagefright* under the title of *Bloody Bird*

dancers from other parts of Italy who were in search of a room in Rome. A long line of roommates alternated for years and the best one was a handsome Brazilian boy with an impossible name shortened to the nickname of "Genius." He was great fun and whored around a lot, playing hard to get with two rich guys who were fighting for his pretty dark ass with shots of champagne and trays of caviar, so our fridge could compete with a millionaire's.

When we resumed shooting there was more of a "hurry up" atmosphere, and Massaccesi became the cameraman, something at which he was very skilled.

One of the last scenes saw all the corpses maniacally arranged on stage by the killer as statues in a museum, and a cat was supposed to sniff at our entrails and blood and then wander away. But thinking he was the reincarnation of some Egyptian god refused to take orders from some vulgar human being. Sometimes even a pretty ugly street cat can rise above its station in life. With the excruciating heat the animal entrails spread around the set were stinking to hell and we stayed motionless for hours while everybody in the crew was attracting his Feline Majesty with treats to convince him to do his job, which he finally did.

Stinky and sweaty, we were so happy we completed our six-week schedule and parted. I was convinced the movie was going to be a success as indeed it was, and the award won at the Avoriaz Horror Festival opened the door for Michele to make more movies to come.

Chapter 23
A Role Can Change a Life

After this tiring but also exciting movie interval, theater was awaiting me with the second season of *Bedroom Farce* and two new productions, one with the Tolentino amateur group and the other with the Sardinian Theater, the main theater company on the island.

The Tolentino amateur company, which had participated in *The Courtesan*, was mainly composed of men, for the most part middle-aged, and this gave me a bizarre idea: staging *Arsenic and Old Lace* with the two principal actors in drag as the angelic killer aunties. At first they were perplexed, but then accepted the challenge and invested some money in buying the scenery from a professional company, which had staged the play in the recent past. Amateurs can rehearse only in the evenings and for a short time, so each new production takes months to be staged, and I was going there every two or three weeks for a weekend to watch the improvements, make my corrections and instruct the company for further scenes.

In the meanwhile the Actors Society was to present *Bedroom Farce* in Rome in a larger theater and then on going out on tour.

We rehearsed a few days to refresh the production and successfully opened at the Teatro Vittoria, this time using the curtain so that poor Nick (Gianfranco) could pee at his convenience. As with the previous season we had a full house every night, and a great amount of applause and laughs, and among the latter a very strange one that puzzled me for days.

In a successful comedy, laughs become a part of the script as an extra character speaking his lines; you know when they are coming and you must learn neither to indulge them nor ignore them, not to spoil and make inaudible what follows. I was there every night, sitting at the end of the pit, and I was perplexed when night after night I noticed that just the left section of the audience was laughing for no reason during a scene between Nick and Jan, the Alessandra character. After a while I moved from center to left and, to my utter surprise, I could see in the mirror behind Nick's bed what the audience was laughing at: the reflected image of our light technician passionately kissing and petting with his girlfriend. The stupid boy (a substitute for our usual one) was working in the balcony from a production room, and considering he had nothing to do during that long scene, he had thought it wise to invite over the girl for some rump, not in the hay but on the lights console, without considering that they both were visible in the mirror. I scolded him severely, but couldn't help seeing the humor in it.

If we had been in London or New York, we could have stayed in the Teatro Vittoria for months, but the Italian theater system is sadly based on subscribers and, after the scheduled five weeks, we had to make space for the upcoming production and left for our tour, during which I had to fulfill a promise I made to all the male actors. If they were required to work in a movie or T.V. production,

I would substitute for them. I had (still have thanks God) a portentous memory and knew all the lines from rehearsing, so I went on stage as old father Ernest in Florence and had a lot of fun, even if hardly coping with Giannina Salvetti's Delia, my stage wife, who tended to laugh at any minimal change or accident. She thought my Ernest utterly funny and, if she hardly restrained herself in our scenes, she only half suffocated her laughs when we were in darkness and the action switched to one of the other rooms and our bed was positively shaking from her hiccups.

But the unforeseen event that was to change everything happened when I substituted for Tito Vittori, as Trevor, the egotistical but charming and childish womanizer who causes all the misadventures in the play, along with his wife Susannah, played by Claudia Della Seta, a neurotic, post-hippie woman passing from yoga's self-assured mantras to hysteric fits.

My first night in the role was in a little town in Tuscany. I got there by train in the afternoon and had a quick rehearsal of my scenes. I was relaxed and planning to play Trevor in the same way Tito had done, as to say following my own instructions as a director. But as soon as I spoke my first line it was as though the real Trevor took hold of me and I played the part with subtexts, actions and comic timings that I had never considered. I wasn't doing anything "consciously," but as a possessed actor I could have quoted the great dancer Vaslav Nijinsky when he was scolded for his unbecoming miming of masturbation at the opening night of *Afternoon of a Faun* that caused a scandalized outcry in the 1912 Paris audience. "It wasn't me, it was the Faun." But my audience was causing a revolution … it was a crescendo of laughs and applauses, two or three times greater than what had ever happened with Tito. My partners were somehow electrified by the changes and responded by giving their best, and the little town in Tuscany got the best performance of the play since its start the previous year. At the end we had endless curtain calls and meeting people in the wings; Franco Clavari, generally very thrifty in compliments, reflected positivity in his eyes, and told me this had been a great lesson in acting. Trevor is a very physical role and I had played it stretching even more the character's neurotic bounce; I was exhausted but I knew something great had happened.

Show business has its cruel laws and poor, blameless Tito never got his role back full time. I kept being Trevor for three years and, even if it sounds crazy and hyperbolic, playing him changed my life.

Trevor had a special mix of gentleness and manhood, childishness and cynicism, calmness and brutality that made him the heterosexual I would have been if I did not have an inclination for men as well as women, and these characteristics slowly passed from the role to the actor and I know deep in my heart that without playing Trevor I wouldn't have married and had a son.

We kept touring for a while and started making plans for a new production, while *Bedroom Farce* was receiving a triumphal reception everywhere. In Genoa, maybe the most refined town in Italy for theatergoers, the box-office had to send people home and at curtain calls the audience was thronging in front of the stage to shake hands with us. At the last performance a huge banner said in capital letters, "Come back soon."

Other changes in the cast occurred. Gianluca Favilla was more interested in a movie career and didn't want to be tied to theater tours; he was a good actor but he tended to overact and I didn't miss him a bit when I bumped into Mauro Marino, one of the best actors I have ever worked with, who became a steady member of the company after his good rendition of Ernest. Lucilla Salvini got pregnant and she didn't want to tire herself out since sections of the tour were on a "one day one place" basis, so the Kate role also saw changes, as well as the Susannah character, because Claudia Della Seta was fidgety and each new boyfriend led her to new adventures, new countries and even new religions. Then Stefano Viali was called for military service (still mandatory in Italy at that time) and, if the army was kind enough to allow him to perform in Rome and give him some leave, he wasn't nevertheless available for the whole tour and so I had to take his role and call Tito back to play Trevor temporarily. The show suffered a bit from all these alternations, but the audience kept responding with enthusiasm.

Ayckbourn had been our lucky star considering the amount of great plays he had written, I was positive in selecting another one of his for our next engagement. *Absurd Person Singular* was a masterpiece, but the complicated scenery was still a major obstacle, so I thought of *Confusions*, which was a very smart relay of five different plays interconnected by one character passing from one to another. It had a cast of only five and, if each situation needed a different setting, it could be allusive and I was sure to find a cheap way to solve the problem. The company agreed on my choice and we scheduled it for the next season, to be alternated with *Bedroom Farce*, which was far from having fulfilled its potential.

For the time being, after the tour was over, I left for Sardinia to rehearse *Little Things*, a one-act play with two characters by local playwright Enzo Giacobbe. It was a minimalistic account of the difficult relationship between a man and his sister and I didn't find it exciting, but I had accepted the opportunity to open a door for potential assignments with the Sardinian Theater, which was an interesting company and was also running the schedule for hosting tours of other groups on the island. But when I started rehearsing in Cagliari, Sardinia's capital town, I got more than excited when finding a rare jewel in young actress Isella Orchis. The Sardinian Theater didn't think much of her and had confined her to minor roles and only God Almighty knows why, because she was a natural phenomenon. In personal life she was a sportive and cheerful big puppy reminding me a bit of a girl scout and her conversation was matter of fact and even banal, but as soon as she was on stage she was struck as though by a flash of lightning and the very Muse of Theater got into her, making her body vibrant, her face radiant and her voice full of a thousand shades. She mesmerized me and totally out-staged her partner, who was by the way her companion in life. I definitely wanted to work with her in something more momentous and thought she would have been a wonderful Yerma. After the successful opening of *Little Things*, I related my idea to the company general manager and he was enthusiastic about the play, but he told me that it was hard not to give such a big role to their usual leading actress. I replied that for me it was either Isella or no one else, and he said he had to think about it.

The ageless Valeria Valeri

In the fall of that year I also got my first call as a director from a major theater company, which based its productions on a famous thespain couple consisting of Valeria Valeri and Paolo Ferrari. They wanted her to star in a French play from the 1950s, but when I read it I found it utterly stupid and quite unbecoming, because it was based upon a woman's pregnancy; Valeria Valeri had erased her birth date from every offical document, but her pregnancy would have nevertheless been first page news as an event, impossible for science and nature and obtainable only by religious miracle. As a young director being offered an important professional assignment, I should have shut up and done my job, but it wasn't in my nature. Movies as an actor were and still are always fun for me, even if they aren't first rate, and as a stage actor I can accept some compromises. But as a theater director I can't work on something I dislike or don't respect because my brain just closes up and I feel like spitting on an altar. Theater was born as a religious rite and something sacred in terms of quality should always be there, even if you are representing a farce.

I played this entire situation quite diplomatic and stated that I had a much better play for them and respectfully asked them just to read it. It was another Ayckbourn work, his first success *Relatively Speaking*, and it was a farcical mechanism as perfect as a Swiss clock. They were old theater foxes and immediately saw my point and agreed to perform in it. It had been already staged in Italy many years back and it had been translated by Luigi Lunari. Considering Mr. Lunari had translated *King Lear* for Giorgio Strehler, I assumed he was reliable for Ayckbourn, but I had to reconsider my assumption when I read his Italian version during a train trip. Not only was all the humor lost and the lines sounded awkward, but also there were ridiculous mistakes as though created by someone who didn't know the language. When, at page 12, a stage direction said that the Ginny character was saying her line, "putting on her dressing gown," and Mr. Lunari, tricked by the word gown that sounds like the Italian "gonna"(skirt), translated it with "putting on her skirt." I opened the train window and threw out the script. I re-translated the whole thing but I signed it under the name of Lunari, to avoid a diplomatic incident. Needless to say that he didn't blink an eye, because what interested him were mainly the royalties. From there on I never staged anything in English or French that wasn't translated by me or by Masolino D'Amico, one of the few Italians to be trusted in the business and a long-time friend. Sloppiness and ignorance of foreign languages are unfortunately Italian trademarks, as well as conceit, and it would suffice to say that Salvatore Quasimodo, acclaimed poet and Nobel winner, translated *Macbeth* without knowing a word of English: his wife was translating it literally and he was adding the poetic touches (but with no verses and rhymes ... this would have been too demanding).

Rehearsals were a bit hard because of a generation gap. If Paolo Ferrari was clever enough to understand that the play had an "English" style to be respected, Valeria Valeri attempted to play it in what she called the "French" style, as to say underlining comic effects, making unnecessary actions to attract attention and blinking to the audience. This was exactly what had caused Ayckbourn to be unsuccessful in Italy. She was also overly concentrated on her dresses and in looking younger, and she desperately asked Aldo Buti for a skirt that "follows me when I walk," as to say, vaporous. He humorously answered that if he was to invent a skirt that stayed in place when she moved, he would surely win the Tony Award for best costumes. With a lot of patience and a great help from Ferrari, who had been her partner for ages and knew how to handle her, I got to guide her in the right path at least 80 percent of the time. The remaining 20 percent arrived when, after the opening, she realized that the other actors, in following my directions, were getting huge laughs. From there on she chased me behind the wings asking how she had to say a certain line. Oh, actors!

All in all the play proved to be an immense success and I was booked for their next production.

1988 started with a one-day assignment in a movie by Ruggero Deodato, *Phantom of Death*. I was pleased to meet Ruggero again, but I was convinced the cameo role of a priest (for once a good guy) would not add anything to my career. It didn't, but it gave me an exceptional thrill in working with Michael York. I loved him as Thybalt in Zeffirelli's *Romeo and Juliet* and in his leading role in *Cabaret*, and I was curious to meet him. We had coffee before shooting and a pleasant chat about some theater work he was doing in Los Angeles with Marsha Mason. He was with his wife, who was much older than he was and not particularly attractive, and I thought that it went to his credit that he was a clever man and did not fall for Hollywood dolls. But as nice as he was, I couldn't predict that when playing our dramatic scene electric vibes would erupt from him as though coming from a nuclear engine. He hugged me and I felt a great life force getting into my body; the man had something magical that I never experienced with any other actor.

I never saw the movie (just my scene at the dubbing session), but I cherish the memory of that overwhelming feeling of closeness.

Another engagement, not momentous for my career but very interesting, was the attempt to produce a play in English in Rome for English-speaking residents, tourists and students. Mary Sellers from *Deliria* pulled me into it and the selected play was *Vanities* by Jack Heifner, a very witty study on the life of three Texas girls from high school times and into adult life. The play required no scenery and a small theater offered to host it. I did it for free, but didn't regret that decision one bit. Working with Mary and her friends Dale Wyatt and Gaby Ford, I discovered some great differences from directing Italian actors; they didn't want to be interrupted during a scene, but they would listen to my objections afterwards, always making sure not to stop the emotional flow. They didn't like the idea of the director saying a line in their place to demonstrate what he meant. I respected their views and got into a lot of talking which finally produced a nice result and a success, if even on a small scale.

But the main task for that season was producing *Confusions*, while continuing the tour with *Bedroom Farce*. Along with Alessandro Chiti, the regular set designer of the company, I had devised a very ingenious and spectacular way to handle the five different settings: five rotating parallel sets with some black faces and some bits of the scenery that could be assembled quickly, as in a giant kids' game. There was space inside for a grip or an actor to move them and the final effect with the right lights was phenomenal and repaid us for the long technical rehearsals full of curses, bumps and bruises. I was a silent waiter in the second scene and then my character led to the third one, which was one of Ayckbourn's masterpieces: two married couples are having dinner in a fancy restaurant but

Michael York as the fiend in *Phantom of Death*

are both in trouble because one wife is cheating on her husband with his boss, but we hear their conversations only when the waiter gets close to their table and the conversation fades away as he moves, his impassive professional behavior even during their arguments creating an incredible comic effect. It wasn't easy to get into it and my timing had to be perfect and match the silent dialogue we had written for the actors when I wasn't near them. I was coming and going back and forth, from two doors with trays and a refreshment trolley with grips backstage changing the plates. Being one second late could compromise the whole thing.

During rehearsals I felt that something was missing, but being both actor and director I couldn't tell what it was, so I invited over Marina Garroni and she solved my problems with just one word: "faster." She was perfectly right, and by getting closer to a Charlot rhythm, I had in that role probably my greatest success as a stage actor. When the scene was over I had to frantically change in the wings and become Gosforth, a vulgar pub owner who was the organizer of a local fair; making a mess with the loudspeakers, he revealed to the whole community that he had impregnated a girl, played by Alessandra Panelli, who was engaged with a chief scout, her real boyfriend, Stefano Viali, revealed to be a cuckold. It was the most farcical scene among the five, but unfortunately, as hard as I tried, I never got to play the role more than as a journeyman. Every actor has his limits and Gosforth made me find out that one of mine was coarseness: I was using a Falstaff prop belly and I was scratching my balls while talking to the local charity lady, wonderfully played by Giannina Salvetti, but it was just superficial and not coming from inside: a count Gherardini my ancestor was probably rebelling against. I had no more than four minutes to change my costume and less so to switch from Gosforth to my role of Arthur in the last scene named, "A

The soundtrack album cover to *Phantom of Death*

Talk in the Park," where five characters each address a monologue to a person sitting on a bench, thus leading the latter to escape to another bench and resume the rigmarole. I was the first to speak and I couldn't find a different solution than making Arthur a jogger, because I was wearing his tracksuit underneath the Gosforth costume and I had to justify the fact that it was saturated with sweat.

It was an exhausting play for all of us because we had so many roles and the backstage resembled another play with costumes and wigs whirling all around, but it was great fun. We kept touring alternating *Confusions* and *Bedroom Farce* and opened with the former in Rome in spring, at the Teatro della Cometa (The Comet Theater).

Teatro della Cometa was a very peculiar theater, which had been built in the 1930s by countess Letizia Pecci-Blunt inside her palace facing the Capitolium. She was a patroness of the arts and counted both on the noble blood of the Pecci (Pope Leo XIII's family) and the money of the Blunt, a Levantine family of merchants and bankers. Many personalities of theater and music had performed there and I had seen it as a child and I remembered perfectly the shell-shaped miniature opera house, with sofas instead of seats in the pit and boxes lined with pink silk. But the doll theater was destroyed by fire in the late 1960s, just after countess Letizia's death, and it had never re-opened until 1986, when Giorgio Barattolo, a very rich businessman with a passion for theater, had financed the restoration. Malignant gossips insinuated that the burning had been provoked by the Pecci Blunt siblings, Letizia's son Dino and daughter Viviana, to destroy mama's little toy and build a supermarket in its place, but, whether true or not, they never got the permission to change the zoning and finally decided to rent it to Giorgio Barattolo, who was a friend of Viviana. He was from a bizarre family of industrialists who had prospered in the African Italian colonies but had also been crucial in Italian cinema history, because Giorgio's grandfather had been a pioneer in the business in the silent movie days. Giorgio loved the idea of having his own theater as a Renaissance prince, but on the other hand he was fully busy with his work in the many family companies and didn't have either the time or the skills to make the Teatro della Cometa prosper. Audiences were scarce and productions difficult to assemble, because the theater could host no more than 200 people and box-office incomes weren't appealing. So when *Confusions* attracted a wide audience and he saw his theater packed for the first time, Giorgio looked at us from a different perspective and we soon were offered the opportunity to become the resident company. I was appointed artistic director and Franco Clavari, general manager, while Giorgio maintained his status as president and he had the final word in crucial decisions. I was in love with the theater, which had luckily lost the pink silk in the burning and had been restored in a less mannered style. It was a court theater all the same, but the spacious stage and the comparatively small house were perfect for creating an intimate relation with the audience. Even a whisper would have been heard, thus making possible the movie-style realism that I was fascinated by in that phase of my stage career. I was to remain there for the next 15 years of my life.

Stefano Viali

Chapter 24
A Church for a Movie and One in Which to Be Married

Sardinian Theater had finally agreed on my idea of staging *Yerma* with Isella in the leading role and it was to be performed in two versions, one just with the actors and another on a larger scale in a joint venture with the Cagliari Opera House, with orchestra and choir. The music score was the same beautiful and effective one that Maestro Aldo Cicconofri had composed for the school show in Tolentino and included a lullaby, the washerwomen choir, a religious hymn and the Bull Dance. He adjusted it to be played by a symphonic orchestra and a professional choir, and I started rehearsing in the summer, because the opera version was to be performed in the Roman amphitheater and the prose version in a wonderful Greek theater facing the sea in Nora, near Cagliari.

It was a fascinating project, but many inconveniences arose. On the opera front I had to face the usual Italian slavery to unions and the general sloppiness of whatever state provided financing. When the union delegate was gesturing that it was break time, the members of the orchestra stopped playing in the very middle of a passage and I had to personally fight in the wings with some ladies from the choir who, dressed as Spanish peasants, would take their handbags with them on stage for fear of being robbed. I wanted to play the drama in one long act, but this collided with the Mafia interests of the stalls selling refreshments during the intermission and I was forced to divide the performance into two parts. Other than these shortcomings, the huge open theater wasn't ideal for the actors and, even if they were using microphones, the necessary pathos just wasn't there.

The other version proved equally problematic because, if Isella was phenomenal as I had foreseen, I was forced to cast other steady actors of the company, some of them just average and some pretty awful.

All in all I was tired and depressed and resumed my heavy drinking and that left my liver screaming from consuming the local liquor, which was made of myrtle.

It was just a bad professional adventure in an otherwise good moment in my working life, with the Actors Company becoming more and more successful with the added thrill and new adventure of directing Teatro Della Cometa. But I wasn't happy; love was what I badly missed. When "T" decided to go live with "L," my emotional life became unbalanced, and since Lisa had left me, I hadn't had a new enthralling love life. I was just lazily coping with a relationship with my last housemate, a Sicilian dancer who was much younger than me. He was affectionate and funny as a pup, but we had no interests in common because he was unschooled and superficial, only having fun at discos and spreading dance world gossip. In September I would turn 34 and I feared the loneliness and sadness I had witnessed in so many of my elder gay friends. To be truthful

I had a crush on Franco Clavari, who was gay and in a difficult and quarrelsome long-time relationship with our set designer Alessandro Chiti, but I had understood long ago that I wasn't his physical type and I had resigned to see him as just a friend and the best possible business partner.

My delicate teenage beauty that would probably have attracted Franco had faded away, and I consciously replaced it with a more muscular and manly look, going to gyms regularly and doing some bodybuilding. I was also conscious that my hair was bidding farewell and there was nothing I could do about it. A few years back I went to the best dermatologist in Rome and had a bit of a shock when the man, without even saying hello, had ripped open my shirt. But he wasn't a sex maniac; he was just very busy and wanted to see if my chest hair was growing thick. It was and he explained to me that it's a secondary symptom of "androgenic alopecia,"

Alessandra Panelli as a nun

the scientific name for going bald, which means that it follows a male line from father to son and my father had in fact lost his hair while very young. I was coping with what was left but I detested half measures and I knew that in a few years I would completely shave my head, as in fact I did. Luckily I had the same perfectly round head of my mother and she used to say, "You'll be beautiful even as a skeleton, because you have a nice skull."

When *Yerma* was over I stayed in the island and, weary and moody, I joined Alessandra Panelli, her boyfriend Stefano Viali and Alessandra's cousin Laura in a house by the sea up north that we rented for the month of August.

The rocky beaches in north Sardinia are among the most beautiful in the world, and after a few days of sunbathing and splashing in the green-blue sea, I calmed down enough to see that there was something slightly wrong between Alessandra and Stefano, who had been a couple for some years. Then, one afternoon in a secluded little cove, I confided to Alessandra my sadness and my longing for love. To my utter surprise she wasn't sympathetic, but scolded me instead, saying that I could have all the love in the world if I only were able to see it. I asked what she meant and she bluntly said that she was in love with me. The next thing I remember was the two of us passionately kissing.

I had always found Alessandra attractive and at times I had had fantasies about flirting with her, but she was always in some relationship, and when we had started working together with the Actors Company, I had come to see her just as a very good actress and Stefano's girlfriend. She was aware of my sex life and I had often discussed with her my male relationships, never thinking she had more than a friendly interest in me. As Trevor I had kissed her on stage in *Bedroom Farce* and found it pleasant, but the present passionate kissing on the beach was totally unexpected and shocking.

From then on the holiday was a nightmare, because we were living under the same roof with Stefano, who seemed totally unaware of arising tensions, and Alessandra was sleeping in his bed but kissing me around secret corners. It was like living the disturbing side of a French farce with husband, wife and lover in a tiny cupboard, and I felt guilty about Stefano, since he was a fellow actor in my company and a friend. Alessandra kept telling me that their relationship had been very difficult of late and it would end anyway, but I was nevertheless on tenterhooks hooks and finally left before my time, saying that I was needed in Rome to organize the September season opening of La Cometa with Franco.

It was just a half lie, because there was indeed a lot of work to do. As much as both Franco and I considered the subscription concept a great handicap in Italian theater, we couldn't nevertheless change a rooted system just with our will and had agreed with Giorgio for a subscription campaign with a six-show season. We would open with *Little Shop of Horrors*, produced by the Tolentino company that Saverio Marconi was guiding toward success by producing American and English musical hits, and our company would present *Confusions* for the second time and *Bedroom Farce* at its third Rome round. *Sincerely Yours* was scheduled too and my presence as a director was thus covering a good half of the season.

I told Franco about what happened in Sardinia and he summed it up by opening his eyes wide and uttering, "Oh my God!" He was rightly concerned as a friend of all three parties involved, but he was also concerned about the consequences within the company.

I was utterly confused. I couldn't say I was in love with Alessandra, but she intrigued me and I wished to give the relationship a chance. The thought of stepping into Stefano's shoes was vey disturbing. But egotism prevailed, and when they came back to Rome, Alessandra and I resumed seeing one another and making love. Sex proved to be decisive in our budding relationship, as had happened earlier with Lisa. I felt transcended with an overriding feeling of perfect satisfaction and peace. God knows that I hadn't the least moral or social scruples about heterosexuality being "better" or more becoming than homosexuality, but it was as if my body, in that phase of my life, was finding something that was missing with men.

Alessandra finally talked to Stefano and the bomb exploded. He took it in the worst possible way, feeling rejected and betrayed, but fortunately he didn't talk about leaving the company. The news was spreading faster than winter flu in the showbiz world and gossip was incessant and at times malignant, as it was to be expected. So, all circumstances considered, the offer from Michele Soavi to appear in his second movie, to be shot in Budapest, came as a blessing.

The movie in question was *The Church* and this time Dario Argento was producing, so payment and accommodations were standard professional. My only doubt was about not being in Rome for the season opening at La Cometa, but Franco told me not to worry, and in the first days of September I left for Hungary.

The Church was a very different movie from *Deliria* and the only similarity was in the fact that a group of people were stuck in a confined space, facing horrific events. I never asked Michele if he had seen Bunuel's *The Exterminating Angel* and I would guess he didn't, but surely he was fascinated by this literary and cinematic claustrophobic topic. If the horror in *Deliria* was caused by the realistic presence of a serial killer, the church now in question was haunted by demonic and surreal creatures from the beyond, generated by a massacre of heretics in the Middle Ages, depicted in the film's opening sequence. They had been buried on the spot where the cathedral was built and their souls were now creeping out of their grave for revenge in an atmosphere that was more related to Fulci horrors than to the gory Argento thrillers. There was also a touch of *Cannibal Apocalypse*, because the characters were spreading this devil possession by scratching each other.

A Spanish poster for *The Church*

The problem with the script written by Argento with many un-credited collaborators was, in my opinion, that there were too many irons in the fire and the space dedicated to the description of fearful monsters right out of a Bosch delirium left a very limited space for insights of the many characters that were thus only superficially sketched. My character of the Reverend was vague and undefined with a too subtle homosexual hint that would have needed more attention in the writing. Furthermore the whole story was too complicated and with too many references and the final result was confused. Once again logic had little interest for Michele and it was clear that his heart was in the many figurative quotes, from ancient sorcery literature to Goya's nightmarish black

A very young Asia Argento, as she appeared in *The Church*

paintings. I didn't have time to talk to him about the script, but I honestly was just happy to be out of Rome, in a town that I was curious to visit and with friends such as Michele and Barbara Cupisti, who played the leading female once again.

Budapest, among other things, is renowned for its many spas. Turkish baths and hot water swimming pools were a tradition dating back to the days of the Ottoman invasion of Eastern Europe, a war won by Vlad Tepes, aka Count Dracula. Our hotel had a spa too, and as soon as I arrived, I went down to the basement to see what it was like. I got the visceral feeling of being punched in the stomach in the men's locker room at the sight of finding a perfect, statuesque, naked black man. The hotel was quite big and I didn't immediately relate his presence to the movie and only afterwards I found out that this semi-God (who never even looked at me) was Hugh Quarshie, who played Father Gus.

Alone in the sauna my mind was sweating as well as my body. Was it right to have a relationship with Alessandra or with any other woman if the sight of an attractive male body was so deeply unsettling? What should I do? Should I repress one side of my sexuality in favor of the other? And was it possible to do this? I finally decided that it was not sensible to think too much about it and that time would tell.

As with *Deliria*, *The Church* was an ensemble movie and, even if the characters did not have an important function, each character was bound to be seen as background dressing in every sequence, so the whole cast was on set almost every day and, in the huge shady cathedral, I could study my fellow actors while relaxing and waiting.

Fan-made artwork for *The Church*, designed by Silver Ferox

Luckily Hugh Quarshie was always fully dressed as a clergyman and his sexual spell was thus considerably diminished. He was a very nice person and with a solid theater background, and I discussed a lot of Shakespeare with him and specifically the issue of Othello's blackness, a role he had had the privilege to perform, even if he was unconvinced that being of African origin didn't add an inch to its potential. Thomas Arana was also theater schooled and, when he had settled in Italy, he had been the producer and a leading actor in the internationally acclaimed theater company Falso Movimento (False Movement), based in Naples, but I had very little to do with him in the movie and, as it had happened with David Brandon, he spent a lot of time alone. In minor roles there were Lars Jorgenson, a handsome Swedish model, Rubenesque Antonella Vitale (who I suspected was having an affair with Argento), and Micaela Pignatelli, who I socially knew since the Tessari evenings. But the two most peculiar cast members were the youngest and the oldest, Asia Argento and Feodor Chaliapin.

Asia was 13 and appeared in several movies. She was in that very peculiar Lolita moment when a little girl develops into a woman, and if her body was already fully ripe, her attitude was still that of a child, but with a hint of playful seductiveness, such as when she insisted she desired to sit on men's laps to play

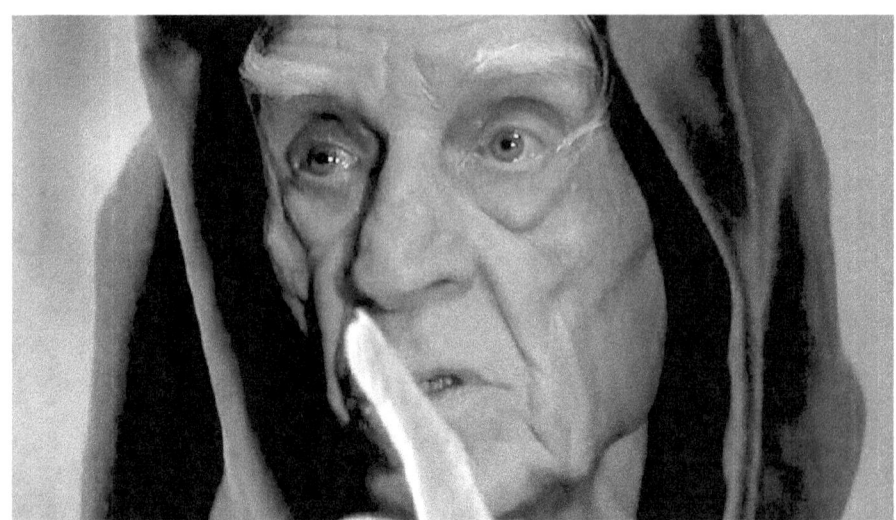

Feodor Chaliapin, Jr. as he appeared in *The Church*.

horse, her miniskirt usually up to her belly. I was her favorite for such games and, remembering my experience with Lisa's sister, I wondered if I had something especially appealing for younger teenagers on their way to becoming very liberated women.

On the other end of the tree of life, Feodor Chaliapin, Jr. was 83 but positively looked 120, and if his bony wizard face was perfect for his role of a mysterious Bishop, his memory had completely gone and he couldn't remember even a short line. When he was in a scene prompters were just everywhere, under a table, behind curtains or jammed at his feet in the pulpit where he was preaching, but he was utterly deaf and couldn't hear them. In a dinner scene in which he had a long line, I finally was forced to re-act a trick I had used once in *Atlantis Project* with an Egyptian guy who didn't speak English. When the camera was on him, I said my line and then silently mouthed his, so that he could read it on my lips. But his lack of memory wasn't just related to lines, and one afternoon he went to the bathroom and came back with his zipper open and his shlong in full sight. Everybody was too embarrassed to mention it to him and he just stayed that way for a while, until he realized the situation and just put it back where it belonged with a little giggle. I must say that his wife surely must have had a very stimulating marriage life.

The crew was pretty large but Michele was steadily in command as he had been with the smaller one in *Deliria*, and Dario Argento was always by his side. I read that they had a difficult relationship while shooting *The Church* and that Dario was imposing himself and his ideas on Michele, but, on my part, I never got such an impression and I can state in a court of law that Michele was in high spirits. Seeing him with Dario was like watching two kids play with their favorite Lego design. As with Michele, Dario was skilled in technical jobs and liked doing things with his own hands, showing a real passion for set life that I

Barbara Cupisti as she appeared in *The Church*

found very refreshing: few words and a lot of facts. I was meeting him for the first time and I found that, despite his mad serial killer looks (never has a horror director had features more becoming to the genre), he was a jolly man, very warm, open and full of funny anecdotes. His way in relating to Asia on set was very positive, at the same time friendly and paternal.

I was having a nice time when, suddenly, a phone call from Alessandra brought a black, rainy cloud over my head. We were phoning each other often and all seemed fine, but one night she sounded terribly upset and told me that there was gossip that I was going to bed with both Giorgio Barattolo and her. I laughed with all my heart and that caused a scene on her part, saying that I didn't understand her embarrassment and discomfort in becoming the stupid girl who was cheated on by me. I couldn't believe my ears and tried to make her reason. I had been openly bisexual my whole life and Giorgio was rich and gay. The gossip was to be expected, considering that so many theater companies in Rome would have liked to be in our place. But she insisted and I told her I was who I was and she had known about my lifestyle from the beginning, so either she made peace with it or it was indeed going to be a serious obstacle to our relationship. She calmed down a bit and agreed on coming to Budapest to visit me soon after the beginning of the season. I went to bed puzzled and surprised. I mean, she had been a close friend for many years, how could she think my past could be erased? The truth was that I never gave a shit about what people were thinking and I assumed it was just the same for her, but I was wrong and a more attentive reflection on the issue would have avoided many sorrows and misunderstandings to come.

I was spending off set time with a small group that included Michele, Barbara, photography director Renato Tafuri, Lars Jorgensen and Micaela

Pignatelli. We were spending time in the sauna right after shooting to relax, and then we were going to dine on caviar, which in Budapest was cheap because of the economic closeness to the Soviet Union. Vodka was a must and we were often tipsy and singing on our way back to the hotel, like a bunch of students on a school outing. In our rooms Cristalivitz was taking care of our excess in eating or drinking. It was a local mineral water and the fizziest on Earth, bound to make you digest even a rock if you survived the shock of the first sip. When Alessandra joined me she immediately got familiar with the others and was warmly welcomed. Michele was radiant about our love story and told me my girl was great. We also had time for just ourselves and visited Budapest, which was a very beautiful city with lots of monuments and churches. But on closer scrutiny, I found out that not a stone was authentic. As was true of many towns in central and Eastern Europe, they had been razed by bombings during the war and were rebuilt exactly as they were, with Russian money.

The Communist influence was visible but not as strong as in other Eastern countries because Budapest had always been the Las Vegas of Soviet Russia and the severe members of Russian "nomenclature" used to go there to enjoy prostitutes, strip-tease shows and other Western pleasures that were as a matter of fact openly available, even in our hotel. But I was very disturbed when, in a supermarket, I was spotted as a tourist and invited to jump the long cashier line. I was bringing money into the country so I was entitled to privileges that I wouldn't have dreamed to ask for. And for the same reason the many luxury shops from Adidas to local antiques were open just for foreigners and forbidden to Budapest residents. But I was only interested in the music shops that sold wonderfully cheap audiocassettes of classical music and opera from Hungaroton, the local music publishers. The country had a long tradition in opera and ballet and I discovered great singers I had never heard of because they were confined on that side of the Iron Curtain. One year after the fall of the Berlin Wall, decades of restrictions and oppression passed away.

While Alessandra visited we made passionate love almost every night and tensions seemed to fade away. She told me the *Cometa* opening had been a success and the subscribing campaign was booming. The future looked radiant.

Filming went on without incident and after Alessandra left I had my most interesting scenes, pretending to play a wonderful gigantic organ and then dying as if overcome by a mysterious dark presence: one of the many unsolved points in the screenplay.

When I viewed the finished movie as not a horror fan, but instead attempting to judge it from a literary point of view, I reluctantly concluded that it was a demented piece of crap. On the other hand, if I viewed it as a fresco or a series of paintings in a museum, it was a masterpiece. And anyway when a horrible primitive fish jumped on Lars' face, it was confirmed that as a spectator I was not a fan of horror. I almost died of a heart attack and I never ever understood why on Earth one would pay a ticket for that. As for me, 40 cigarettes a day was doing the job slower and more pleasurably.

When I got back to Rome, Alessandra and I officially got together. She didn't move to my place, but she was there almost every night and the huge loft was all to ourselves because I had announced the new situation to the Sicilian dancer and he left immediately, not without robbing me of some old tie brooches that once belonged to my grandfather. I didn't complain and took it as a punishment for having treated him a bit like a toy, an attitude I tried avoiding for the rest of my life.

We started thinking about resuming work with the company and we prepared for the difficult task of coping with Stefano on a daily basis. Then, just as we had started refreshing *Confusions* for the tour that was preceding its second round at La Cometa, Alessandra one afternoon told me that she was pregnant and that the baby was undoubtedly mine, probably conceived in Budapest.

I was thunderstruck with the most intense feeling of joy I would ever experience and I could have kneeled in the parking lot thanking both the Christian God and the old She-God of life.

As a matter of fact I was aware that Alessandra was not using the pill or any other contraceptive and, on my part, I wasn't wearing condoms, but I was idiotically convinced that I was sterile just because no pregnancy had occurred with my previous girlfriends, not all of them mentioned here and not all using an IUD as Lisa had.

I had no doubts about keeping the child, but after a while, I also asked Alessandra to get married and, with hindsight, this last step was indeed rushed. The fact was that deep in my heart I was, and still am, a man of the 19th century who kisses ladies' hands, likes waltzing and marries a woman if he gets her in trouble. When faced with modern habits I didn't like, I used to joke and say, "Count Gherardini is haunting me," but this time my great-great-great-grandfather who had committed suicide after losing all his possessions on the gambling table, because that's what a gentleman does when he can't pay his debts, was talking to me for real and he had a modern counterpart in doctor De Pascalis, my shrink. I had stopped therapy some two years back, but on this special occasion I asked for an appointment and de Pascalis openly encouraged me to take the big step.

Official announcements were made to friends and family and the reactions were at times surprised but generally positive. Only Alessandra's father, a very peculiar man I will later describe, asked in bewilderment, "But wasn't he a faggot?" The subtleness of bisexuality escaped his generation's range of understanding.

A very bizarre and unexpected reaction came from Marcello Mastroianni, who was the best friend of Alessandra's father and had adored her mother. We were in a friend's house and we casually met in the kitchen where I was looking for mineral water and he for ice to add to his whisky. Suddenly he grabbed me by my shirt, pushed me against the wall and hissed into my face: "Make her happy and I will love you for life, but make her suffer and I'll kill you." Marcello was the most sympathetic man on Earth and I was positively bewildered, but I promised that I would do my best and he kissed me on the forehead and let me go.

The fact that we were expecting a child wasn't bound to improve things with Stefano and we faced the first day of rehearsals after the announcement in quite a state of tension. But the God of Theater helped. That day we were going to work on the *Confusions* bit called "Gosforth's fete" that I already mentioned briefly and, too busy with reality, we didn't realize that on stage the situation was exactly the same as what we were experiencing in life: Gosforth (me) gets Milly (Alessandra) pregnant and she is Stewart's (Stefano) girlfriend. As soon as Stefano stormed on stage, fuming with rage in his Boy Scout outfit after finding out about the pregnancy from loudspeakers, we looked at each other, had a clear vision of the incredible mix of fiction and reality and started laughing ourselves to tears. The whole company joined in and it was hard to resume rehearsing for a good hour. It was indeed a blessing, because two seconds took care of grudges that could have lasted forever. From there on our relationship with Stefano was considerably relaxed and even more so when, after a while, he embarked upon a steady relationship with another woman who was to make him a father in two years' time.

I was mad with joy about the baby, because it was unexpected and because I had always loved children and most especially newborn babies. I had tenderly babysat Marina and Massimo's first son Gianmaria and sang lullabies to many others, finding out that I had a fantastic ability in putting them to sleep with some repetitive old French songs my grandmother had taught me as a baby. During the *Confusions* tour we visited Lucilla Salvini and her husband, German sound designer Hubert Weskemper, and I passed an entire afternoon with their son Federico, about nine months old, holding him with my eyes lost in that profound and amazing way that only infants have, staring at you. Look at a newborn baby in the eyes and you'll see Eternity.

We got married on February 6, 1989, on a Monday because we were on stage at La Cometa with *Confusions* and it was our only day off. On my expressed wish we had a religious ceremony in the little romantic church of Saint Sebastian in the center of the Palatino Roman ruins; to follow the tradition I didn't sleep at home the night before so not to see the bride, and I was put up in the D'Amico house. Silvia was, by the way, Alessandra's witness along with her cousin Laura, and mine were Massimo and Marina's mothers, the former having been a real mother to me after the death of my own. An uncle of Alessandra's who was a priest presided over the celebration; he was a bit on the senile side and another young priest was prompting him, which added a touch of humor to the otherwise moving ceremony. To the notes of the trio playing Mozart's *Così Fan Tutte* (All Ladies Do It), Alessandra's favorite music, the lyrics comforted us saying: "Gentle be the breeze, calm be the waves and every element smile in favor on their wish."

I had insisted on a church marriage, because, in a very personal and controversial way, I felt as though I was a Christian-Catholic, with a much stronger emphasis on Christian. Religious education had been a fight ground for my maternal grandparents and my father. I was baptized because they would have died of sorrow if I wasn't, but my father would not allow any kind of rite to be observed, such as First Communion, in the belief that those matters must be decided by each individual when they grow up and he didn't want me to attend Mass with my grandparents, not when in their care. I had a sort of theatrical fascination for the music and the church atmosphere, but what induced me to receive First Communion at the age of 15 was a real religious need that got me after my mother's death. Since then my relationship with the Holy Roman Church was changeable and I alternated phases of devotion to harsh criticism toward the repressive doctrine, most especially about sexuality. I was at peace with my conscience because the words of my first confessor about homosexuality were rooted in my heart: "Where love is no sin can be." Not all church members agreed with the Pope, so why should I? Growing up I concentrated more on this world than in the world to come and got more and more fascinated by Jesus Christ and his message of "here and now" action, compassion and charity. His words were bizarrely matching the ones of a mundane Spanish playwright of the 17th century, Calderon de la Barca, who wrote a phrase that I always hang somewhere in my houses: "Either this might be reality or a dream, only one thing matters: do good. If it's reality, because it is, and if it is not, to acquire friends for the awakening moment."

We held a reception in the foyer of La Cometa, organized and offered as a wedding present by my stepmother Fabiola, and then we left, not for a honeymoon, but to go on tour with *Confusions* and *Bedroom Farce*. Alessandra was five months pregnant and some precautions were called for. I insisted that she take a train for long travels and I changed some of her physical actions on stage, specifically in the famous comic scene in *Bedroom Farce* where Nick, unable to move because of his back, falls on Jan and traps her under his weight. Gianfranco Candia's muscular body falling on her belly wasn't indeed advisable.

Chapter 25
Life and Death

Living with Alessandra in the confined space of hotel rooms proved not always easy and I found out that she was hyper-sensitive to noises and light. Our first marital row exploded one night because I was fidgety and woke her up just by switching on the reading light to go to the bathroom. Pregnancy didn't help her moodiness, and I had the impression she was often studying me, as if suspecting God knows what if I was just silent or melancholic, as I at times had been my whole life. I tried to do my best to adapt, but I couldn't avoid having the same personality I was born with; if I was Jekyll marriage wasn't bound to turn me into Hyde and vice versa, and she had known me for years (the best and the worst) before promising to love me forever in front of God. Was close friendship so different from marriage? Do people change as if touched by a magic wand on the altar? I hoped that time would smooth out the rough edges.

In the meanwhile I was taking care of her as much as I could. If we were in the same car I smoked cigarettes leaning out of windows in a way that would have pleased De Angelis if I had been on a helicopter, and I wonder how I wasn't cut in two by a passing truck, a death that would indeed have honored my horror demises.

Lodgings and food were at times a problem as when we toured in central Sardinia, going from one little village to another in an atmosphere that was very Yerma-like, as to say frozen in some undefined country from another century. No hotels, but just a few inns with some rooms and no restaurants, let alone the pressure of finding one open after the show. We were living on ham and salami sandwiches and I feared I was to father a little piglet. Finally one night a local culture counselor invited us to dinner at his home and, sure to get a proper dinner at long last, when we arrived at his place his wife said: "We thought you would enjoy a buffet of our sliced salami and cheeses ..." Most theaters didn't even have a proper stage and audiences were quite peculiar and composed mostly of old women dressed in black and small children. I feared that English humor meant very little to them and that they would throw their chairs at us after the first 10 minutes, but I had undervalued the fact that Sardinians are one of the most clever populations on Earth and somehow they understood at least some of the ridiculous problems of British middle class and laughed and applauded.

Our season ended with *Bedroom Farce* at La Cometa, outdoing all previous box-office records of the theater and I left for Tolentino, where I had to rehearse the second play I was directing for the Valeri-Ferrari Company after the incredible success of *Sincerely Yours*. It was difficult to find good plays for them because Valeria's age, as much as she tried to hide it, made it difficult to see her in romantic affairs which most plays for a pair are based upon, so I finally selected *Look Who's Talking*, by Derek Benfield, an English farce that was almost the photocopy of *Sincerely Yours*, but not as subtle and refined. It was actually funny, opened successfully and was to be performed for the next two seasons.

Johnny with wife Alessandra Panelli and son Giacomo (1989)

At that point we had just to wait for our child's birth. We knew by then it was to be a boy and I was glad about that because it meant that the surname Lombardo Radice wouldn't die with me. As a matter of fact the official name had originally been Lombardo, a very common name in Sicily, and following the Spanish usage the mother's family name was added at each generation.

My grandfather Giuseppe had been the son of a Lombardo and a Radice, but when he became famous the unique surname of Lombardo Radice was used for his books and it passed to my father and then to my brothers and me, even if documents were always saying just Lombardo. To solve the tangled situation, after my father's death, Marco and I made a request to officially add the Radice, while Daniele refused because of despising a family that, in his opinion, had abused and rejected him. His children were then just Lombardo and Marco hadn't any offspring, so the only hope of having the surname survive was in me having a boy. All this sounds very Jane Austen-like, but, as I said, some of my values are definitely from another age.

Alessandra had insisted on the house being restored, and if I saw the point of having a third bedroom for an au pair girl, I had been a bit annoyed by her statement that the house had "too much of a past." In fact it did, but it was my past and the idea that she wanted to erase it didn't go in a direction I liked. The renovation was also very expensive and I had to ask for a bank loan. My writing career had just recently taken a big step forward with the inclusion of Marina and myself in the writing team of *I Ragazzi del Muretto* (The Boys at the Wall), a teenage series that was Rai Channel 2's flagship for the near future, but it didn't pay well enough to completely change the structure of the loft, install parquet floors and build two verandas in the terraces, one as a dining room and the other as Alessandra's study.

Because of the construction we moved to Alessandra's place, which was situated in a separate section of her father's large house. Since the death of his wife Bice Valori many years back, my father-in-law had lived alone with Alessandra's former nanny, a sweet woman named Benigna, but he was mistreating her despite the fact that she had a weak heart. Very recently even her patience had come to an end and she had retired in her home village, leaving him in the care of housekeepers he always found unsatisfactory and soon fired or they left of their own will, one after the other.

Paolo Panelli was one of the most peculiar characters to be found and he would deserve an entire book just for himself. I will just say that, adored by at least three generations of T.V. audiences for his surreal comic talent, in private life he was totally detached from reality, egotistical to the extreme and even ill mannered when he thought that his starring role as a comic allowed him to make whatever personal and unnecessary remark to people. He lived self-centered and suffered from acute O.C.D., requiring objects to be in a certain place, superstitious rituals, and he had a passion for carpentry, something in which he was, in my opinion, much better skilled than in acting. It has to be said that his life and the life of his wife had been devastated by the death of a baby boy, born before Alessandra, who caught incurable meningitis just as Bice fell pregnant with her. Paolo had depended on his wife for everything, from professional to practical life and was used to being pampered and to having all his whims satisfied, from coffee at a certain temperature and only in a special cup to a complicated bells system of his invention he used to signal what he wanted without talking to house helpers. When Bice died of cancer quite young, Paolo was devastated because he had worshipped the Earth she walked on, but he immediately decided that

Alessandra was to take care of him as her mother had done. Of course she thought otherwise and coped as she could, trying to find a balance in between showing affection and not being devoured by her father's demands.

Such a father hadn't left her without psychological consequences. Just one year earlier she had asked my brother Marco to suggest a good psychologist for her and she was now in therapy.

My father-in-law's fame didn't seduce me and I didn't intend to indulge any of his whims, so the first time he asked me to make his bed I answered by offering to teach him instead, and this episode and a few others made him detest me and nickname me "the Nazi." All this considered, plus the fact that Rome was already quite hot, I decided to rent a villa by the sea in Tuscany and have Alessandra reside there the last two months of pregnancy.

The comic eccentric, Paolo Panelli

She had been on stage until the seventh month and she needed rest. Her cousin Laura, an ancient Greek scholar who I liked very much, came with us to drive the car in case of an emergency and we settled in Talamone, awaiting the restoring of my house which was proceeding, but not as fast as promised, which is always the case.

It wasn't a happy choice. The villa was very beautiful and the sea breeze was indeed better than the torrid Roman heat, but we were very isolated and differences between our temperaments flared to full sight. During my whole life I had tended to be by myself a great deal and I had been eager to meet others and to be brilliant and conversational only on scheduled occasions or when working. Alessandra took this attitude as a lack of interest for her and was often gloomy and offended by the fact that I wasn't very eager to make love because of her advanced pregnancy. She felt undesired and her constant need to be reassured and desired was frustrated by my behavior. In a few words, I was a very independent individual and she was not.

Her reaction was to overdo things and tire herself too much by swimming or sailing a little rented boat. She adored the sea and was skilled in all forms of beach life, including fishing. The result was that on the morning of July 14 in the village of Talamone, in a phone booth, her water broke 15 days before her due date and we had to rush to Rome, some 200 kilometers south, and Laura's presence proved essential, because she drove the car very well masking her concern for the responsibility. We stopped at a hospital near Talamone and were told that we could go to Rome safely, because labor hadn't begun.

It never did.

We safely arrived just before midnight at the clinic just outside Rome where her gynecologist was based and not a single labor contraction occurred; the doctor decided to do a caesarean. I insisted on witnessing the birth all the same, but he refused saying that it was surgery and I couldn't be allowed in. I thus waited all alone in a room, smoking like a chimney, and a few minutes after 1 a.m. on the 15th a nurse introduced me to my baby boy, who had graciously decided to arrive on the same birthday as his grandfather Paolo. To be true he looked a bit like him too, which is not exactly a compliment, but I can say it without worries, considering how handsome he turned out to be when growing up. He was crying, but he immediately calmed in my arms. The name of Giacomo had already been selected; Nicola was also considered, but out of sheer vanity I had preferred the boy to have my same initials and that of his grandfather Giuseppe.

I gave him back to the nurse after signing some papers and went to see Alessandra, who was groggy and dozy from the anesthesia, but happy all the same. We slept a few hours and in the morning we received the visit of granddad Paolo and took a few photos, each person holding the baby as a happy family. It was quite obvious that the sight of his grandson made Paolo think about his lost baby boy and I felt sincere empathy for him. I then went to Rome to get necessary supplies for Alessandra and the baby.

As soon as arriving at the house I tried phoning my family members to make the announcement, but nobody answered. I was a bit puzzled but I kept trying and I finally got hold of Susanna, the younger of Fabiola's daughters. Hearing my voice, she started to stammer and when I told her the baby was born before time she said: "Oh my God … Oh my God …". I asked what was the matter and she, pour soul, had to carry the terrible weight of informing me that on the same night Giacomo was born my brother Marco had died of a heart attack in Cortina, a mountain holiday location where he was with his wife Marina. As I was trying to reach them, all family members were trying to reach me, which had been impossible because no cell phones existed at the time and they knew I was in Talamone in a house with no phone. A friend on holiday nearby had been sent to find us, but we had already left.

I put down the phone and I stayed transfixed for a few seconds, then I began to shake and fell on the floor. I was too shocked to cry, and I was unable to think of what to do. Without even being conscious of what I was doing, I dialed Franco Clavari's number and managed to tell him what had happened: the greatest joy and a terrible sorrow occurred at the same time. He just told me: "Don't move. I'll be there right away." He materialized in less than 15 minutes with Alessandro Chiti and got the situation well in hand. Susanna had told me that Fabiola and my aunt Viv had been on holiday near Cortina and were already there; it was obvious that I had to leave as soon as possible. I decided to take a sleeping car train to Cortina the next night. In the meanwhile the T.V. had Marco's death in the news, because, besides being a valiant therapist, he

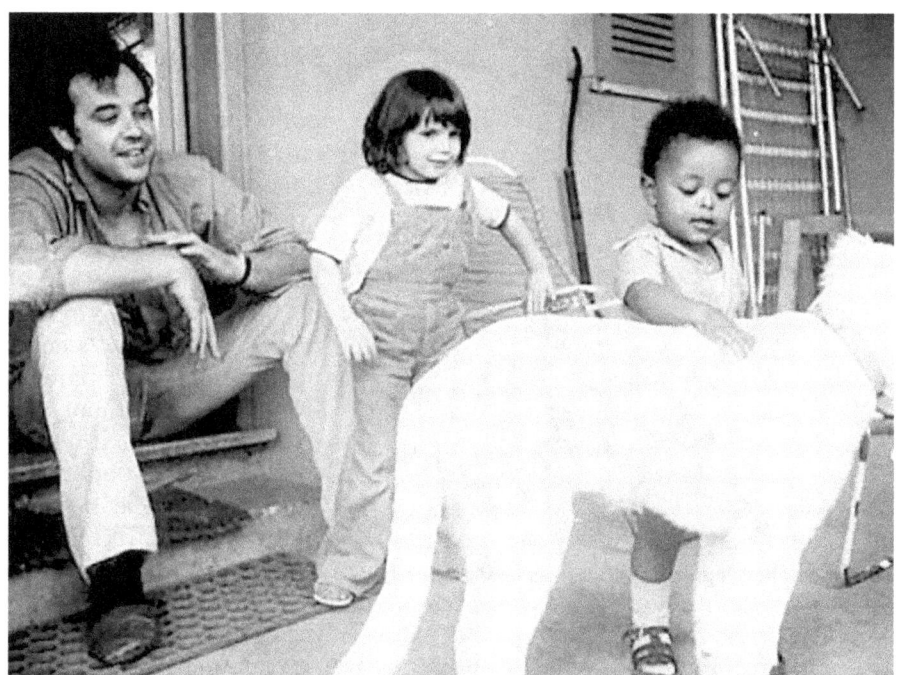

Marco Lombardo Radice with foster son Fetsum, nephew Cristiana and dog Blu

(along with Lidia Ravera) had been the best-selling author of *Pigs With Wings*, a book that analyzed the entire age of juvenile rebellion in Italy during the 1970s. Friends who had Alessandra's place phone number started phoning up and I had to give everybody the same rendition of life and death.

But the most awful thing I had to face was going back to the hospital to tell Alessandra the bad news before she heard it from somebody else.

I did and at first, seeing my expression, she feared something had happened to the baby. When I told her she was transfixed as I had been and then cried. She had loved Marco too, even if the acquaintance had been very brief.

The day went by with people visiting in a surreal mix of joy and sorrow. A group of old beloved friends from school days took me out to dinner and I then tried to sleep but I couldn't, so I smoked and cried the whole night, sitting on the floor of a balcony.

My mind went back to Marco and to the wonderful influence he had on my life. My family had been normal and sometimes even exceptional on the surface, but had been quite disturbed underneath the sparks of cleverness and culture. But he had been a steady rock, helping me with my school exercises and gently yet firmly guiding me out of many problems during teenage adolescence. He had silently protected my relationship with "T" and never judged anything by societal "morals," but only by "ethics," as to say honesty and good behavior toward society. When I had my first dramatic spell of depression and anorexia at the age of 18, he had taken me with him into his house and fed me with Campbell's soup from a spoon as if with a baby. And he had selected Dr.

Fetsum Sebhat, Marco's foster son, is now an acclaimed singer.

De Pascalis for me, because Marco thought he was the best doctor for my case, even if his very strict colleague didn't approve of his revolutionary methods in directing the teenage section of the psychiatric hospital where he worked his whole life.

I had done things for him too, even if in less essential fields. When he separated from Marina (without ever divorcing), I started buying him shirts and underwear to improve his scientist look. Once or twice, seeing how stressed he was from his total dedication to his patients, I dragged him on vacation, which meant for him laying his huge body on a beach chair underneath a beach umbrella and reading some psychiatry book while sipping a Martini, but at least sleeping decently and eating properly were part of the deal. But, most of all, I had been his slave for whatever side activity concerned his teenage patients. If he thought that it was important for the doctor-patient relationship that some of this patients were aware that he was from an old and important family, he would call me and say: "I'll come for tea, with a young friend" and that was the cue for me to take out the best silver and china and act like Count Gherardini. I just did it … I never asked why. If a boy or a girl had some interest for show business in any form, I was called in and, on his request, I took into the Actors Company a new stagehand, a 17-year-old boy suffering from a hysteric form of epilepsy; he is now a very good movie actor and completely cured.

This wouldn't have been possible without Franco Clavari, but I found out by working shoulder-to-shoulder that Franco was the person closest to Marco that I had ever met. Many other dropouts and lazy boys who did not come from Marco's hospital entered the company as grips or light helpers and are now successful professionals. Not without cause, when Franco arrived to take care of things after the news of Marco's death, I had told him in tears: "Now, I only have you." At 35 I was left without reassuring male-father figures in my family and I had to cope somehow.

At the station a little crowd of friends was waiting for the sleeping car and among them my uncle Pietro Ingrao. But what made my heart lose a beat was seeing that Fetsum, Marco's adopted Eritrean child, was also there with his mother, a political refugee whom Marco had taken in when the boy was a few months old. After some years they had moved to Germany, where she had relatives, but Marco had visited often and Fez, as we called him, had always been with our family for Christmas and summer holidays, and this was precisely the cause for him to be there. But nobody had told him that his beloved "Baba" had passed, only that he was ill. It was impossible to have him arrive to find him dead, so I gathered the little forces I had and told my 12-year-old black nephew that I had phoned Cortina and got the news that Marco's conditions were critical and there was little hope he could survive the night. This done I closed myself in a compartment with my friend Massimo, Marina Garroni's husband, and cried in his arms the whole night.

It is impossible and too painful, even after so many years, to recall the desperate sorrow in the hospital morgue. The steady group of teenagers that Marco had cured by letting them be part of his personal life were there, among them Alberto, who had suffered from a hysterical paralysis and had been cured by continuously being in physical contact with Marco, who held him 24 hours a day, as a mother ape with his little one. He had then gone to live with him and, as with Fez, he hadn't been legally adopted, but was considered his son in every sense. To make my readers understand the level of Marco's skills as a therapist, I'll relate that Alberto is now a psychiatrist himself and the father of two children.

In the garden outside the morgue, I stayed by the side of my sister-in-law Marina, who had always been a very fragile person. Her love story with Marco had been momentous and, even after separating, they had kept seeing a lot of each other and continued celebrating the holidays together, as with this last tragic occurrence.

At the funeral in the little cemetery, I said a few words of hope, announcing that my son had been born on the very same day of Marco's death and that I intended to educate him by his example. I then quoted Horatio's farewell to Hamlet:

> Now cracks a noble heart. Good night, sweet prince:
> And flights of angels sing thee to thy rest.

And I left him there, in his simple grave, circled by high mountains covered in perennial snow.

Chapter 26
The Theater Years of a Not Ideal Husband

I had very little time to mourn Marco's death, because in September I started rehearsing *Poverty and Nobility* by Eduardo Scarpetta, the most famous farcical writer of the Neapolitan tradition, and which had been filmed in a movie with Totò and Sophia Loren. The leading actor was Carlo Giuffrè, a comedian with a long theatrical pedigree and known to genre movies fans for a bunch of sexy comedies with Edwige Fenech and many other curvaceous beauties.

Neapolitan, as many other idioms in Italy, is not a dialect but it is actually a different language. If spoken fast and with the traditional old vocabulary it can be totally incomprehensible to people from other areas in Italy. As brilliant and witty writer Ennio Flaiano used to say: "Italian is a language only spoken by dubbers," and to give an idea of how true it is, I will recount the first time I went to the U.S.A. as a teenager. I was in the subway and two old ladies behind me were speaking fast; I couldn't understand a word and I was wondering if American English was that much different from the British I had learned since infancy. When I heard the word "belìn" (dick), it made me understand that they were Italian and speaking the Genoese language; they were obviously two immigrants who had stuck to their native idiom.

The Neapolitan in *Poverty and Nobility* was somehow Italianized, but still very savory and vivid and I tried to keep it as it was and did my best to master it so as to direct the actors. But it was useless, because Carlo Giuffrè didn't intend to let me do my job. The Dr. Jekyll in him had called upon me to refresh a worn out comic tradition with the British humor he had so loved in my direction of Ayckbourn's plays, but Mr. Hyde compelled him to push me aside and direct everything himself, leaving me the tasks of being interior decorator and light director. It was very frustrating and from there on I was very cautious in accepting offers by leading actors who confuse directors with butlers.

It was the beginning of a long phase of my life dedicated to theater, both as director and actor, and considering this book is mainly about my movie work, I won't go into details of the many productions.

From 1990 to 1997 I staged 16 plays and an opera as the director. I acted in four plays and translated from English all the ones I dealt personally with, and many more for other directors, one of them in French. Titles included three more different versions of *Bedroom Farce* for other groups or acting schools, one more of *Sincerely Yours* for Carlo Alighiero and Elena Cotta (whom I also directed in Ayckbourn's *Woman in Mind*), and two more new Ayckbourn plays for the Actors Company (*Just Between Ourselves* and *Absurd Person Singular*).

The Scarborough play writer was my favorite, but I had very satisfactory encounters with other English authors such as Willy Russell, Martin Worth and Peter Yeldham (whose *Lighting Up Time* I staged both in English and Italian) and Charlotte Keatley, the author of *My Mother Said I Never Should*, which I consider one of the best plays I read in my whole life and probably provided me with my best direction ever. She came to the opening, and considering it was a woman's play, I was very stupidly expecting something post-feminist; the young woman I met at La Cometa was the miniaturized version of the perfect English Rose and I could have fallen in love, but she was otherwise engaged and close to marriage.

The only two Italian plays I dealt with were the musical version of *Pigs With Wings*, which I directed and wrote with Lidia Ravera, who had been my brother's co-author for the book, and *Fegatelli*, by Maurizio Donadoni, a genius and unpredictable actor and playwright. It was about a movie crew shooting the last details of a demented T.V. series and I had incredible fun both in directing it with Donadoni and in playing the gay make-up man.

American writers were also very much to my liking and I directed plays by Tom Griffin, Peter Keveson and John Pielmeier, but my vote for best author went to A.R. Gurney, Jr. My production of his *The Old Boy* was a very simple version for a gay festival, but *The Dining Room*, which I directed for the Actors Company, was considered by an important critic "a staging to be studied for a long time" and the skills of the actors in playing so many different characters in the space of one night were shown in a sparkling and glamorous light.

Carlo Giuffrè was directed by Johnny in *Poverty and Nobility*

The Actors Company in its steady formation (Alessandra Panelli, Giannina Salvetti, Barbara Porta, Mauro Marino, Stefano Viali, Gianfranco Candia plus Claudia Della Seta and myself at times) was indeed a powerful and amazing stage-war machine and an absolute exception in the Italian theater landscape. We were so used to being on stage together and so great was our complicity that we could mount a play in 18 days, from first reading to opening night. The audience and the critics adored us and it was a great shame and a huge loss that such an artistic heritage went belly-up after some years for personal reasons, the main one being the marital crisis between Alessandra and myself.

I think that in this book I indulged too much already not only in recounting my theater adventures, but also in going into my personal life, but it is nevertheless at times impossible to divide private from professional, as for the reason I slowed down my acting career for some years and indulged directing, translating and writing for T.V.

Alessandra and I did the best we could to disperse the gloomy atmosphere that Marco's death had cast on our marriage, and we tried to concentrate on the joy of having a child. But we had to work and, even if we had accepted the idea of leaving the boy for long periods, we had no grandparents or other family members to rely upon for taking care of Giacomo if we were touring. Paolo Panelli was hardly capable of taking care of himself and my stepmother Fabiola was already burdened with frequent babysitting of Susanna's daughters. Anyway she was too old to take care of an infant the whole day long. The few others left were working hard, nicely lunatic or both.

We hired an au pair Swedish girl and, when Giacomo was just five months old, we left for a little town in Tuscany that had agreed on hosting the rehearsals and opening of *Just Between Ourselves*, our new Ayckbourn production.

Coping with our first au pair we fully realized that the first thing to look for in a steady babysitter is ugliness. Alex, the Swedish girl, looked right out of a beauty contest and her only interest was deciding who to date in the long line of boys in the area gathering at our door as wild famished wolves. Other girls followed, some better than others, and some just terrible, but even having a nanny with us didn't work, as the already hard task of touring became a nightmare. As it happened, when we closed *Just Between Ourselves* in a short time (too clever and melancholic for audiences already made demented by Berlusconi's T.V. empire) and we revived the perennial *Bedroom Farce*, matching it with *Absurd Person Singular*, our long-time dream come true and a huge success.

We were forced to make our personal residences into makeshift hotels, so as to cook Giacomo's meals and we, thus, got separated from the rest of the company and became more and more secluded in a restricted family set that didn't allow us to receive fresh air for creativity because we were doing the same job and doing it in the same place. What were we supposed to talk about if we were together 24 hours a day? Just the trivia of everyday life and its many inconveniences: morose babysitters for lack of night time fun, Giacomo's increasing nervousness from being moved back and forth and our own lack of any kind of personal space.

I must admit that I resented the situation much worse than Alessandra. I had been totally independent my whole life, free to eat, sleep, read or whatever else at my leisure and I felt trapped. I didn't even have time to go for a walk, because my free time from playing or moving from one town to another was dedicated to writing.

The Boys at the Wall first series was a success and two more followed, along with many other commitments: a tearful medical series about a pediatrician, a legal one centered on a woman lawyer and so on. In other words, T.V. rubbish created to pay the bills that theater work was far from taking care of. I tried anyway to write at my best.

Marina Garroni was always my writing partner and we usually worked hard together, first in inventing plots, and then we each wrote specific episodes. When on tour I was writing either in the confined space of a residence (with Giacomo playing, crying or involved in whatever noisy activity a little man is indeed entitled to exercise his lungs with) or in dressing rooms. Both situations were bound to produce continuous interruptions from Alessandra or the babysitter asking for advice or stage managers and stagehands having problems with the scenery. Unfortunately I hadn't inherited my father's wonderful temperament and his supreme ability in doing many things at the same time: writing a mathematics theorem with one hand, holding the phone with the other while talking politics and playing horse with a child. I was sadly like my mother and often needed silence and time for myself.

Was I hysterical? Yes, I was. But I was too good mannered and too introverted to let off steam with scenes of manly cursing. I was no Gosforth, as my scarce ability in the role had demonstrated. I had a couple of fury spells, but they were too realistic and offending to make things work better.

Giannina Salvetti was another member of The Actors Company.

I kept all inside and reacted by subtracting: less and less talking, less and less smiling and, most of all, less and less lovemaking. A very harsh Neapolitan proverb states that: "The cock doesn't like worries" and almost every male reader, apart from a few professional porn actors or a few others provided with more testosterone than average, will agree on that.

In a diabolic spiral of frustrations and misunderstandings, my lack of ardor increased Alessandra's jealousy, which had been on alarming levels from the very beginning. She suspected anyone of the male sex between 15 and 60 who crossed my road, came to my dressing room or was in my life in any form, and I just couldn't live with that. My virility suffered and the circle closed as a dog biting its tail.

The fact that her jealousy was deeper and more morose and wild in regards to men was also quite hard for me to understand. In that phase of my life I wasn't cheating on her, but even if I had, wouldn't it have been easier to deal with if her "rivals" were people totally and utterly different from her and thus not bound to instigate competition and lack of self-confidence? In my quite extensive experience in love affairs with straight or bisexual men, it was generally the other way round, as confirmed by the words of a great friend of mine when I had a short and tempestuous love affair with her husband. She was a great lady and after a while summoned me to her place and told me: "If my husband cheats on me with another woman I am bound to cut off his balls and scratch her face with my nails, but if he does it with another man and most especially with a good friend, such as you, I honestly couldn't care more than if he were out playing soccer. The only thing I want is that nobody gets hurt." Both her husband and I were as a matter of fact getting hurt and the story ended with no consequences. They are great friends and always will be.

But, starting from Alessandra, I was to find out that indeed a minority of women are more offended by a homosexual extramarital affair than by a straight one, the reason being exactly what is more relaxing for the majority: to compete with something unreachable. It takes all sorts.

For all these reasons, but mainly because Giacomo was literally suffering in leading a life unfit for a little boy, as soon as he was ready for kindergarten and *Bedroom Farce* was finally over, I decided to withdraw from *Absurd Person Singular* and stay in Rome as much as possible with Giacomo and the au pair girl of the moment, so allowing Alessandra to do the only job she had and she was great in. She was just acting while I was doing other things, and it seemed fair to me that I was the one to renounce being on stage. Gianfranco Candia thus took my role of Geoffrey in *Absurd Person Singular* and, to be honest, he played it much better than I did.

I didn't cast myself in other productions of the company, I concentrated on the T.V. series I was writing and willingly accepted a few roles in movies, among them the cameo one in *The Sect*, which marked my third and last collaboration with Michele Soavi.

Chapter 27
How to Destroy an Escalator and Live Happily Ever After

I must admit that when Michele announced to me that he was to make another movie and that he wanted me to be in it, even if just a cameo role, because I was his lucky charm, I was pleased for the token of affection, but since I was fully busy with the kind of life I just described, I didn't even read the whole script. I was in a short sequence at the beginning and died at the end of it. What followed didn't look momentous, but anyway I wouldn't have said no to Michele for any reason. And to be true I never saw the finished movie either, just my scenes at the dubbing sessions. But I have a vivid recollection of shooting in Germany (but I can't remember what town it was) and in the Rome subway station of Furio Camillo, a place that wasn't ever the same after my passage.

Even if only on screen for a few minutes, my character was not banal. It was a guy affiliated to a satanic cult and who spots a fugitive member in the street, follows her home, murders her and tears out her heart (offscreen). He then takes the subway with the heart in his pocket (the funny side of many horror pictures ...), a very unlucky thief tries pick-pocketing him and the heart falls on the ground creating horrified chaos among the passengers. He escapes and a policeman chases him along corridors and escalators, and when he is trapped, my character forces the gun held by the policeman into the cop's mouth and he shoots himself dead. Bingo!

The interesting side for me was the sect membership, something that had always fascinated me as a concept totally opposed to my critical spirit and emphasis on free will. I decided to concentrate on the void: watch without seeing, becoming utterly obsessed by a sparkling red light just as the princess in *Sleeping Beauty* was when the witch hypnotizes her and guides her toward the spindle (one of the best Gothic horrific scenes in a Disney animated movie). Watching the Disney movie today, I think I got my inspiration for how to play the scene from here.

The three days in Germany were fun, with Michele adorable as usual and Dario Argento (once again producing) at his best, both in telling jokes and anecdotes at the dinner table and in acting as grip or prop man on set. He insisted on personally breaking the milk bottle just bought by the victim and spill the stage blood on the milk in slow motion, an effect that was indeed much more impressing than the unseen knife cutting the flesh.

My only problem arose in the first take in the street scene, because I had to hold a three-month-old baby who was playing my son, and then pass him to my wife so to follow the former sect member. The baby wasn't supposed to cry in the arms of his father, but my alarming looks made him think otherwise. Fortunately we were arriving in a car and, before getting in sight of the camera, I presented the baby with my singing talent, pulling forth the boring French

Cover art for the German VHS release of *The Sect*

repertoire, and he fell asleep on the spot as many more had done before. If you are desperate about a sleepless child, go to YouTube , search for "Aux Marches Du Palais" (Yves Montand sang it) and play it to the baby or learn it and sing it yourselves. It will work every time.

Back in Rome, the long sequence in the subway didn't prove as easy.

The production had rented the Furio Camillo station for three nights and we started shooting around 11 p.m., as soon as the passengers of the last train had left. No special problems arose on the train as we filmed the attempted theft and the beginning of my mad escape, but from that point on a steadicam was employed, the first I worked with in my career and it was very different from the quite light ones of nowadays. It was terribly heavy and thus carried by a gigantic cameraman.

With time I got to love steadicams very much, because they allow you a fluid action and free movements for quite long sequences, but, as a christening, the one in *The Sect* was not the best to wish for, nor was the action, which required running among a crowd of extras. When shooting with a steadicam the actor and the cameraman must work as two dancers in a "pas de deux" in a ballet, and timing and coordination are essential. After a while the poor cameraman, burdened with that sort of medieval torture machine, and I found a good mutual understanding, but the extras were always in our way and not able to cooperate. The cameraman stumbled and fell twice, always protecting his valuable possession before thinking of protecting himself, and we had long breaks in the torrid heat of the tunnels. At each take I was giving back the bleeding heart to the guy who played the thief, and the disgusting bit of entrails from a sheep

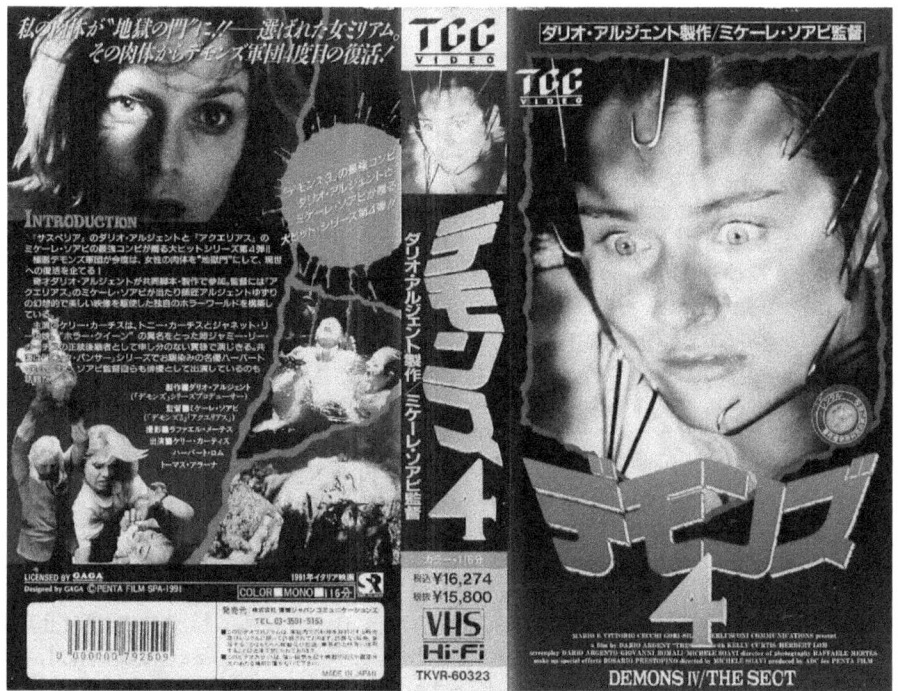

Cover art for the Japanese VHS release of *The Sect*, where it was titled *Demons IV: The Sect*

or some other animal only grew more smelly, but the uncomfortable situation didn't prevent me from seeing the humor in it; only in a movie or in an actual cannibal tribe two can human beings keep exchanging a putrescent heart as if it were a normal and rather boring routine.

For the first time I saw Michele nervous and shouting; after the first night shoot began time was running down and we had to leave before the subway reopened at six in the morning. A final fall left the cameraman injured and another one arrived, but at that point we had reached the escalator and Michele wanted me to jump on it from the ground to the highest step I could reach. I accomplished the request, but not without a few bruises on my ankles. But each time I landed on the escalator it stopped and got stuck. The man from the subway company in charge was furious and yelled at me not to jump, but I told him to yell at Michele and Michele pretended not to listen or just disappeared into thin air (which was a special skill of his). The sequence "jump—escalator blocked—man yelling" went on and on, and when the production manager kindly suggested to me to jump "in a lighter way," I, quite kindly, suggested to him to go and screw his mother. This was just before the subway man, all red in his face, was about to have a stroke. I finally managed to get on top of the escalator without blocking it, and we could move to the last part, with me committing suicide. A protective metal plate was applied to the back of my head and then the small charge of explosive and the stage blood that had to squirt out in slow motion as I dropped dead. The fact that the little bomb was not in the trajectory of my eyes relaxed me in comparison with my death scene in *Cannibal Apocalypse*, but nevertheless I was nervous and very tired and I didn't fall on the ground as slowly as Michele wanted. It was the first and last time he scolded me on set.

My participation was over, but strangely enough I kept passing by the Furio Camillo subway station for many years to come because Franco Clavari had found a cheap rehearsal place in that neighborhood and, as God is my witness, the escalator I had jumped on never fully recovered from my violent use of it and was out of order 90 times out of a 100, so that I could proudly say to my fellow actors of the Actors Company: "It was me!"

The Sect was a last in many respects … the last movie I ever did with Michele, and one of the last horror movies to be produced in Italy with a professional budget. It was also the last horror movie for Michele as a director. He directed *Cemetery Man/Dellamorte Dellamore*, but that was a very special and different type of thing (being very good and funny in my opinion) and not at all a genre movie. He was desperate because there was no role for me in it and phoned me to say how sorry he was. It was very sweet of him and I told him not to worry, but in the following years I was a bit puzzled by the fact that he never called me when he successfully switched to T.V. crime dramas and police miniseries, soon becoming number one in that area. Directors are unpredictable and Michele is no exception. Maybe I was too tied to his horror movie past and he wanted to completely jettison that aspect of his career, or maybe we were too close for him to see me in roles very different from what I was in life.

Anyway I bore no grudge and I still love him very much, even if, over the years, his airy attitude has elevated itself to an unreachable quality and to get hold of him by the phone or by email is more difficult than contacting His Holiness the Pope.

In Italy the season of horror movies dried up and only Dario Argento kept doing one once in a while. The thousands (maybe millions) of horror fans that are on Facebook or other social networks testify that the reason was not a change of tastes in the audience, but just changes in the movie system, which got destroyed by T.V. networks.

Not a single frame of a movie is shot nowadays in Italy if not supported by T.V. money and networks don't invest in genre movies but only in prime time family stuff or in a few "author" movies to be worn as a flower in the buttonhole at Cannes or Berlin festivals. Producers just became a fearful category of executive people who take the money and use it, but not without keeping a good share in their pockets.

Do I despise them? Yes, with a few exceptions, I do. Very much.

When I wrote a four-episode movie for Italian singer-dancer-T.V. hostess and national star Raffaella Carrà, the producer asked me to send him episode four even if he hadn't paid for the previous three. I said that I wanted to be paid first for the work I had already done, and he answered that he couldn't because Rai hadn't paid him. At that point I saw red and suggested to him to sell or pawn that Cartier watch that he wore on his wrist. A diplomatic incident of biblical proportions followed and my agent (who was dear, iron made and good-hearted Carol

Levi) told me that if I were to say something like that one more time, she would kick me out in a flash. I bowed my head because I couldn't afford to do otherwise, but I kept thinking I was perfectly right and I would like very much to see the resurrection, from a Fulci cemetery, of old-school producers like Franco Palagi (*House on the Edge of the Park*) who weren't dandified but were coarse and at times utterly ignorant but loved movies and risked their own money.

A very young Raffaella Carrà

Another reason for independent productions disappearing and never having a chance for success is that no effective tax shelter law was ever made and investors were not motivated. So, if I kept doing independent movies in the U.S.A., the U.K. or Germany. Whatever genre project I am asked to get involved with in Italy (very few, I must say) disappears after a short time or gets stuck in a perennial limbo.

I wasn't fully aware of all this when I bid farewell to *The Sect* and the Furio Camillo subway station, but it was in the air.

The other three movies I did around 1991 and 1992 were a T.V. film in two parts called *A Cold Place Deep in the Heart*, directed by Sauro Scavolini, *Ricky and Barabba* by Christian De Sica and *Body Puzzle* by Lamberto Bava.

Cold Place was a provincial story of spoiled kids dealing with drugs. Kim Rossi Stuart starred in it, while I played a corrupted local nobleman. We shot in the wonderful town of Perugia and I was glad to be with Kim, because he was one of the few exceptions in the new wave of young movie and T.V. stars. He fitted perfectly the definition a critic once labeled Vivien Leigh: So beautiful she wouldn't need being talented and so talented she wouldn't need being beautiful.

Christian De Sica was a friend in personal life and an enthusiastic follower of the Actors Company, so he knew how good I was in comedy and called me for the cameo role of an acerbic and snobbish director of a deluxe hotel, the manager who had to deal with comic Italian star Renato Pozzetto and Christian himself not wishing to pay the bill. It was fun and all T.V. channels keep broadcasting it morning, evening and night, so it helps not being forgotten.

Body Puzzle was a horror/thriller and definitely fit into my genre career because it was directed by Lamberto Bava, an acclaimed director and the son of director Mario Bava, "the man who started it all" for Italian horror cin-

Italian poster for *Cold Place in the Heart*, an Italian T.V. movie

ema, along with Riccardo Freda. As with *The Sect*, I never saw the finished movie and I have only a vague recollection of reading the script. What I remember is that I was an antiquarian, I was gay and ambiguous and I was either on a horse or with Tomas Arana, and the horse more firmly stuck in my mind because it was the first time I was riding in many years and I was glad to find out that it is indeed the same as with the bicycle, you never forget.

After *Deliria* I was offered quite a lot of gay roles and it pissed me off, not because I didn't want to play gay characters, but it was once again typecasting me in one more way as frail, neurotic, violent and cruel. But my mind was very much concentrated on the theater and I must admit that, even if I was always professional, my attitude toward cinema in those years was very much in the Woody Allen state of mind: Take the money and run, most especially if I got short roles or cameo ones.

While I was dealing with gay roles, my marriage was going to rack and ruin and Alessandra (who wasn't aware of what I was doing in movies out of understandable disinterest in genre things) would have seen a sinister aspect in this coincidence.

We are now very good friends and the proud parents of 28-year-old Giacomo, but, if we were to re-discuss the reasons for the end of our marriage (something we carefully avoid), she would state on her deathbed that it ended because I liked men and I would state on my behalf that it happened because, as a couple, we were totally incompatible. She was jealous and I was not, but I had little patience with jealousy in others. She was very dependant and I was desperately free. She cared about what people said or thought and I didn't give a shit.

To her honor, I must say that while I stayed just the same, for the best and for the worst, up to this very moment, she changed a lot and did a hell of a good job on self-improvement. Therapy of course helped, but she was also determined and she was a woman. After Alessandra I refused to deal with another woman in a relationship, not even if asked by the Archangel Gabriel to procreate and bring forth on Earth the new Messiah, but I nevertheless state that women are in many respects much better than men, that they can change while men just can't. Women should understand this fundamental difference and stop asking their partners to do what nature, culture, history or the sum of the three made impossible for them.

To save my marriage I tried resuming therapy and I went back to Dr. De Pascalis, only to be thunderstruck after a few months by his sudden death in a car accident. When I had ended the first cycle of therapy he told me that after a few years either the patient quits or he becomes somehow a therapist himself, and I had that in mind when I butted heads with the woman therapist I had tried consulting after De Pascalis' death. I had enough knowledge to understand she was a bitch and could have destroyed whatever self-confidence I had acquired.

Lamberto Bava
Body Puzzle

In the early summer of 1992 I had a long break from my difficult family life, because, even if very poorly paid, I accepted the assignment to direct an opera at the Fermo Festival. It was *The Indiscreet Curious*, a little 18th-century comic piece by Pasquale Anfossi, which entered posterity only because Wolfgang Amadeus Mozart, as a token of his esteem, wrote three wonderful arias to be inserted into the work of his colleague, a common practice at the time.

What was complicated and fascinating at the same time was that if the musical score had survived, the libretto was composed of bits coming from different sources and it didn't make sense as it was. Months before starting rehearsals I worked shoulder to shoulder with young Maestro Roberto Soldatini to assemble a revised version, and what came out wasn't indeed a masterpiece like the Da Ponte librettos for the Mozart operas, but a nice simple farce to go along with good solid professional music enlightened by Mozart's three little pearls.

In Fermo I met the cast and, as a pleasant change from the tragic *Cinderella* in Montepulciano, I was very pleased because they were extremely good both as singers and as actors and among them there was a valuable diamond: Greek soprano Jenny Drivala, who looked a lot like her compatriot Maria Callas and sang wonderfully.

As with Callas, Jenny was thin and elegant, always perfectly dressed in sober high fashion outfits that emphasized her aristocratic demeanor and a waistline that would have made Scarlett O'Hara proud of Mammy's efforts in tightening her corset. She bore a refined culture and spoke five languages. She was an early riser as I was and while having breakfast together, we could discuss poetry, movies,

theater and politics, switching from English to French and from French to Italian. She was also fluent in German and of course Greek, but unfortunately I was not.

I was mesmerized by my Diva and it was obvious that she liked me a lot, but our relationship stayed friendly and professional until I found out that the tenor, the only missing component of the cast, was bound to arrive very late because of a previous engagement. He had love duos with Jenny and she needed to rehearse her movements, so for a few days I doubled him on stage, with the piano maestro singing his bits. And ... in a sort of retaliation, what Alessandra had feared could happen with a man occurred for the first time with a woman.

The tenor finally arrived in the shape of a fashion model who sang like an angel. He quickly learned what I had done in his place and the opera opened with a great success, which awarded my efforts not only as a director but as a set designer, because there was no money to pay one and, with the help of the stage manager, I sketched a simple but ingenious system of geometrically-shaped hedgerows that could be combined in different ways.

Back home, I didn't tell Alessandra about Jenny (and never did as a matter of fact—she will find out by reading this book), but we were nevertheless forced to face our marital crisis.

We discussed our situation and tried to develop our marriage into a more free and friendly relationship. She had a couple of affairs with former boyfriends that I had never met, and I had some gay adventures. Neither she nor I received very positive vibes. Furthermore, Alessandra was increasingly unhappy and anguished about leaving Giacomo for long intervals when she was touring, and she knew the child missed her badly. They had a very intense relationship, maybe more intense than what is usual and healthy between mother and child, and Alessandra projected on him all the need for affection she wasn't getting from me. Someone very wise once said that the best thing a father can do in the early years of his son's life is to keep the mother happy, and I definitively failed at that end. I loved Giacomo very much and had enough feminine nature to perform some of a mother's tasks, but I had to work hard because the financial management of the family was extremely expensive and, if working at home writing, I would lose my patience if Giacomo interrupted me and wanted to play Lego with his father instead of the babysitter.

The worst moment arrived when Alessandra, in a break from theater, was hired for a movie to be shot in Kenya. A new au pair girl had just arrived, she was African and very sweet, but she spoke very little Italian and Giacomo hadn't seen a black person before and he was afraid of her. He cried, yelled and refused to be near her if I wasn't present.

I had an urgent writing commitment and I was desperate, so I finally begged Lella (an actress from Saverio Marconi's company in Tolentino, who Giacomo liked very much) to come to my rescue. In all this, Giacomo got the flu and Lella made the terrible mistake of telling grandfather Paolo, who, because of his son's death as a child, would get hysterical whenever the boy had a minor ailment.. He manifested his distress by phoning literally every 10 minutes, asking with his peculiar clucking voice: "How is little Giacomo?" Little Giacomo, having a temperature, just wanted to be with his father and was crying because his throat ached. The 10th phone call produced a tantrum that was to remain permanently in our family annals and in the memory of many show business people who knew both Paolo and me.

Me: (Already knowing it was him) Paolo?
Paolo: How is little Giacomo?
Me: (Calmly) Look Paolo, you are an actor, so I'll explain this to you in theater terms. The title of the play is "The Child Has the Flu." The star is Giacomo, who has a temperature. I am the co-star because I take care of him. (Suddenly I go berserk and start yelling like crazy): You are a fucking extra and you must not break my balls!

I admit I was cruel but God knows he stopped calling.

Chapter 28
Freedom and Drama

When Alessandra came back from Kenya, the crisis between us came to a head, and we decided to split.

Her father had just paid her a share of her mother's legacy and so she bought a little mini-apartment just around the corner, and I moved there, leaving the house to her and Giacomo. My new place was just a room with a little kitchen, some open space and a bathroom, very much in the style favored by hookers of both sexes and, as a matter of fact, some of my neighbors were in the business, one of them being an outrageous Brazilian transvestite. It was fortunate that I had the habit of doing everything in my bed, because God knows that there wasn't space for a desk or a dinner table, but I didn't complain. My books were in the old house and I had free access and took Giacomo to kindergarten every morning on my moped. He wasn't tall enough to sit behind me, so he was standing in front and at times he fell asleep just dropping his little head, made disproportionately big by the helmet.

Whatever tension that came from separating didn't last long. We had been friends for years before marrying and it wasn't difficult to redirect our relationship. I was constantly available to be with Giacomo and I supported mother and son financially as I had always done. No legal step toward divorce was made because we couldn't care less and just wanted to breathe and move forward.

I was intoxicated by my regained freedom and I had a short season of flirting with many different men and going to gay saunas without remorse, and in one of them, on Saint Valentine's Day, I met Camillo. He was a Sicilian actor, some years my junior, and the sweetest and kindest person to be found. He was warm and protective and in his big arms I experienced once more the feeling of a little boy in need of paternal affection. We had a relationship that lasted for two years, but, after marriage, I wasn't ready for monogamy and I often cheated on him. He suspected it and didn't make scenes, but I could see he was suffering and after a while I preferred not feeling the guilty party and we broke up, only for me to regret it, from time to time, in the saddest moments of loneliness. But at that time I was close to being 40 years old and I was trying to grab my vanishing youth by its skirt and make her stay as long as possible.

But the most momentous event in those years was "T's" resurrection. We had kept being sporadically in touch and I knew he was totally fed up with "L," even if they had had a second child, a boy who had bewitched "T," even more than his daughter.

We had played happy fathers at our children's birthday parties without resuming any form of intimacy, but strangely enough, because he was no Florence Nightingale, he visited me almost every day when I was in the hospital with hepatitis, feeling very poorly. Deep in my heart there was a special place that was only his and I knew that my life would have been entirely different if a steady relationship with him, even if free and open, had been possible. A sonnet by English poet John Clare I had casually found in an Ayckbourn play and a few lines depicted perfectly my feelings toward "C."

I loved you, though I told thee not,
… Thou were my joy in every spot
My theme in every song …

Even if he knew perfectly well, I had never told him openly that I loved him and I had been very careful, maybe too careful, not to scare him away with overwhelming demands.

I was very happy to have him back in my life and the bitchy part of me opened more than one bottle of champagne in apprehending that "L" couldn't pass through doors because of the horns on her head and that he had currently a side relationship with a former girlfriend I had met and who was now married. The guilty lovers hadn't a place to indulge in forbidden pleasures and I willingly volunteered to let them use my little apartment when I was out. Did I feel pity for "L"? Not an ounce … I had warned her and in my opinion she was the perfect specimen of woman who justifies every man becoming gay or a heartless Casanova or both.

As I had known would happen, "T" and I had sex after a very long time and I melted in his hands, totally mesmerized by a body and a scent forever tied to the very beginning of my love life.

If it wasn't surprising that I was still attracted to him, aged but very much the same, I was totally stupefied by the fact he was having sexual desires for a body so different from the slender, androgynous one he had been attracted to as a young man. But you don't look a gift horse in the mouth and I just accepted the fact as a blessing.

Even if I was on friendly terms with Alessandra, I didn't feel like working together with her on a daily basis, and I thus let another director take care of the new productions of the Actors Society. It wasn't a wise move and it slowly led to the end of the group, which was finalized when Alessandra decided to stop acting. She had been the iceberg that formed the top of the company, because of her famous surname, and selling a show without her became impossible. In those years Italian theater was definitely surrendering to the power of television … any tits-and-ass whore blowjobbing a politician was most likely playing Anna Karenina on the little screen the following week and was then allowed to be on stage and tour intensively because provincial audiences wanted to see her (or him) in the flesh.

A great part of Alessandra's decision was tied to the fact that she was tired of touring and leaving Giacomo for long periods, but there was also a more profound longing for something less frivolous than the stage world. She had been part of the cast of *The Great Pumpkin*, a wonderful movie by Francesca Archibugi inspired by the professional life of my brother Marco and, dealing with handicap and mental illness, even if on a fictional basis, made her wish to employ her skills in that field. I supported her in this decision and for a year she didn't work at all, but studied to get a diploma in social sciences and earn the title of head of community. She then started doing theater with handicapped people, both physically and mentally, and she founded an association, which is still active and producing amazingly good shows and many activities in cooperation with hospitals and institutions.

With Alessandra steadily home I resumed some stage acting and Marco Mattolini directed me in two productions: *Alibis of the Heart* and *2005 The Last Act*. The latter was a witty farce set in a futuristic world where theater has been prohibited by a Fascist regime, but my character, a General with playwriting ambitions, was secretly paying a troupe of Neapolitan actors to produce one of his demented works. It was fun and it caused one unforgettable event to happen.

We were performing in Naples at the Diana Theater, a huge space with 2,000 seats, and I was ready in the wings for my first entrance, preceded by the yelled salutation of the dictatorship, which instead of "Hail Hitler!" was "To Him!" I uttered the cry and my voice just cracked and disappeared. No falling scenery, blackout or memory void in a fellow actor had ever scared me on stage, but that time I was lost. I couldn't utter a sound and my partner in the first scene was a former T.V. dancer totally unable to help me in any way. Luckily there was a microphone in the wings for a song to be performed later and I managed to grab it and whisper my lines in it, but it was a disaster and after being stuffed with cortisone I tried giving up smoking and switched to chewing nicotine gum … it didn't last long, also because new responsibilities and serious economical problems were awaiting me.

After Marco's death the little group of young patients closer to him had developed a strong attachment to me, and through them and some of Marco's colleagues I started doing some social work. Like Alessandra I needed some other activities besides theater and movies to feel useful in the world.

I helped with schooling a group of young people living in the Magliana (the same ill-reputed suburb where Nando and Sergio lived in the days of my youth) and over the years I was gratified by the fact that I could be of some real help, not only in education but also in personal life. Fabio, whom I met when he was 19 and a violent hooligan in search of trouble, is now a good tattooist and a happy father, and Marula, the most studious and clever of them all, improved her English to the point that, right after graduation, I could ask my agent Carol Levi to try her as a receptionist. She was to stay in the office permanently and made a good career, becoming Carol's personal secretary until her sad demise a few years ago.

Acting was still fun for me and social work fulfilled more intense needs, but what allowed me to live without money problems and support my family was writing for television. But, bizarre as it might seem, it was precisely a contract for more than a hundred million lire that led me to sell the big beloved house where Alessandra and Giacomo were living and that was still "mine," not only in property but also in affection, and not in any other country other than Italy could this have happened.

As I already explained Rai was, and still is, state property and there was a law saying that every contract for more than a hundred million was to be approved by the board of directors. But the board was politically nominated and in those years Italy was dealing with its worst political crisis of the century, governments were coming and going and no board was steadily in charge, so the contract for the third series of *The Boys at the Wall* couldn't be signed. Enzo Tarquini, in charge of the fiction department of Rai 2, faced Marina Garroni and me (who were to write more than half the episodes) in a very resolute and even harsh way, saying that we should work all the same or leave.

I thus worked for more than a year without receiving a penny and I was forced to take out a second loan with a bank, the modern and socially accepted formula for loan-sharking. In a few years it became harder and harder to pay the loans and survive and I was forced to consider selling the house, which was definitely incredibly too large for just Alessandra, Giacomo and a babysitter. I told Alessandra that with the income I would pay my debts and buy a smaller house for her and Giacomo and, considering she was going to live in it, I let her choose it within a certain budget.

She was addicted to the very expensive area where my house was located because it was the same neighborhood in which she had grown up as a child and thus, instead of preferring a larger place in a less bourgeois neighborhood, she finally selected a house that I personally found awful. It had a very little backyard. She was fond of gardening and the yard made up somehow for the two big terraces we had at my place, where she had the opportunity to grow fruit trees.

But she was never to live there, because as soon as the deal of selling the old house and buying the new one was completed, a terrible event fell on us all and led to consequences that changed the lives of many people, closing the circle that had started with Maria Luisa falling from a chair on the first rehearsal day of *Bedroom Farce*.

As I already recounted, Lucilla Salvini had been called in her place, but after marring Hubert Westkemper and having a child, she retired and was now expecting a second baby boy, an event we were all looking forward to with joy.

The fact that her son Federico was less than a year older than Giacomo created an off-work bond of friendship between Alessandra and Lucilla, and they saw a lot of each other and spent more than a long holiday together in Alessandra's father's summer place, with Hubert and I coming and going because of work.

But right after delivery, shortly before Christmas of 1995, Lucilla had a sudden and unexpected hemorrhage. The private clinic she was in underestimated the situation and she died in less than an hour at the age of 37.

I got the news by phone from Alessandra in tears and I remained speechless and horrified. I was somewhere on the last days touring *2005* and there was nothing I could do but curse "the show must go on" tradition. I just calmed down remembering that my father-in-law Paolo had been performing in Milan when his son died in Rome and he went on stage that very night.

As soon as the tour was over, I rushed to Rome and put myself at everyone's disposal. Alessandra wanted to go to Florence to help Hubert and I took Giacomo for a few days to Castiglioncello, Paolo's summer place. Answering his questions was one of the worst experiences in my whole life. He was six years

Hubert Westkemper, sound designer, is on the left.

old and the mother of his best friend had died at childbirth. Was there a way to answer to his "why?" when I myself couldn't find a reason for that neither in nature nor in religion? With Giacomo I adopted the same wise attitude of my parents, when explaining death to a little boy. You get old, you are weak, you are tired, you just sleep and don't wake up anymore, without any suffering … Children generally face death at first with their grandparents or some other old relative, and they are hopefully grown up enough when they get to understand that the Dark Lady doesn't indeed kiss only the weak and the old. Lucilla was young, healthy and ready for the greatest joy in a woman's life, so what was "good" or natural in her death? I was forced to tell him that there were tragic exceptions and that we should concentrate on the newborn baby because it was what Lucilla would have wished for. But I could see that Giacomo's mind was deeply troubled and his heart was aching and there wasn't a single thing I could do about it. I guess every parent will understand the sorrow and the frustration that summed up to my own, concerning this tragic event. But at times you can't protect your children from life and this was one of those times.

Poor Hubert was in the worst possible situation one could imagine. He was a widower with a seven-year-old boy (Federico) and an infant (who had been named Cosimo) and he had to resume his work as sound designer immediately to support his kids. I had never been really close to him, even if I had been one of the first show business people he had met when he had arrived from Germany back in the 1970s, but I felt an enormous empathy for him under the circumstances and I told him to act as if his family was my family. He had work to do in Rome and he didn't want to leave the children in Florence in care of Lucilla's parents, destroyed by the sorrow caused by the death of their only daughter. So he and the children were Alessandra's guests in my former house and she bent over backwards to make their life as jolly as possible and be a substitute mother for little Cosimo, a blond angel with immense blue eyes who took my heart the very first time I held him in my arms.

In the space of months, from Christmas to summer, the friendly care and affection toward a friend hit by a tragedy developed into a stronger feeling. When I joined them in Castiglioncello, Alessandra told me that she and Hubert were in love and wanted to live together.

The Ayckbournian circle of hazard, life, love and death was completed. If Maria Luisa hadn't fallen from a chair and broken a leg, we would have never met Lucilla, and a new family would not have been able to face life after such a terrible tragedy.

Chapter 29
I Am the Third Fairy and Madness Is My Name

As later events confirmed, Alessandra and Hubert's decision to live together seemed a bit rushed, but at that moment we were all happy about Love fighting Death, as in one of the *Triumphs* of Italian poet Petrarca.

But the house I had just purchased for a family of two and a nanny wasn't of course large enough for two adults and three children, so they rented a place in the same neighborhood and I was forced to go live in a house I hated, so as to let Alessandra rent the little one.

It was the start of a sort of enlarged family life. I was often at their place to take Giacomo and Federico to the movies or McDonald's, and Alessandra and Hubert got to the point of allowing me to have the three children, so she and Hubert could travel together on work trips or if they just needed to relax and have a short holiday by themselves.

On the professional side, the D'Amico family proved once more crucial in determining a new step in my career. Caterina D'Amico, the younger sibling, was in charge of the National Cinema School and she wisely thought that the graduating students needed a theater experience. She called me for this task and I decided on an umpteenth version of *Bedroom Farce*. Working in the school I met other teachers and got along so well with them that we decided to create a new acting school connected with La Cometa. We wanted an international approach to the endeavor and involved Nicolai Karpov from the Gitis School in Moscow as director of the movement and acrobatic section, Alan Woodhouse from the prestigious Guildhall School in London as chairman of the voice department, and I got the acting professorship.

I had taught acting in the Tolentino School and found it very rewarding from an emotional point of view, but doing it on a daily basis with young, potential professionals was even more exciting and I dedicated myself to it with great passion and enthusiasm. I also found the time to write my first book *Handsome and Unreachable*, which was a satiric "do it yourself" instruction book for gay men wanting to seduce straight guys. It was of course largely inspired by my story with "T" and it garnered a little crowd of fans all over Italy.

I also kept doing social work and a psychologist I met during this time introduced me to Alan, a 15-year-old punk right out of juvenile care, who needed medical attention because, from time to time, he was spitting blood for no apparent reason. His father was in jail for life because of bank robbery and homicide and his mother was a schizophrenic and alcoholic, who progressed to the point of having him not attend school after the fourth grade. Taking the boy, who looked like a wild caged animal, to some doctor friends was the first step toward a difficult, at times desperate, but ultimately happy story of fostering him and struggling to make him choose life instead of death (which he was courting in many ways, from drugs to mad motorcycle driving). I won't tell about this in detail, because I think this will be the primary material for my next book, if God is by my side.

But to win the game with Alan I had to survive one of the darker moments of my life, once again connected with "C."

When I moved into the new house our relationship grew more and more intense. He had broken up with the married former girlfriend and he miraculously wasn't in any other relationship with a woman. He got the habit of coming over to my place every morning after taking his son to school. He made me coffee and we often had sex. Once, while making love, he had the most unexpected violent fit and

Russian Nicolai Karpov joined the staff of the new acting school. It was associated with La Cometa.

shook me wildly, saying, "You are mine, understand? Only mine!" But he also got romantic and once arrived in the middle of the night and brought me a rose, picked from a garden on the way; he woke me up by caressing me with it and for the first time whispered, "I love you."

We also talked about ourselves on a more rational basis and we agreed on the fact that one of the reasons we were not able to have life-long relationships in the past had been the deep-rooted awareness that we had each other to rely upon, as a safety net against loneliness.

I couldn't believe my heart. Was this really happening after so many years? I was 43 and he was 50. Was this a benign destiny intended to make us live together for the last part of our life?

I treated this new relationship as a precious glass cup from some remote Chinese dynasty, but even if we carefully avoided behaving like lovers in public, "T" was confronted with two realities and two aspects of his personality that he found difficult to reconcile: his being the straight father of two children and my lover of 30 years.

The consequences weren't immediate and back in Rome we resumed our usual life. Over the years "T" put to good use his skills in whatever handiwork and had started a small redecorating firm. I visited him among dust, debris and the smell of paint as I had done at the very beginning, when he was 19 and earned pocket money by working as a mason and I joined him, studying and doing homework while sitting on bricks or paint buckets.

Then, one night, he told me, half bored, that there was a woman who was chasing him and he didn't' know what to do. And at that point I probably made my worst mistake by telling him to do as he pleased. I should have told him that perhaps we should concentrate on one other and sort out what was still difficult to decipher between us. Maybe he wanted a "property statement" from my part ... maybe ... maybe ... it's easy to be wise in hindsight. I saw our relationship as the repetition of an old script, since I had 30 years of docility behind me and I feared that acting possessive would have distanced him from me.

It was the other way around. A supposed one-night stand turned into a steady relationship and he literally disappeared from daybreak to dusk. I thought it was temporarily, but weeks ran by and he stopped visiting and calling. I was shocked and, for the first time, also furious and offended. But I was also deeply hurt and reacted by not eating. Sleeping became difficult too and I begged my doctor for some strong pills; I started abusing them to anesthetize my sorrow.

Alessandra's father died in May 1997 and with the money she inherited she bought a huge, luxurious house where the family moved. But there was some work to be done and, without my knowledge, she called "T" to take care of it and it was at her new place that I finally met him, once I went to pick Giacomo up. I didn't greet him and pretended not to see him and this led to the final act. He stormed into my place the next day while I was drowsy from sleeping pills and he insulted me in the worst possible way. I was crying and I understood less than half of what he was shouting, but at the end of it I found myself holding the home keys he had thrown on my bed before storming out.

I got out of bed, and I looked at myself in the mirror ... and it happened.

> She left the web, she left the loom,
> She made three paces thro' the room ...
>   from *The Lady of Shalott* by Alfred, Lord Tennyson

I didn't utter a word and I also didn't take a boat to Camelot (another line from the poem above), but the mirror did crack from side to side and I became crazy at that precise moment, and for a few months I had the same look as my character had in *The Sect* and the red light guiding me into the void was death.

I stole a prescription from my doctor and switched from the already strong sleeping pills I was taking to Roipnol, a powerful and dangerous hypnotic drug, which was outlawed a few years ago by The World Health Organization.

If during the day I more or less managed to be Jekyll and do what I was supposed to—writing, being with Giacomo, taking care of Alan, teaching the Magliana kids and being at the acting school—at night Hyde was taking hold and I was plunging myself into an inferno inhabited by hookers, filthy old clients, drug dealers and sadists who were more than eager to pay good solid money ... I didn't need to play their dirty games. It was the real *City of the Living Dead* and I lived there until dawn, when, considering death hadn't arrived, I often drove back home on my moped in the wrong lane, drunk, stoned and desperate.

Aside from the devilish red light I always had "T's" face in front of me, both caressing me with a rose and shouting insults. I hadn't been able to keep him by my side, so I wasn't worth a cent and I needed punishment. The voice of madness is only rarely the voice of truth.

I almost stopped eating and looked like a skeleton, but there was no older brother to feed me Campbell's soup anymore. It was crystal clear to anyone that I was in danger and people close to me didn't know what to do as I avoided them as much as possible. Only years later I learned that Alessandra and Franco Clavari had thought of having me lawfully committed.

Before that happened, two different forms of love saved my life: the rough, powerful love I received from a man and the paternal love I felt for Alan, who had just me to rely upon.

The man in question was named Fabrizio—better known by the colorful nickname of The Bandit—and he was the leader of a small gang of derelicts who circled like vultures around some of the sordid places I was frequenting in search of trouble. One of them was named Vincenzo, and he was from Naples, had witnessed a Mafia killing and had been shot in the back, survived by a miracle, with two holes the size of a coin an inch from his spine. He was suffering from excruciating back pain and, to calm it, he had become addicted to heroin. Fabrizio was his best friend and, as much as he wasn't Saint John the Baptist, he hated heroin more than the cops and had thus sheltered Vincenzo in a locked room, the only family key firmly in his hands. This shock therapy worked and, when I met them, Vincenzo was clean, but the pains were occasionally still there and Fabrizio, having heard that I was a masseur, asked me if I could help him. I did what I could and one night, without having suspected that Fabrizio had a sweet tooth for men, I found myself flattened against a wall with him passionately kissing me.

He was 10 years my junior and many inches shorter than me, but he took my life in his powerful fist and, not without a few slaps in my face, he prevented me from committing a disguised suicide. No drug dealer was to sell me stuff, especially Roipnol, and no dirty old man with sadistic instincts was allowed near me. He had a reputation for not being a "just talk" type and in a flash I found myself in a dark void filled only by his affection, care and passionate lovemaking.

I never knew in what illegal activity he was involved and where the stacks of money he always carried in his pockets were coming from. He did not tell and I did not ask. Only once he involved me in a translation session from English to his thick Roman dialect with some Dutch guys. They could have been executive managers working for some corporation, but of course, they were not. The meeting happened in a nightclub close to the Via Veneto with champagne on the table, lousy music blaring and sexy strippers in the background. It was like being in a B-spy movie and the whole conversation was disguised in a horse-based code, so I would not understand what they were dealing with. It satisfied me that it was not heroin and I was sure about that fact because of Fabrizio's ferocious hate for whoever was selling or consuming it. He strictly followed the precepts of the old criminal underworld he had grown up in: no harm to women or children, no heroin and loyalty to friends.

What was sure was that he always carried a lot of cash and used a great part of it to help people, playing the role of a modern day Robin Hood. He surely wasn't using much money for himself because he was always dressed in worn military fatigues and drove a Renault from the late 1970s. But he didn't think much of money and had very personal ideas about what could or couldn't be done to earn it.

Giuliana Lojodice played the Anne Bancroft role in Johnny's version of *Agnes of God*, which he directed.

I had carefully avoided telling him and his friends that I was in show business, knowing that they watched very little television and Fabrizio was only addicted to children's cartoons that he watched in a sort of religious trance.

But while I was spending my time with them and slowly getting back to my right senses, I was engaged in doing my first commercial, a spot for Sanbitter, a non-alcoholic aperitif, set in ancient Rome, with gladiators, the Emperor and me in the leading role as the Emperor's secret adviser. Fabrizio saw it and questioned me about it. I made up a story, saying that one of my massage clients was in the business and opened a few doors to get me a job. He asked how much I got paid and when hearing I had earned the not despicable sum of five million lire he snorted and said in his wonderful Roman dialect: "Five million to be a clown in front of everybody? If you had only asked me I would have given you twice that amount!" From a different perspective his ideas about acting didn't differ much from my grandfather Jemolo's point of view.

As I said, another great help in me coming out of my deep depression was Alan and his need to be taken care of by someone not as desperate as him. He was street smart and much older in life experience than his age typically allowed, and he could see that there was something wrong with me. Little by little I weaned myself from Roipnol and accepted a theater engagement directing *Agnes of God* by John Pielmeier, a play that was famous for the movie version directed by Norman Jewison and starring Jane Fonda, Anne Bancroft and Meg Tilly.

I took Alan with me for the last rehearsals before opening in a theater summer festival in Liguria and, on the way, we stopped by Raffaella Carrà's Hollywood style villa in Tuscany. I was writing for her and there were things to discuss.

Meeting in person an Italian T.V. idol (the equivalent to Oprah Winfrey in the U.S.A.) mesmerized Alan, and she was incredibly nice to him and personally cooked a filet because he didn't like the sumptuous fish and mussel buffet she had prepared. She warned him about the incredibly powerful hydro-massage in the Olympic swimming pool by saying: "Watch your dickie!" and he splashed in it for hours while I was discussing with Raffaella the mini-series she had to star in. When I checked on him he looked at me with sheer joy in his eyes and told me: "If it's a dream, don't wake me up."

Giuliana Lojodice, who played the Anne Bancroft role in *Agnes of God*, was famous enough for even Alan to know who she was, and she was twice as nice. Dealing with Alan for a week, she got to talk to him about his future, his past and his problems as a grandmother would have done. The same thing happened when, back in Rome, I took him to a one-man show by Gigi Proietti, a comic actor every teenager worshipped, and then the three of us went out to dinner.

It might seem fairy tale-like and sugary, but meeting these stars and being treated as a person of importance made wonders in Alan's improvement toward a normal life, and I will be always grateful to them for helping Alan. Show business stars can be egomaniac and whimsical, but they have their good points, and experience taught me that generally the more famous they are the more sensitive they act toward people in a difficult situation. You need a heart to get into the soul of an audience.

Chapter 30
I Only Sit on a Throne

I convinced Alan to attend a special school for adults who had abandoned their formal education as children. It stated that in only one year one could earn a middle school diploma. It was an exceptional case of a public institution that worked; teachers were patient and caring and he liked the school, even if, to prevent escapes, I had to take him there, wait for him and then take him back home.

My total presence was for him a guarantee that I really cared and the headmaster was kind enough to let me use an empty classroom where I could write while I was waiting. He was staying with me in Rome from Monday to Friday and he returned to his mother in a little town nearby on weekends, mostly to be with his girlfriend, a nice and amazingly beautiful girl who was very helpful in Alan's process of reintegrating back into society and whom I shamelessly bribed with gifts and attentions.

But in the spring of 1998 I had just to hope that he would keep going to school by himself because I was called to work in a period T.V. movie based on the classic love story of Tristan and Isolde (Yseult, Iseut, or whatever name different versions of the story use). The title was *Heart and Sword* and it was a real blast, because Titanus (number one in Italy and run by movie tycoon Goffredo Lombardo) was producing. The company paid extremely well and my character of Baron Andret, villain and usurper, was first rate. It was a coproduction of Italy, France and Germany and I was almost the only Italian actor with a major role. The T.V. movie was to be shot in Brittany for exteriors and then interiors were to be filmed in Rome and it sounded like a real wonderful occasion for me, with just the shortcoming of leaving Alan for about two months.

With Titanus everything was first rate, beginning with the wonderful costumes designed by Nanà Cecchi, whom I knew very well because she was a cousin of the D'Amico siblings. And the fact of knowing her well allowed me to beg her not to make me wear, among my many costumes, a leather cloak with a huge piece of marble mounted on the front; it was beautiful but it weighed a ton and it didn't fit my idea of Andret being a vulture. Nanà understood my point and provided me with a black wardrobe and a large mantle that could float around me as a dark cloud. But I refused that cloak, which proved to be a very wise move, because

Costume designer Nanà Cecchi

it went to German-English actor Francis Fulton-Smith (now famous for his character of priest detective Father Castell) and, even if he was much larger and more muscular than I was, by the end of the movie, during a riding sequence, his horse stumbled and bent on one side and the weight of the cloak made him fall like a sack of potatoes. He ended up in hospital with a broken arm.

Just by auditioning I knew that director Fabrizio Costa was totally prepared, so, very unwillingly, I accepted his request of growing a beard for the role. It made me look much older and the skin underneath got itchy, but it was definitely good for my performance and it avoided the necessary two extra hours at make-up to apply a fake one.

With a salt and pepper beard I got to Brittany and settled in the enchanted town of Saint Malò, which is a peninsula, perfectly round-shaped and circled by walls erected in the 18th century that are perfectly preserved as was the whole town; not a single house was built in modern times. It is entirely surrounded by the sea and the tide phenomenon was just amazing. A little hill a mile from the town (which hosts the grave of French poet Chateaubriand) became an island in the space of less than an hour and loudspeakers were giving an alarm signal in time for people not to walk on the land anymore; incredible as it might seem, some people had drowned in the past.

German-English actor Francis Fulton-Smith

My fellow actors weren't stars, with the only exception of Pierre Cosso, who had a moment of incredible success as a teenager's idol when he played Sophie Marceau's boyfriend in *La Boum* ("Ready for Love"). Tristan was played by German actor Ralf Bauer and, in my opinion (shared by the director as I later found out), he was completely wrong for the role. He was tall, well into his 30s and completely lacked the boyish charm the role needed, but he obviously had influential friends in his country because the German share of the production selected him. He was, anyway, an agreeable chap with the only fault of being both very brave and very accident prone and, while jumping from walls or plunging into a well, he got hurt more than once and slowed down the schedule. On the other hand, young French actress Lea Bosco was the most perfect Isolde one could have imagined, with flawless white skin, blue eyes and a cascade of

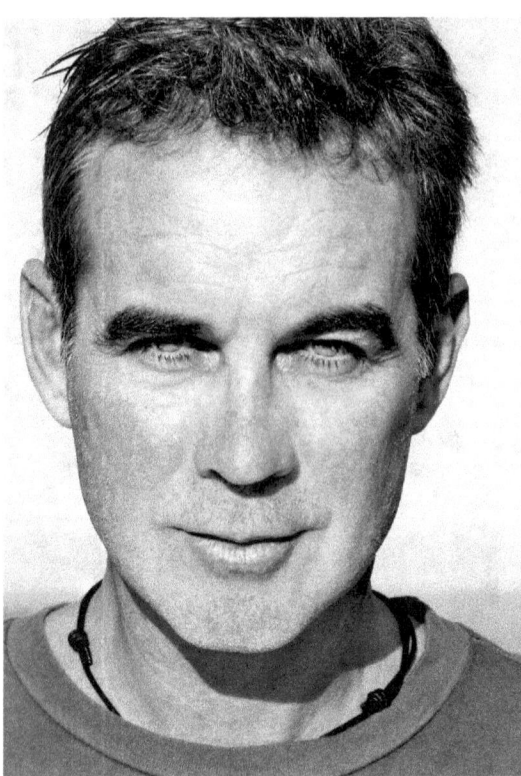

The only "star" in the cast ... Pierre Cosso

blonde-reddish curls that were right out of Dante Gabriel Rossetti's re-interpretation of the Middle Ages. King Mark was Joachim Fuchsberger, a good professional but a bit too old for the part, and there was a cameo role for Maria Schneider, but I never met her because her scenes were in a different location and were shot later.

The story took place somewhere around the turn of the first Millennium and our sets consisted of some castles on the Brittany coast, a few of them with a movie history such as the one where *The Vikings* with Kirk Douglas had been shot. To me it was like a dream come true because I had always adored period movies full of adventures and battles and I was finally making one. At the end of the movie there was a big battle scene and Baron Andret, who had usurped King Mark's throne, had a final duel with Tristan, which led to his death and the freeing of Isolde, who had refused to marry him and had been consequently condemned to be beheaded. It was to be shot many weeks later, but rehearsals for every single duel during the battle started immediately and they were as hard as they were exciting. The stunt coordinator was an expert in fighting and duels from different ages and he and his team taught me the ritual dance that a medieval duel actually was, with a code of pre-scheduled moves and countermoves made exhausting by the weight of the sword (a real one) and a special way to place your feet, which thank God resembled the fourth position in ballet. If I weren't shooting, I had one hour training a day and one hour additional for riding, and I needed the refresher course because I had many scenes where I had to ride.

Fabrizio Costa, who reminded me a lot of Deodato, proved to be even better than what I had first thought, and he is surely one of the best directors I ever worked with, especially for his inventive camera movements, which made each take both a dance and a challenge. My idea of Andret being a vulture materialized in circling the people I was talking to, and Costa often matched this with a circular movement of the camera in the opposite direction, which emphasized the effect: for once acting and camera technique were going hand in hand.

When Easter came, Alessandra and Giacomo visited me (very generously hosted by the production) and we had a wonderful 10 days of sightseeing around Brittany, which included a visit to Mont Saint-Michel, the amazing castle-monastery that according to the time of day and the tides is either on land or an island. Since infancy Giacomo had a marked dislike for the acting profession that separated him from his parents and he wasn't excited about seeing me with armor on, but liked very much my gray horse, who was not only beautiful and well mannered, but also one of the best actors I worked with (or *on* in this case). The horse was movie trained, understood perfectly both the words "action" and "cut," and moved and stopped by itself, but he was also capable of going exactly on his mark after one rehearsal, even if it were quite far from the starting position. Needless to say I loved him dearly; I bribed him with carrots and sugar and at the end of the day I often helped the stable boy in washing and feeding him.

Director Fabrizio Costa

When Alessandra and Giacomo left, I resumed using my free time in writing fiction and at times (having by then a laptop) I did it also on set, and it's a pity nobody took a picture of a medieval warrior in full armor and helmet typing on a computer some tearful T.V. series. At dinner I was always with a small group that included Fulton-Smith, Pier Paolo Capponi (the other Italian actor with a big role and in need of help with his English) and Stefano Corsi, Flora Mastroianni's nephew, who in the movie was my evil accomplice as a hunchbacked sorcerer. Fulton-Smith was very attractive and, even if he was straight, my long experience told me that he wasn't unattainable, but, with my gray beard, I didn't feel like a possible prey for a ladies man and I was contented with his pleasant company and his many funny stories, my favorite being the following:

A man enters a pet shop full of wonderful colored parrots and he starts asking for the prices.

> Man: How much is the blue and red one?
> Owner: It's five thousand dollars, sir.
> Man: Oh, my God!! What does he do for that price?
> Owner: Well, sir, he can recite *Hamlet* by William Shakespeare, the whole play.
> Man: That's amazing! And how much is the green, orange and purple one?

The dramatic death of Baron Andret (Johnny) in *Heart and Sword*

Owner: Oh, it's $15,000, sir.
Man: $15,000?! And what does he do?
Owner: Well, sir, he can recite *Hamlet* and Chekhov's *The Seagull*.
Man: That's incredible! And what does the multi-colored one do?
Owner: He recites *Hamlet*, *The Seagull* and *Doctor Faustus*, both in German and English. It costs $40,000.
At this point the man spots an ugly gray old parrot, losing its feathers, and asks for the price.
Owner: Oh, sir, the gray one costs $100,000!
Man: Jesus! And what does he do for that sum?
Owner: Nothing, sir, he's the director.

Day after day and scene after scene, Baron Andret, using my body, had schemed against Tristan and put him in a bad light with his Uncle Mark after apprehending by sorcery Tristan and Isolde's guilty love. He had then usurped the throne and was sitting on it to witness Isolde's execution, when Tristan and his men arrived and the big battle started.

Each pair of fighters had carefully rehearsed their duel, first with a stuntman and then with the actual partner, as I had done with Ralf Bauer, but we had fought in an empty space and nobody had prepared us for the utter chaos that took place when every section was put together.

The first take was a very long shot of the whole scene from a hill with no rehearsal and when action was called I found myself dueling with Ralf, an inch from other fighters. There were swords, knives and spears moving wildly everywhere, frightened peasants running away in all directions and terrorized horses madly galloping on the muddy ground. Ralf and I tried our best to fight as instructed while looking to each other in puzzled fear, but when he finally stabbed me to death in the space of a second, I pictured horse's hoofs viciously stepping on my face and, instead of falling on my back as Costa had told me, I fell on my stomach, thinking that an actor's more valuable part is his face and that it was better to be crippled than disfigured.

Lunch break with Johnny and son Giacomo while shooting *Heart and Sword* in 1997

The mad horses did pass an inch from me, but luckily with no consequences, and when "cut" was finally called I was unharmed. Not so Pierre Cosso, who had received a spear blow in his thigh. Once again, acting is not always risk free…

The battle was my last scene in Brittany and I went back to Rome having the pleasure of meeting Roberto Benigni at the Paris airport. I had known him quite well in the 1970s, when he was struggling for bread and butter in off-circuit theaters, but he was now right in the middle of the triumphal success of his *Life Is Beautiful* and, if there's one thing I hate, I hate struggling to be acknowledged by famous people. So, in the business class lounge, I didn't greet him, but he recognized me and we warmly hugged and had the most pleasant chat.

Back in Rome, I had some scenes at the Rome studios and the most important one was my attempt to induce Isolde to marry me and thus reinforce (with her queen status) my usurpation of the throne. We were in Isolde's bedroom and Francesco Bronzi created a wonderful period space, but he hadn't thought of what was happening just outside the door, in this case me storming in with some 10 soldiers fully armed. We were to wait for our entrance in a sort of narrow box-like room and it took all my ability to fit in the extras and me in what could have been a sequence from a gay orgy, with faces, crotches and bums in the most bizarre angles. Our entrance was preceded by a short scene between Isolde and her maid, and that day Lea Bosco, who was quite inexperienced and only 20 years old, decided to play "I am so sensitive" diva-like and continuously stopped and cried. At the fourth interruption I stormed out of my uncomfortable hideout and scolded her in front of everybody, both in French and Italian for the crew to understand. I said that if she wanted to be a star she should begin with being professional and respectful of others. Nobody dared contradict me, not even Costa who was very fond of her, and back in the box-like room I was greeted by the enthusiastic approval of my soldiers, who acted as Britons but were in reality from the Rome suburbs. The emotional crisis did wonders for the tension between us and I successfully crafted what I had thought the night before: changing some lines slightly to transform them into blank verse, similar

The cast of the Italian T.V. mini-series (from left to right): Stefano Corsi, unidentified player, Pier Paolo Capponi, Joachim Fustberger, Johnny and Francis Fulton-Smith

to the style created by Shakespeare. Nobody would have probably noticed, but it gave the dialogue a sort of inside music that I found very becoming for a love-hate scene from the Middle Ages.

I kept doing this in some other period movies which followed, because Baron Andret was just the beginning of the "royal side" of my career, not putting my arse on anything less than a throne, and the following character was a king for real and not a usurper, when I appeared once more in a Fabrizio Costa T.V. movie, *The Courier of the Czar*.

But before I stepped into the costumes of Feofar Khan, king of the Tartars, a great change happened in my life because of Alan.

Even if during my absence he had gone to school one day out of three, Alan succeeded in getting a diploma and, as a present, asked for a puppy. I diplomatically got him to change his choice from aggressive breeds such as the Rottweiler or Pit Bull and he finally fell in love with a white Labrador named Jack. The dog basically lived with me, because Alan didn't trust his mother to take care of him if he were out. I had many cats in my life, including a female Siamese whose best pleasure was to climb the stockings of my female friends out of jealousy, but Jack was the first dog I lived with since Archimedes, my mother's dog, and I had been quite negative toward the poor soul because of my mother's open statement about liking him much better than her sons. At first I accepted Jack just for Alan's sake, but I got to love him very much, even if he was too lively for me and was never tired of walking and running.

And I was quietly reading with Jack at my feet one night, when Alan stormed in, disheveled, with a bleeding cut on his forehead and a desperate expression.

I was surprised because he was supposed to be with his mother in a little town outside of Rome where she lived, but what had happened was that he defended her from her alcoholic and violent companion and had almost killed the man, who was now in the hospital. It wasn't the first time something like this happened.

While taking care of his cut I understood that, if I wanted to save him and allow him to continue on his current path he had set by going to school and getting the diploma, I had to take him in with me permanently and remove him from his crazy mother, her punk boy friend and the everyday risk of going to jail for killing him.

We discussed it, but he positively refused to live in Rome. He was scared of its vastness; he liked the country and, most of all, Alan wanted to be close to Valentina, his girlfriend.

I took a major step and rented a house in Aprilia, which was the town in his area better connected with Rome, and I selected a big place five minutes from the station that faced a park where Jack could run free. After consulting my lawyer, I made Alan's mother sign a paper in which she accepted his living with me. He was 17 and it was useless to embark upon legal fostering for just the one year left before his majority. Now with two houses and coming back and forth from Rome, my lifestyle became sky-high expensive, but I was earning solid money and I could afford it. I was to pay much higher prices in terms of affections and social position in the theater world.

Fabrizio was offended by my decision that was settled upon after I politely vacillated concerning his request of him and I living together. He had said that he was tired of the street life and he wanted to open a garage with the money he had saved. It was hard for me to believe these good intentions would last, because he was used to living at night and never woke up before noon, but even if it was true, I couldn't imagine Alessandra's reactions if I had permanently settled with someone like Fabrizio and involved Giacomo in my ménage. And if I wanted to guide Alan with a firm hand I should stop mixing with exactly the same kind of people I wanted him to get away from. It was the end of my love story with The Bandit, and as much as I tried to find his whereabouts in years to come, I never saw him again.

Giacomo was also going through a very difficult period, and so was Federico, Hubert's eldest son. While Cosimo was still unaware that Alessandra wasn't his real mother, the two older boys had been pushed too hurriedly into a new family life. One of the boys was missing his mother's love and the other boy missed not only his dead mother, but also his grandparents and Florence. And as for Giacomo, he was also confused about the relationship between his mother and me. Why had we separated if we were on such friendly terms? And if she was with Hubert, what was my sexual orientation and love life all about? He was almost 10 years old and the concept of homosexuality as it existed in the world was crossing his mind. I would have explained all this to him many years back, starting with my love story with Camillo, who was perfectly decent and loved children, but Alessandra had forbidden me to do so, saying he was too little and would not understand, but I thought she was committing, in my opinion, a major mistake. My fostering of Alan didn't improve things because Giacomo was of course jealous, and I was living part-time in Aprilia, which made seeing him more difficult.

We decided to send both boys to a psychologist and for me this meant disaster, because after a while Giacomo's therapist said that the boy needed to make order both in his mind and life. I wasn't to mix with Alessandra's family anymore and see him alone, and most likely not with Alan, who was still too disturbed to have any positive influence on Giacomo. I don't know if the doctor was right or wrong, but I know that I positively hated him because I was plunged into the nightmarish world of divorced fathers eating at restaurants and going to the movies, and with the aggravating circumstance of living mostly in Aprilia, where the last train from Rome departed at 9:50 p.m.

Feofar Khan (Johnny), king of the Tartars, in *The Courier of the Czar*

On the work front I let go what was keeping me in Rome on a daily basis and concentrated on writing, which I could do in Aprilia, and acting in movies, because it was well paid and the work was compressed into a defined period of time. I thus stopped teaching and I resigned from the artistic direction of La Cometa, but the latter choice was also the consequence of the end of the Actors Company as a resident group. Without it my functions were much less interesting and Franco Clavari, who kept producing shows for different stars, tended to use La Cometa as an exchange value on the tour market. At times I was forced to host into the season some productions that I abhorred, just because Franco's productions were hosted in other Italian theaters.

In the long run both moves proved to be terribly wrong, but I hadn't a crystal ball to watch the future and it was just what I felt I had to do at the time.

I willingly accepted Fabrizio Costa's second movie offer, *Michele Strogoff, il coriere dello zar*, once again produced by wealthy Titanus with French and German investments, to be shot in Slovakia for a much shorter time than *Heart and Sword*.

As it had happened with *Liala*, I tried reading Jules Verne's book, but as a novel, I found *The Courier of the Czar* incredibly boring, which surprised me because as a boy I loved some of his books. Perhaps they were edited versions for children or tastes just change in growing up.

Different from Saint Malò, the location in Slovakia was just awful. It was a huge dilapidated palace in the middle of a park that had belonged to some local gentry and it was perfect as the eagle nest of a nomad king, but it was in the most remote countryside with just a little village close-by and a couple of very spartan hotels for tourists visiting the palace, which wasn't happening at the moment because it was winter. It was snowing almost every day and the temperature was often below zero. Nobody in the hotel spoke a word of English, just their native language, and at times a little German, so both Lea Bosco (who had again the leading female role) and I were clinging to the skirts of German actress Esther Schweins, who could help us order meals from the menu.

There was absolutely nothing to do on the days I wasn't on set and I wasn't even busy with writing, so I was just going to a gym in another village in the area, which had a wonderful large sauna, very relaxing but free of whatever side activity.

Boring myself to death, I had more time than usual to concentrate on my character of Feofar Khan, who was less extensive than Andret had been, but still very interesting. He was a proud warrior king fighting against the Czar for his ancestors' land and in doing so not backing away from trying to kidnap the Czar's son or employing, at his service, the traitor general Ogareff, who he greatly despised but nevertheless made use of. Not a villain then, but just the dignified and even iconic enemy of the hero of the story, Michael Strogoff, who, at the end, after defeating him, out of respect allowed him to commit suicide to prevent being arrested. My totem animal was of course this time a lion and as a lion Feofar Khan had a vain side, which showed in his ambition to be photographed by a funny French guy, whom he kept imprisoned for the purpose, which led to some comic interludes. All in all a very good role, with many shades of nuances to work on and a great look created by the Tartar tail of hair at the back of my shaved head. I also enjoyed a sumptuous wardrobe embroidered in gold and completed by a huge heavy white fur coat that was to be used only in one scene, but I always had it with me as a defense against the terrible cold of the unheated castle. With a throng of servants, a personal guard, my private harem of wives and a eunuch to control them, I felt indeed very regal and I royally froze myself to death until the very end of the movie, when I could return to warm Italy.

In 1999, the end of the century delivered a wonderful gift to my "extended" family, because Alessandra and Hubert had a child, a handsome boy called Davide. Now they could say, as Doris Day had in *Please Don't Eat the Daisies*: "Dear, my children and your children are beating up our children!" Davide's birth had a comic-legal side, because Alessandra and I had finally asked for a legal separation only after she found out she was pregnant and thus, for Italian law, the child was to be considered mine and I had to disclaim his paternity. The procedure implied a blood test for both the baby and me and we went to the doctor as one big happy group. While Hubert was parking the car, I went in first holding Cosimo, who by coincidence had my white skin and blue eyes. With a look of complicity the doctor whispered to me: "You are the real father, aren't you?" and I jollily answered: "No, I am the fake one."

Chapter 31
King of the Jews

In Aprilia the struggle to motivate Alan toward a healthy and fruitful adult life was at times exhausting, because the boy was taking three steps forward but two back, and if this meant one step in the right direction I was at times desperate and in need of help and good advice. For that reason I resumed therapy with a new psychologist, Dr. Fabozzi, a tall man as thin as a feather and as elegant; in his study I let go a lot of pressure about many sorrows, from Marco's death to "T"s" deserting me, and I received good help, not only for guiding Alan, but also for myself.

In the meantime my royal career was proceeding and I sat on a modern industrial throne as the iconic Supreme President of a multinational corporation who watched after his employees and addressed them from omnipresent screens: a comic emphatic version of Gianni Agnelli or Henry Ford. The movie was *Honolulu Baby* by Maurizio Nichetti, an extremely refined director and actor in the Charlie Chaplin tradition, who was directing commercials for a living and made movies only once in a while, when he felt inspired.

After that movie my throne became a holy one, because I was cast in the cameo role of Pope Pius the 12th in a T.V. movie about Padre Pio, the controversial monk who had the stigmata and performed miracles. Strongly thwarted by the section of the Roman Church led by father Agostino Gemelli, he was later canonized as a saint by John Paul the 2nd in 2002.

As a matter of fact I was the protagonist of a historical mistake, because the scene I had with Father Gemelli (played by Mariano Rigillo) had occurred

between him and Pope Pius the 11th and that was what the make-up artist knew. So when he saw me he was bewildered, because Achille Ratti had been a short sturdy man with a round face, while I looked much more like his successor, Prince Eugenio Pacelli. We decided not to create a problem and I was made up as the latter and wore his thin metal-rimmed glasses.

The production of *Padre Pio* was by Lux Vide, the wealthy and most influential production company just behind Titanus, and it was with them that I got to the pinnacle of my royal career in the role of King Herod Agrippa in *Saint Paul*, one of the last episodes of the Bible series that Lux Vide (strongly tied to the Vatican and dealing a lot with religious subjects) had started shooting 20 years back in the same Moroccan town of Ouarzazate, where I had been with *Atlantis Project*.

Johnny as Pope Pius the 12th in *Padre Pio*

I auditioned for the role and I wanted it so badly that I took with me some make-up and an oriental embroidered shirt. I changed in the bathroom and went in front of the camera with black pencil around my eyes and my skin darkened by a brownish powder. The latter proved unnecessary because Herod was of Greek ascent, but I got the role and in due time I left for Morocco, far ahead of my shooting schedule, because money wasn't a problem and the production preferred to have costume and make-up fittings on location.

Just before leaving, I formalized the selling of the much-hated house I bought for Alessandra and the purchase of a new one that I loved very much, but it was in need of restoration. I made the deal benefitting from the fact that I still rented the Aprilia place and thus had a roof over my head before the new house was completed. It was a small-detached house in the working class neighborhood and student community of San Lorenzo, not far from Termini station. I got it quite cheap because it was facing the historic Roman cemetery of Verano, and apparently people didn't want to live with a reminder of death in full sight. I had no problems in living in the real house by the cemetery and I laughed at the pun of Marina Garroni, who, considering the house was on Verano street, stated that it was "an address for eternity." I intended it to be so, because I was sick and tired of moving.

Johnny as King Herod Agrippa from *Saint Paul*

Ouarzazate had an airport and the connection was in Casablanca. The flight on Royal Morocco in business class was just perfect and in Casablanca there was a wonderful Arabian waiting lounge with big cushions to lie on and rest. Only later on I found out that I had been lucky in not getting stuck suddenly either in Rome or Casablanca. Royal Morocco Airlines is private property of the king and if there are not enough people on the flight to make it profitable, it can be cancelled on short notice.

When I got out of the small Ouarzazate airport, I thought there had been some mistake and I was in some other place. The small town had gone and given way to a metropolis full of modern buildings, lights and hotels. The cause of this amazing transformation was Lux Vide and the fact they constructed huge studios and employed hundreds of people to work on building sets, work as extras or work in the different technical departments. The movie industry had attracted tourism and visiting the desert was now highly fashionable.

If local people were now richer, the new lifestyle had its shortcomings. Not only were tourists heartily invited to see the medina, but gay harassment was positively everywhere and even boys age eight or 10 were caressing their crotches with a lustful smile when in sight of a male tourist walking alone. In my first days there I was stopped on the street by a 15-year-old (pretending to be 18 or so) and a much younger boy who offered me an "Arabian massage"; I bought them a Coke and severely scolded the older one about what he was doing and even more about involving a child, but I knew it was all for nothing. In North African countries the sex abuse of children by older relatives is a deep rooted habit, so why not make a profit out of it with naughty tourists?

After completing the fittings for make-up and costumes, I could have kneeled in front of the head of each department, because I looked just terrific with a red curly wig, a red beard, skin smoothed by perfect make-up and my eyes underlined in black. The two hours that the beard needed to be applied, almost hair-by-hair, was absolutely worthwhile. At 46 I wasn't feeling handsome anymore (if I ever did, regardless of what people thought), but if I had been allowed to parade in everyday life made up as King Herod Agrippa and dressed in his wonderful robes, my self-esteem would surely have improved a great deal.

Aside for the short scene as the pope, the character was the first historical one I played, and I asked to see a cultivated priest, hired by Lux Vide, to be sure that every detail connected to religious rites or historic accuracy was spot on. Without getting into details, what came out in my character was a flamboyant and very theatrical man who had been punished by God's thunderbolt when he arrived at the circus games dressed in gold and so dazzling that people saluted him as divinity. The episode wasn't unfortunately in the script, which instead revolved around his prosecution of the first Christians right after Jesus' death and Saint Paul being considered the worst enemy of the new religion. But, even if the character's stagy death wasn't depicted, whatever I was doing went over the top, from receiving the High Priest while bathing and being manicured by my slaves, to slaughtering Saint James the Apostle in front of the crowd on the stairs of my palace. Herod Agrippa was also openly bisexual and, during a banquet scene, including a dance performed by a half-naked black boy and a similarly half-naked black girl, I stated that I desired to have a private meeting with either him or her … or both, a quite risqué line for religious prime time, but a line I fought to have maintained. Another line I adored was connected with him not being a Jew and not giving a shit about religion in general and only acting according to the wishes of the Roman Empire. When he got Saint Peter arrested, he could not make head nor tails about his real name being Simon. "Peter … Simon … two entirely different names … these Christians are crazy," I spoke in an annoyed tone to the High Priest.

It was anyway a character to be carefully studied and rehearsed to find a balance in between stagy and exceedingly over-the-top and tedious, and I knew that when an actor is too enthusiastic and pleased with the funny side of a character, over-acting is waiting at the door. The animal I had selected was this time a snake, but it wasn't easy to perform snake movements with costumes and jewelery that weighed some 10 kilos, so I asked the costume department to lend me a robe and a mantle to practice in the hotel and I got into spiraling exercises by the swimming pool, insouciant of the bewildered looks of the attendants.

Director Roger Young was almost invisible because he was either in control from a remote production room or in his apartment in the hotel, but the few instructions he gave me made sense and went exactly in the path I had decided to follow.

As was my character, the production was larger than life, where 10 or 20 people in each department reconstructed vast sections of Jerusalem and Rome. It was impossible not only to get to know them all, but also to see how many they were because some were working in separate buildings. Because I was in search of a quiet spot to have a cigarette, I bumped into Antonio Margheriti's daughter, named Antonella after her father, who was working in the prop and special effects department; we warmly hugged and talked about Antonio and my great love for him.

There was also a crowd of extras and being on set was like walking in a busy shopping mall. I missed a bit the intimacy and friendly atmosphere of smaller crews, but I was feeling very star-like in having a personal chauffeur and a personal assistant on set, always asking if I needed this or that. As a matter of fact I just needed to sit perfectly still, breathe calmly without drinking or eating, just sipping a mix of orange juice, honey and mineral salts. It was the end of June, the heat was beyond imagination and I had to try to not sweat so as not to spoil my make-up … not an easy task if you are wearing a wig, two robes and a mantle, a crown and as many necklaces, rings and bracelets as a Tiffany window.

It was a dry heat though and I didn't find it unbearable, but not so some of the others, and once I grabbed at the last moment old English actor Jack Hedley, who played the High Priest, as he fainted in the middle of a scene.

There were once again production investors from many countries and so the cast included Johannes Bandrup as Saint Paul, Thomas Lockyer as Reuben (a fictional character who was at first Paul's best friend and then his enemy after conversion), Barbora Bobulova as Reuben's wife, Daniela Poggi (who I knew well because of her many years in the theater) as Mary Mother of Jesus, Ennio

Fantastichini as Saint Peter (cursing wildly while learning his lines in English) and Franco Nero as Gamaliel, Paul's former teacher in the Synagogue.

I knew Franco quite well because he had been an Ayckbourn fan, had seen many of my productions and also because, with other mutual friends, I had been to his place to watch the soccer World Championship in 1978. He was very nice company and not a bit pretentious about his star status, which was emphasized in Morocco because the king was a great fan of him and had invited him to the Royal Palace, where a huge poster of *Django* was displayed in his private room. I knew about his many love stories and his success with women, but at the time we were shooting *Saint Paul* he was 60 years old and I couldn't imagine his courting a girl could ever achieve the shameful level as it happened with Barbora Bobulova, who was 30 years his junior.

International star Franco Nero

One day at sunset I was in the hotel swimming pool alone with Barbora when Franco arrived, crouched by the pool and started making verbal passes at her, not in any way coarse but yet quite open. I diplomatically started on my way out, but Barbora looked daggers at me as if saying, "Don't you dare leave me alone," and so I embarrassedly pretended to swim not far from them. She tried to be playful and nice, but Franco was so insistent that at a point she said: "But Franco, I could be your daughter!" He didn't lose a beat and answered with the most perfect Italian nerve: "It's scientifically proved that the perfect age gap between a man and a woman is exactly 30 years." I dived underwater as not to laugh loudly in his face. By the way Barbora was having an affair with Johannes Brandrup, who was as handsome as a Titian portrait and with a perfect athletic body, while Franco's face was still amazing, but his body ... had seen better days, so to say.

There was a friendly atmosphere among we actors and fair play was maintained even when we watched the final soccer game France vs. Italy for the European Championship. Christian Brandel, who played Saint James, and other French actors in minor roles were of course supporting their country, and so were the Moroccans, because of the old colonial bond. It was a hard fight and France won, but no row ensued and we all went to dinner together as we were often doing.

Barbora Bobulova: "But Franco, I could be your daughter!"

But I was also spending a lot of time wandering around by myself and during one of these walks I got into a wonderful adventure just by refusing to buy a djellaba (the traditional Arab tunic).

A young boy about 20 stopped me in the street and asked in a broken French if I were interested in the tunics he was carrying. They were awful, in tacky bright colors, badly cut, but the one he was wearing was instead very beautiful, even if a bit worn out, delicately embroidered and in a very rare shade of grayish blue. I told him that the only one I liked was his and he laughed and said that he too liked what I was wearing, which were Nike shorts and a Nike t-shirt. Without hesitating a moment I asked him if he wanted to make "barraka" (an exchange) and he opened his eyes wide to what looked to him the best possible deal in the world. So we got behind a bush and exchanged our clothes. He was much thinner than me, but the shorts had elastic at the waist so it wasn't a problem and he was just radiant.

He thought I was a chap who deserved to be better known and he invited me to visit the shop he was running with his two older brothers. On the way he explained to me that they were from a nomad desert tribe and they were just occasionally renting a shop in town to sell stuff. His name was Sahid and his brothers were named Mohamed and Ahmed, and they were very amused and pleased about the clothes exchange.

At first sight the shop was very similar to the many others in town and the merchandise displayed wasn't very interesting, but when I sat down and accepted a cup of wonderful mint tea, Ahmed, the middle brother, who seemed in command and spoke good French, showed me what they were really trading: very beautiful and quite valuable jewels that were safely kept in hidden boxes. Some pieces were indeed interesting but too expensive and I didn't want to go into the long bargaining Arabs are so fond of doing. But while I was politely refusing to buy anything, a couple of middle-aged American tourists got in and the wife seemed very interested in what Ahmed was showing me. They didn't speak French and Ahmed didn't speak English, so I volunteered to translate, and in doing this, I doubled and at times tripled the prices Ahmed was making. I had dealt with enough urban punks to be street smart and I had gathered that these people were rich. They bought three or four pieces, and when Ahmed took the money, I blinked an eye at him signaling not to register any surprise. As soon as the Americans left, Ahmed explained to his brothers what I had done and they sat around me with smiles from ear to ear, inquiring if I was to stay in town for long and if they could have the honor to have me as a guest in their shop in the future. Arabs are never straightforward in giving words to their thoughts, but I understood very well that the hidden meaning of the questioning was: "Are you available to come back and help us sell again?" The situation amused me and both Ahmed and Sahid were very good looking, so I explained that there were days I was engaged with my work, but that in my free time I would be very glad to be in the shop with them.

By the time I met them I was halfway into shooting and for the second half of my staying in Ouarzazate I spent all my free time with them, and I even slept at their place if I wasn't needed on set the following day.

As I thought would occur, Sahid made passes at me and I was a bit embarrassed because he was less than half my age, but he was so sweet and delicate (and so handsome) that "why not" prevailed. One of the many good things about Arab countries is that middle, and even old age, aren't seen as less sexually attractive but quite the other way round as if, by a magic transmigration, the wisdom and force of the older was passed to the younger when having sex.

I was fully aware that bisexuality is deeply practiced and accepted in North African countries, but I was nevertheless puzzled in seeing young soldiers walking hand in hand when off duty and more so when Sahid wanted to do the same with me and got to the point of kissing me on the lips in the market square. As much as I had openly lived with many gay relationships, the idea of kissing and hugging in public with a man was very disturbing, but I reflected and saw the good points in the Arab way. We Westerners talk a lot about gay sex and they never openly mention it, but as for action, they are probably more open than us.

As an example of not talking about the subject, Mohamed, the older brother who was close to 40 and very religious, once employed some 2,000 words and complicated phrases to basically tell me that Allah didn't approve of what his little brother and I were doing, but considering I was a Wise Man (the word he employed contained a bit of holiness, out of his good heart), both Allah and he would close an eye. He was to be married soon, and when I inquired about his wife to be, he simply answered that he didn't know her. I was speechless at the very idea, but he explained to me that his mother had chosen her for him and he trusted her and that, after all, if the girl was good in cooking and in giving birth there wasn't much else to ask for. Considering how their society and family life was structured, it made sense.

During the day we were at the shop, chatting, smoking, drinking mint tea and of course selling and many a time my translations with English-speaking tourists proved financially helpful. Being a professional businessman, Ahmed at a point offered me a share of the profits that I helped make, but I politely refused saying that I didn't need the money and I was doing it just out of friendship, and this made me even more exceptional and "holy" in the money-allured eyes of the three brothers. At night we were going to their place and settled in the huge terrace, where I was served and revered as a guest of honor and treated with delicious couscous, fresh fruit and the best hash joints to be wished for in hippie paradise. And sleep came while watching the most beautiful starred sky I ever saw.

Those days in Ouarzazate were some of the best in my life, but they came to an end.

I filmed my last scene on the stairs of the palace, addressing a crowd of 1,000 extras. This sequence was indeed emotional, since I never recited these lines on stage: "Friends, Romans, countrymen …" The end of my engagement was announced by loudspeaker and I got the greatest "end of movie" applause I ever received.

In saying goodbye, severe and unreachable Roger Young paid me the best compliment I ever received from a director when he told me "With most actors, if you say 'less' they just do nothing and if you say 'more,' they then go into terrible overacting, but you are like a musical instrument and a director can play you on the exact note."

When they discovered I was leaving, the brothers asked me to follow them on the Big Caravan that was to start soon. The traditional yearly migration of trading nomads from Morocco to the Ivory Coast, passing through the Mali desert, takes two months traveling on camels.

For someone as crazy as me it was a great temptation, and I made a few inquiries about medical care, and Ahmed matter of factly answered that if minor diseases occurred or even snake bites, they had better cures than Western medicine, but if I were to have a stroke or a heart attack, I would die. I then said that if I were coming I didn't want to be a guest, but I wanted to work and, after some serious thinking, he said I could feed the animals.

It could have been a great experience, but what about Alan and Giacomo? Could I afford to just think about my pleasure in that delicate moment? No, I couldn't and in saying no I was helped by the ironic memory of Bertolucci's *Tea in the Desert*, with me as a male version of Debra Winger, half-prisoner and half- lover of a nomad leader.

I kissed my friends goodbye, and they presented me with a wonderful thick silver bracelet with enamel inlays. It was intended as a man's jewel, but I dared wear it only a few times at bizarre summer parties, yet it's one of my dearest possessions, as is the grayish blue tunic that had started it all.

Chapter 32
From Riches to Rags

Back in Aprilia, I found out that Alan had maxed out the credit card I had forgotten and left behind before leaving and that I told him on the phone to put in a safe place; at some point the little punk had spied the secret code behind my back when I was using it and this was his way to punish me for being away, even if I had left him provided with all the money he could need. He knew pretty well how expensive my life was and how much I needed to work, but a disturbed young mind doesn't work logically and this was just one of the many contradictions in his feelings. Mainly he loved me because I was taking care of him but at the same time I was the living proof that loving him in a paternal way was possible and that his parents had deserted him in not performing the tasks of which I took total responsibility.

I scolded him severely and cut down his weekly allowance of pocket money, but the solution wasn't as simple, as he was not taking care of our dog Jack. He had wanted him as a toy, but he never walked him and when I was away the poor dog was using the kitchen terrace as a toilet and the neighbors were justifiably in revolt. I got a letter from the administrator of the building saying that it was either the dog or us and I was forced to give Jack away, carefully selecting a family who had a house with a big garden and a female dog of the same breed. But my heart was bleeding and this is probably the only thing I will never pardon Alan for.

In 2001 I started writing a new T.V. series about a primary school male teacher. It was a comedy, it was successful and a second season followed, but I didn't know it was my last engagement as a screenwriter.

In the same year Silvio Berlusconi became Prime Minister once again after his first success in 1994 and during the electoral campaign I openly exposed myself against him, by banding with thousands of other people and employing more personal and showy gestures, such as hanging a satiric poem on the Pasquino statue (the place were Romans were expressing their secret feelings towards those in command since the Renaissance) or giving the finger to the security cameras in front of his Rome residence.

I don't want to play the "politically persecuted" card, but it's a fact that he was not only the owner of his private networks, but also in political control of Rai and thus the absolute master of the entire Italian T.V. system. But as much as not writing anymore produced my financial ruin in years to come, even now, when at times I don't have the money to buy food or cigarettes, waking up and knowing that I don't have to prostitute my brain in writing shit is a joy and a relief.

I never got why so many people thunder against the prostitution of bodies, when the prostitution of minds is in my opinion much worse and just everywhere, from journalists writing the opposite of what they think to directors and writers producing movies and books only for economic success. Actors are also involved

in this, but they are more the instruments than actual minds in control and their work is anyway somehow connected with prostitution since the very beginning of time.

But as for writing T.V. fiction (Italian T.V. fiction), I would prefer to sell myself on the street, as I did at times, than be held responsible for creating that slime. The only problem being that a blow-job earns much less than the tearful, sugary monologue of a mother asking the Virgin Mary to save her child. You can write shit until you are 100 years old, while the request for sexual services dramatically drops with age.

But in 2001 I didn't know that I was at the end of one aspect of my working career, and SACT (the T.V. and movie writers guild I was associated with) sent me to represent Italy at the jury of the Banff T.V. Festival in Canada.

It was a fantastic experience; I met many great people and screened eight or 10 hours a day in all categories, from miniseries to children programs. It was exhausting but very interesting. Without my intervention, Italy won in the social documentaries category for a documentary abut the tobacco industry and its ambiguous bonds with the State, but the Italian producer of Zeffirelli's *Traviata*, running for special cultural events, was positively pissed at me because I didn't want to support his production. With all due respect to Franco Zeffirelli, I thought it was awful and patriotic solidarity is not a priority of mine.

The only bad thing about going to Banff was that the 12-hour plane ride back and forth left me crippled, and from then on I decided not to accept overseas invitations if not in upgraded business class accommodations. The leg space provided by airlines was shortening year by year, but I wasn't and my back had given me some serious troubles in the past.

Another event of that year was my "blink an eye and you'll miss it" participation in Martin Scorsese's *Gangs Of New York*.

Sheila Rubin (who sadly passed away a few years ago) was an enchantingly witty and very bizarre American woman who had settled in Rome many years back and was working as a casting agent for English and American productions. She liked me very much and was often calling me, and I thus auditioned for the huge Scorsese production everybody in town was talking about, and I got the brief role of the actor playing Mr. Legree in a stage production of *Uncle Tom's Cabin*. I read the very interesting script and studied the few lines my character had, but then, because of the movie's extreme length, the lines of the actors in the play were cut. At this point my agent, dear ladylike Emanuela Di Suni from the Carol Levi office, didn't want me to do it, but the generous payroll hadn't changed and I was very curious about the reconstruction of 1860 New York that had employed for months hundreds of people in the Cinecittà studios, and I so accepted.

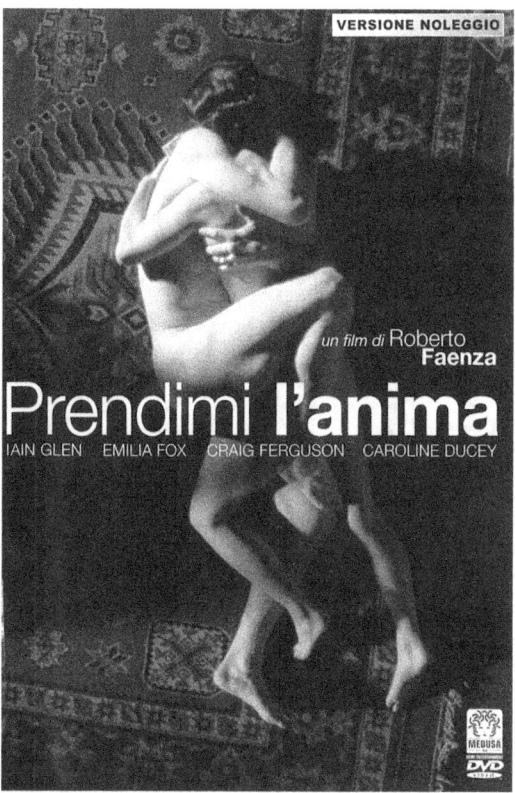

The Italian cover art for *The Soul Keeper*, directed by Roberto Faenza

I had thought that *Saint Paul* was a big production, but what I saw on the set of *Gangs of New York* was beyond imagination, especially the reconstruction of an entire town, with buildings, squares, streets, theaters and the harbor, with two ships anchored and scads of people employed. The small group of actors employed in *Uncle Tom's Cabin* had an assistant just for ourselves; we were warned not to walk around the set alone, not to get lost, and our assistant led us on a brief guided tour of that miracle of the movie industry.

I worked the 10 days it took just to shoot that scene and I only saw Scorsese from a distance when he was directing Daniel Day-Lewis and Leo DiCaprio, who were in the audience watching the play. A second unit director supervised our sequence while Scorsese was working at another location.

In 2002 I went to Moscow as the only Italian member of the cast of *The Soul Keeper* by Roberto Faenza, a director I highly esteemed who had finally realized his long-time dream of filming the story of Sabine Spielrein, a patient of Gustav Jung who had become his lover and created a major scandal in the psychiatric world. She then became a psychologist herself and founded a kindergarten for mentally disabled children, which at one point was closed by Stalin. Being a Jew, she ended her life in a concentration camp during the war. The film featured a wonderful script and the movie came out as a masterpiece. Even if in

the cameo role of the army officer who closed the kindergarten dramatically, I am very proud of having appeared in it. During a dinner Faenza bluntly asked me what the fuck was I doing in Italy, considering that I didn't look Italian and spoke good English and thus could get lots of work abroad. It was indeed a very good question and the answer involved my attachment to theater and my private life; the former had dried out because after the glorious years of the Actors Company, Italian theater didn't seem to be very interested in me and the latter, my private life ... I still needed some commitments to be honored, like seeing Alan and Giacomo walking on their own two feet without my constant support.

Lux Vide and my lifelong friend director Andrea Barzini hired me for one episode of the *Don Matteo* series, starring Terence Hill in the role of a detective priest. I honestly don't know what I did, because I was feeling like shit, incredibly weak and falling asleep even on the floor of my dressing room. As soon as the job was over I found out that I had Hepatitis A, caused by food; it was probably sushi that I discoveed in Canada that conquered me. Fortunately it wasn't as bad as the previous B infection and I got cured at my San Lorenzo house in Rome, which was completed and very much reflected my taste even if it was spartanly furnished. In the last move I had given Alessandra all the valuable paintings and silver I still had, including a wonderful centerpiece with the "N" of Napoleon engraved on it, this piece having been in my grandmother's house. San Lorenzo was saturated with poor people, and I was very open in my acquaintances. I didn't want to encourage anybody to a criminal act by providing temptation.

In 2003 I portrayed the Governor of 1870 Rome as Cardinal Renzi in *The Pasquino Night*, directed by Luigi Magni, an old lion of Italian cinema who had dedicated his movie career to describing the dramatic years of transition from the papal temporal power to the annexation of Rome during the new-born reign of Italy, precisely in September 1870 when the story of the movie was taking place. Magni had a great talent for comedy and he was the only director in my career who showed me what he wanted me to do by doing it himself first. This was simple yet extraordinary in the Italian landscape.

After that the abyss of poverty opened at my feet. No more writing opportunity occurred after the second series about the primary school teacher, my bank account shrank every month and no new movie work was in sight.

Johnny as the Governor of 1870 Rome from *La notte di Pasquino* (aka *The Pasquino Night* in the U.S.A.)

I was forced to leave the big Aprilia house and, since Alan didn't want to live in Rome, I rented a little place just for him, but I confronted him with taking the responsibility of taking care of his life and finding a job. In the long run the crisis proved a positive shock and he slowly found his way of independence. He is now 35, he keeps changing jobs and girlfriends at an alarming rate, but he supports himself and I can say that, all in all, I did a good job with him.

Back in Rome, I rolled up my sleeves and found a job as a waiter in the café inside San Lorenzo's little park.

I was paid 30 euros a day for eight hours' work serving tables, and I was hired because of the many tourists who passed by and my skill with languages. It was very hard work and the owners were not always kind, but I didn't complain, because at that point my only aim was not to starve and, much more importantly, not allowing to starve the greatest love of my life, a beautiful creature who wasn't from the human race but from the much more evolved race of dogs.

After the sad experience with Jack, the idea of getting a dog was as far from my mind as climbing Mount Everest, but one day at the tobacconist I saw a man holding in his arms a German dachshund puppy and, with due respect, I felt exactly as I had when seeing for the first time Antonella Interlenghi in Savannah: pure, absolute love.

I had never seen a dog of that breed, but in the space of a week I had Tommy with me; I bought him from a breeding farm that specialized in dachshunds and I selected him because he was black with red paws and beard instead of the most common brownish gray, and because he was all alone in his cage since his little sister had left the day before. Buying him cost me the only savings I had, but it proved worthwhile even if he had been 10 times more expensive. People bragging about their dogs are even more boring than people bragging about their children, so I'll cut it short with saying that never in my life had I loved anything so much and never was I so loved. At the time I am writing this, he is now almost 13 years old and has a young companion named Audrey.

My situation improved when my uncle Pietro Ingrao, now in his 90s, hired me as one of the secretaries he was allowed to have as a former president of Parliament. I had a salary and my job was writing under dictation his letters, articles he was writing for newspapers and chapters of the autobiography he was working on. Old age hadn't undermined his cleverness, his clear political vision or his iconic status of moral leader in the eyes of many, not only among leftists. His wife, my father's sister Laura, had died, and even if he was now alone after more than 50 years of marriage, he fought depression and was still eager to be active in the world.

The job with Pietro was part-time and tied to his being alive, so I didn't quit my waiter's job and I was so scared about being short of money that I accepted a third job in theater in a small production of Thomas Bernhard's *The Hunters Brigade*, directed by Emanuela Giordano. I found comic success as a former Nazi general in a wheelchair.

Another important event of 2004 was the start of my friendship with some Rumanian immigrants who were experiencing a difficult life in my neighborhood. They weren't yet EU citizens and a Fascist law from the Berlusconi government put them at the everyday risk of being arrested and deported in the so-called "Immigration Centers," which were no better than concentration camps. A terrible period of police repression against immigrants followed the bombing in the London subway, and at that point I made a very risky step in stealing a few sheets of my uncle's stationary and signed his name in a statement that X or Y were working for him as a consultant and translator for a book about Eastern Europe. Even though he was a defender of human rights, Pietro would have probably ripped my skin off if he had known, but on two occasions it saved the life of my Rumanian friends. A policeman stopped them, asked for their papers and let them go after reading the letter.

After a while one of them, Marian, came to live with me and it was he who took care of Tommy when I was called to be in *The Omen* remake in 2005 (released in 2006) and finally abandoned my job as waiter.

Chapter 33
A Horror Comeback in Prague

It was Sheila Rubin who once again organized the audition for *The Omen*. The character I auditioned for was Father Spiletto, a small but crucial role in the plot, because it's him who informs Robert Thorn in the maternity hospital in Rome that his wife Katherine has just lost her baby and she had troubles with her uterus and could not have another pregnancy. Spiletto suggests to Robert that another just-born child that lost his mother could be substituted for his son, and Robert accepts the child and gives him the name of Damien. He doesn't know that Spiletto is affiliated to a Satanist sect and that the baby boy is the devil's son.

I hadn't seen the original movie with Gregory Peck, but I knew what it was about and, being in need of work, I did my best and had a pleasant chat with the casting agent of the movie for Italian casting, a very refined English woman who most probably hadn't seen a horror film in her life and thus didn't know who I was. Not so director John Moore, who was a huge horror fan, and in screening my audition immediately recognized me and asked for another one, this time with his instructions.

I got the role and I could have danced in the street naked from joy, because the payroll was excellent and the movie was to be shot in Prague, a town that I had always wanted to visit because of my mother's love for it and her stating it was the most beautiful place in Europe.

I haven't seen all the European capitals (Lisbon and Vienna, to name two, are still missing), but as far as I knew I totally agreed with my mother and I was aghast from seeing Prague's magic concentrated into a quite narrow space (not bigger than Florence I would say). So many wonders, among them the Jewish Cemetery, which seemed to be right out of a Fulci movie because the reduced space allowed for tombstones that over the centuries grew into a sort of graves hill, one fit into the other in the most dramatic way.

It was perfectly possible to visit Prague by walking and I just went everywhere, considering that Twentieth Century Fox was producing the movie and I had been called way ahead of my shooting schedule for costume fittings; if compared to the American major movie company, both Titanus and Lux Vide looked like Cinderella *before* going to the ball.

The only inconvenience was that, thinking they were offering me the best, they put me in the local Hilton, which not only was far from the center, but it was unbearably snobby and disgracefully expensive as all Hiltons are all over the world. I was of course a guest for the room and breakfast and I had a generous per diem free expense account, but I found it offensive to pay 20 bucks for a hamburger. I carefully avoided extra expense and ate my meals at a cheap Chinese restaurant just around the corner. As for snobbery, when the staff learned that I didn't have a credit card, they locked shut my mini-fridge as if I was bound to run away with their peanuts and sodas, with Twentieth Century Fox

not refunding them. Nothing is worst than former Communists just converted to Capitalism.

When I arrived on set in my priest robe, John Moore warmly welcomed me and made me feel as if I was a star instead of just an actor in a cameo role. For the first time I didn't stand in position for lights because there was a guy exactly my height, dressed like me, just hired for that purpose: rich is rich.

Everything was carefully rehearsed and for a long time and during rehearsals I had the strong impression that something about me was bothering Liev Schreiber, who had the leading role of Mr. Thorn. I was right, because after a while he took me aside and very politely explained to me that he had just quit smoking and he was disturbed by the fact he could smell tabacco on my clothes. I said I was sorry, but he very gently said that it was his problem and not mine and we resumed working. When shooting, Liev said something that wasn't in the script and I answered him, thus giving life to a little improvisation that John Moore liked very much and decided to keep. He was a short, plump guy with a beard and he looked right out of a Hobbit village, but what was extraordinary about him was his very open way showing approval by yelling and jumping. But at times he was also very serious and thoughtful and it was clear he was totally taken by his work.

I got back to Rome waiting to be called back for my second scene, when Thorn gets suspicious about Damien's evil powers and wants to know more about the boy's real family from Spiletto. He finds the priest in a remote monastery where he retired after surviving a fire that destroyed the hospital. His face has become a horrific mask because of the burns and he can't speak, but he writes the name of an old cemetery where Damien's real mother is buried and this leads to the final terrible discovery about the child's identity.

I hadn't paid much attention to the make-up aspect of the scene and I was surprised when I was asked to fly to London to make the cast of Spiletto's ravaged face. I was terrified at the idea of going back into the ordeal I had been through in casting my head for *City of the Walking Dead*, but it was explained that modern techniques were totally different and I was anyway offered half my daily salary for each day in U.K.

Julia Stiles and a demonic presence from *The Omen* (2006)

So I made a three-day trip to London and went through the very long and boring proceeding of having each part of my head cast separately; it was at times annoying especially when my mouth and my nose were involved, but nothing compared to the suffocating feeling I had experienced in the past. I was also taken to an optician who had to prepare a special white contact lens for the eye Spiletto lost in the burning.

But if the cast of the head was quite easy, the actual work of putting together the bits and pieces and the final result proved to be the worst experience I ever had on set.

I went back to Prague and from there a chauffeur took me into a little town far up north, close to the old monastery where we were to shoot. I woke up at three in the morning, the make-up procedure started at four and was completed shortly before noon. Each bit had to be applied and perfected with the use of small surgical scissors. It had to dry before starting to work on the next bit. It was just like sitting on a medieval torture chair and, section-by-section, the make-up artists were enclosing my face in something that resembled pretty much the iron mask of the Dumas book. But the man with the iron mask could breathe freely and eat and drink, while my mouth was distorted by a vise probably sketched by the sadistic dentist in *Little Shop of Horrors* and the breathing space of my nostrils was reduced to a tiny hole; even smoking a cigarette was almost impossible, but considering that through my life I had changed the Descartes motto from "I think therefore I am" to "I smoke therefore I am," I somehow managed to light a few cigs during that never-ending working day.

On my request, I had been given a tranquilizer before starting all this and during the torture I quietly moaned as if I were on my dying bed, with a make-

Father Spiletto (Johnny) is disfigured for his sins in *The Omen*.

up assistant holding my hand and whispering "hush, hush." If it hadn't been so painful it would have been utterly comical, and a couple of times I also felt in a state between sleeping and fainting, but my torturers were waking me up because I had to move my head in this or that direction.

When the work was completed and make-up applied, the only thing I could do properly was see, because the blind-effect contact lens had the right graduation and the other one was the one I was normally using. I could thus look at myself in the mirror and the sight was so terrifying that I almost jumped back. If it was absolutely perfect as a horror special effect, it was also true that behind that monstrous mask there could have been me or anyone else ... Demi Moore, my tobacconist or anyone with a blue eye (just one) and an aquiline nose. And I am pretty sure that a greedier and less rich Italian production would have hired for a few cents the first Gypsy passing by instead of a very well paid actor. As a matter of fact the thought of my payroll was the only thing that helped me through the day and I kept repeating the sum as a self-control mantra, preventing me from ripping off the bloody thing from my head.

When I met Liev, he, insouciant of my looks, smiled from ear to ear, showed me a cigarette and whispered in complicity, "I resumed," with the same joy of a Robinson Crusoe returning to civilization after 20 years; it was the only laugh of the day and, of course, just in my mind, because actual laughter would have proved impossible.

The schedule for the scene was two days shooting, but John Moore, who was a very kind man, understood my suffering and did his best to free me after one day, and as much as I needed money, I was very grateful because the very idea

of going through the whole procedure the next morning made me almost suicidal.

Incredible as it might seem, we did use the extra who would have been under my mask, but in the take where my hand was seen writing in close up. It didn't look old and wrinkled as Moore wanted, so an old local woman did it in my place.

When the scene was over and I could unglue the mask from my face, I felt as happy as a whore on a Saturday night, thinking about an Italian poet, the pessimistic Giacomo Leopardi, who stated that "joy is nothing but the end of sorrow."

A couple more takes with a different ghostly make-up concerned a nightmare that Thorn was having at one point and, with a devilish smile, I threw from a balcony in the monastery a broken doll and the ripped pages of the Gospel.

I had one more day to say farewell to wonderful Prague and I then flew back to Rome where I found a bottle of pricey wine awaiting me. It was a present from John Moore, with a note saying what a honor it had been for him to have me in the movie.

I thought it was the sweetest possible gesture and also that I had indeed made a major mistake in undervaluing my horror fandom fame for so many years, beginning with the first hint I had about it in the early 1990s.

Chapter 34
The Past Never Dies

It was a September afternoon and I was rehearsing something at La Cometa before the official opening of the season. The girl from the box-office comes upstairs into the theater and tells me that there is a foreigner who wanted to see me and who refused to leave even if she told him I was engaged. I called for a break and went into the foyer, where I was met by a man and his wife who were right out of a caricature vignette about American tourists, with flowery shirts, shorts on fat legs, a cap, and as many cameras as professional paparazzi hunting Madonna during a topless pose.

He suffocated me in his embrace and told me he was a "huuuuuge" fan of my horror movies and had recognized my name on the posters in the theater windows; his wife, whom I suspect was more into "beautiful" but resilient, kept smiling and nodding at his words as a toy dog hanging on the rear window of a car. I was amused and tried to be as polite and warm as possible and I agreed on taking a picture in front of the theater, pretending to bite his neck vampire style.

I had forgotten about the episode, when, a few months afterwards, I received a letter, addressed at La Cometa, in which an English journalist called John Martin said many complimentary things about my horror film career and asked if he could send his Italian collaborator to interview me for a magazine he wanted to write about me. I agreed and a young and slightly weird boy in his 20s arrived, fitting very much my idea a horror fan, vaguely creepy and dressed in black. What I thought would have been a short thing took three or four hours, because the boy had hundreds of questions, some of them about things I had completely forgotten about, not having seen the movies in question in more than 15 years.

As a matter of fact, I had filed the horror movies of my youth in the section of my brain labeled "things I did to earn money—were fun—are now entirely forgotten." And I didn't take very seriously the John Martin statement that I had fans all over the world. I thought he was emphasizing what was probably a small sect with as many disciples as the one worshipping Stalin's moustaches and less than the one devoted to James Dean's underwear. Anyway I agreed to write an introduction for the book, which said:

Dear friends:

John Martin, who kindly invited me to pen these lines, assures me that I have some "fans." I'm a bit surprised, but I'll take him at his word ... the thing is, after directing and acting in Shakespeare, Molière, Strindberg, etc., never in my life would I have thought I'd become "famous" for the horror movies I did some years (and many hairs) ago.

Shooting those films was fun; I travelled the world and the money kept me through theater (which has always tended to reduce me to poverty), but will you forgive me if I confess that I myself was never a "fan" of them? Nevertheless I am a conscientious actor and always tried to do my best, even when the scripts made less sense than the Telephone Guide. The directors were awful or crazy (or both), and the locations were trashier than the movie itself.

Did I succeed? Do you like me in these movies because I at least try at decent acting, or just because I'm so terrible that I make you laugh? Both ways suit me. To be liked is always good and can be fun, as when .... (At this point I was relating the episode with the American tourist.)

What else can I say? Thank you for your approval, and—especially if you are young—feel free to scream at my movies, laugh at them, get scared, disgusted, whatever by them ... but please do not imitate them! When you go back home, don't eat your mummy ... unless she is unbearably boring, or incredibly tasty!
Love,
Giovanni Lombardo Radice
Or, if you prefer ... John Morghen

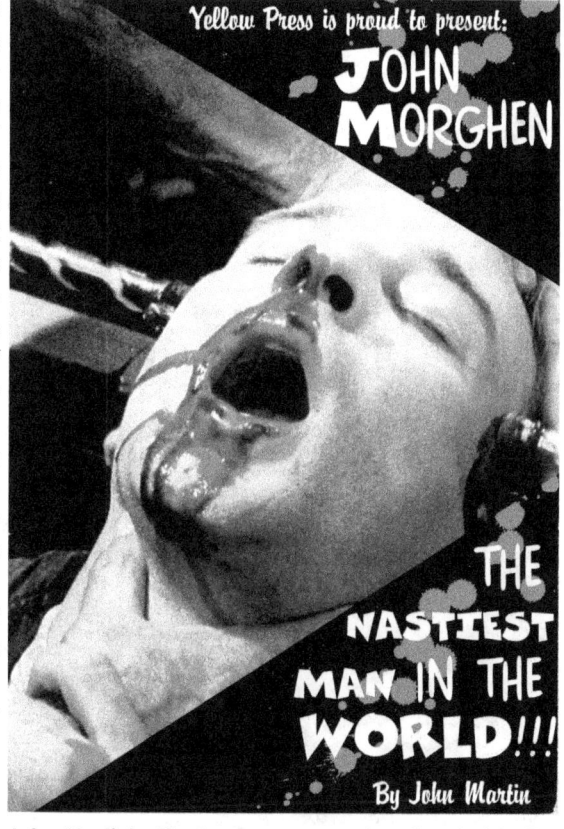

John Martin's 40-plus page magazine devoted to the films of John Morghen (aka Johnny)

When the magazine was published and I received a few copies of *John Morghen: The Nastiest Man in the World*, I thought it was well done and funny, because John Martin had treated my horror past with a great sense of humor and that was pretty much my same approach. Over the years I was less pleased about the fact that the magazine was sold all over the world and is even now on Amazon.com and eBay and I never received a penny, but that's another matter.

La Cometa had a very restricted space for offices and at a point Franco Clavari, Margherita Fusi (our press agent) and I moved into a working space in the much larger Teatro Nazionale, offering them in exchange consulting services, accounting and public relations with the press. I had my own room, filled with the hundreds of scripts of plays I had collected over the years, a phone and an answering machine. And on that machine I one day found a message in English, with the strongest possible American accent and without the speaker taking a single breath saying: "Hi, I'm Sage Stallone, Sylvester Stallone's son; I am making a laserdisc of *Cannibal Ferox* and I would like very much to have you do an audio commentary for the movie. I'll call you back." I had no idea of what a laserdisc was, but that wasn't my first thought; in those days my long-time friend Luca

The late Sage Stallone, the co-producer of the laserdisc of *Cannibal Ferox*

Barbareschi was performing at the Teatro Nazionale. I had seen a lot of him and Luca was notoriously skilled in imitating whomever in more than one language. I was pretty sure it was one of Luca's jokes, and when the phone rang and the same voice went into exactly the same rigamarole, I was about to interrupt and say, "Luca get fucked," when something told me that it wasn't him and the whole thing was true, as indeed it was. Sage explained to me what a laserdisc was and was so insisting that I said yes. I had hoped there was some money involved, but he said that he and his associate Bob Murawski were very poor and, even if it was hardly believable, coming from Rambo's son, I made an appointment for the next day.

The poor producers of the laserdisc came to get me at the Teatro Nazionale with a limo as long as the theater's façade and they took me into a dubbing studio where the whole movie was screened as I gave audio commentary from beginning to end. It was a real shock, because I had forgotten how awful, stupid and violent the movie was. My spontaneous reactions came out sounding exhilarating, and even more if compared to the parallel commentary by director Lenzi, I stated exactly the opposite of what he was stating.

After this very long and tiring work, Sage asked me if I could autograph "something," which turned out to be a crate full of pictures, posters and t-shirts. I mechanically signed "to Jane," "to Mark," "to Whoeverthefuck" and so on, and when my hand was already aching he gave me a t-shirt saying it was for Quentin. "Tarantino?" I tiredly asked ... he said yes and I signed "To Quentin with love." Later on I learned that the American idol of the younger cinematic generation had said very nice things about me in some interviews. At that point my disgraceful laziness was shaken and I wrote him and sent him some recent photos, but I never got an answer and he never tried contacting me when he was in Rome, being more interested in the fading and Botox-filled graces of Edwige Fenech or Barbara Bouchet. Would you trust a director? I advise you with all my heart not to (and the same goes for Eli Roth, by the way), and if I ever become a man who elbows in public places to be acknowledged by a personality, I entitle

Count Gherardini's ghost to come and pull my feet back every night.

Back to Sage, I never saw him again and I was very sorry about his recent death at a very young age, because he struck me as a sad and problematic kid and, even if I never met him, I was also very sorry for his father's loss. But I am fully aware that the laserdisc was converted into many DVD editions, which sold millions of copies just because of the commentaries. Considering "poor" Bob Murawski, as far as I know, is alive and in good health, and I am writing these lines with just a salad in my stomach because I can't afford to buy meat or cheese; if he ever reads this book I want to say, "Hi, Bob, don't you think I deserve a business class trip to New York and dinner at Sardi's?"

American journalist and future agent Mike Baronas (right), arm-in-arm with Johnny

Nothing much else happened on the horror film front since I finally got into the world of the Internet. Being suspicious and stupid about whatever new technology pops up (give me a washing machine different from mine and I'll helplessly stare at it for weeks), I was the last person to have a cell phone and also the last to get a web connection, but, as soon as I was there, I was literally submerged both from the knowledge that there were hundreds of pages about me and my horror movies and from letters and messages from fans and journalists asking for an interview.

Those were the Aprilia days at the beginning of the current century and I was busy with Alan, but I was also spending a lot of time at home and I had time to write back to everybody and answer all the interview requests.

One momentous contact, which was to produce a great change in my life, was with an American journalist, Mike Baronas, who wrote me saying that he was producing a documentary and a book about Fulci and was eager to meet me in Rome, where he arrived in November 2001 with his partner Kit Gavin.

I met them in the very tourist-filled Trastevere area and we went to dinner, only a few days ago, talking about this book. Mike confessed to me that he was so shy as not asking my help in translating the menu and thus ordering just a mozzarella and tomato salad, because it was the only thing he could read. Mike and Kit were as different as Laurel from Hardy and quite funny to look at as a pair, but I immediately gathered that Mike was the serious side of the business, while Kit was enchantingly snobby and vague.

I did the interview for the documentary. I asked Kit, who was English, to read for me with the best Eton accent a Shakespeare sonnet I was working on with some students and I then had a serious conversation with Mike, who raised in front of my eyes the curtain on the reality about the horror fans world: they were millions, my movies were worshipped as religious relics, I was considered an iconic star and there were conventions in many countries (but mostly in U.S.A.) where actors signed photos and posters and … were paid for it!

At this last bit of information, I jumped from the chair both in revolt because Count Gherardini was biting my ass saying it was the most impolite thing thinkable and in excitement, as always when hearing the word "money."

As Figaro sings in *The Barber of Seville*:

What my prodigious talent can achieve when fed by the sweet sound of gold! The mere thought of that powerful metal erupts in my brain like a volcano. And the ideas begin to flow.

But it took a few years before I could silence my noble ancestor and decide to get into the movie convention market.

In the meanwhile I created my website and I agreed on doing DVD interviews and commentaries for the more famous movies from my horror past, but, mindful of the poor deal I made with Sage Stallone and Bob Murawski, I always asked to be paid to do commentaries and once got into a debate with Claudia Cardinale (who was also a Carol Levi's client), because she said that she had always done commentaries for free. This is all very generous, but not very thoughtful because it creates a bad precedent for colleagues in need of money; producers make money from DVDs, commentaries are an added value to the package, and thus celebrities should be paid.

In 2007 I finally agreed to be represented by Mike Baronas for all American and European convention appearances and he was also going to sell my autographed pictures and an "Italy's Whipping Boy" t-shirt on his website.

To get me used to, little by little, the world of horror film fans, in September 2007 Mike first sent me to the U.K. at the Manchester Festival of Fantastic Films, which is a small but very nice convention. I brought Marco Jemolo (my cousin Andrew's son, who wanted to become a director) as my assistant and we had a fantastic time, me in making my first steps in signing autographs and chatting with fans and he seducing every chick in sight. I was struck by the fact that the fans in Manchester were of whatever sex, shape, age and look and not the just the tattooed-pierced-leather kind I had expected. I was very pleased when a charming old lady who could have been Miss Marple told me that she was into vampires and that in her opinion I would have been a fantastic Count Dracula. As a matter of fact the hundreds of drunks in Manchester on any Friday night howling at the moon and zigzagging on the streets as crazy bats were much creepier than any of the horror fans lining up at my table.

A German convention followed and this time Mike came to assist me, and we agreed to a convention tour in the U.S.A. in 2008. Attending more than one convention made it easier to get the business class flights I insisted I have. In Bottrop I met for the first time Catriona MacColl, who I hadn't seen on the set of *City of the Living Dead* because our characters never met in the script. She proved to be absolutely enchanting and we got along famously.

I thus spent two months in the U.S.A. and went to Dallas, Cleveland, Indianapolis and Connecticut. There were of course breaks in between one convention and the other, and I went to San Francisco by myself to visit a friend and I was a guest for some days at Mike's place, where I enjoyed his and his wife's (now ex-wife) company and I made puzzles with his children. The more I knew Mike the more I loved and respected him for his passion in things he was doing and his honesty, both as a friend and as a representative.

Cult actress Catriona MacColl (pictured) and Johnny both appeared on the horror film convention circuit.

American conventions were indeed incredibly larger than the European ones, but the mix of every sort of people was the same with just an added alarming share of the beer-belly type. Over the years I had become almost a teetotaler and I declined many generous drinking offers in hotel lobbies. I enjoyed very much chatting with fans and I was positively surprised at the real emotion of some of them in meeting me. I attended Q&A sessions and screenings of my movies, I gave interviews and I made many friends that I dare not list so as not to offend anybody in forgetting a name.

Signing *Cannibal Ferox* items had been a major issue in my correspondence with Mike prior to attending conventions, but he convinced me that I just couldn't refuse to sign pictures and posters from a movie that was so loved by horror fans, and I decided to catch the occasion to explain to people why I hated just that movie and I always added to my signature something funny, like speech bubbles coming from my mouth in the pictures saying: "Aaargh! Lenzi is after me!" or "Why on Earth did I accept this movie?" But I did not do this on posters, as not to be butchered by maniac collectors, who are much more fearful than cannibals.

At conventions I also met old movie partners like John Saxon (or his mummy, I couldn't tell from the frozen smile) and recently Bo Svenson, as I already said. But it was also a pleasure meeting Malcom McDowell, Robert Englund and

John Saxon also appeared, sometimes with Johnny, on the film convention circuit.

many others. I never saw a Freddy Krueger movie, but the man is fantastic.

In 2011 I was really pissed about missing the *City of the Living Dead* 30-year reunion at the Chiller Theatre convention, but it wasn't my fault and we have only the American Embassy to blame because, when I arrived at the Rome airport, I found out that out of the blue there was a new thing called ESTA to show with your passport before leaving on a flight. It was exactly the same form I had filled many times on planes, with "yes" or "no" answers to questions such as, "Do you plan to kill the President of the United States on your trip?" or "Are you carrying a not detectable nuclear weapon in your luggage?" Such momentous and absolutely clever steps in stopping professional terrorists, but with ESTA you had to show the filled out form at the desk and doing it online cost 15 dollars. Of course I didn't have the paperwork, but I was told not to worry, because I could do it at the airport. But when I got to the designed desk I found out that the site of the American Embassy was under repair and I wasn't allowed to leave. When I filled out the ESTA for my next trip I was highly tempted to answer "yes" to all questions, just to see what happened, but FBI guys haven't a reputation for their sense of humor and less so after the Twin Towers massacre (that I had witnessed on T.V., crying with all the tears I had). Aside from their atrocious and unforgiveable crimes, terrorists are also responsible for turning typical plane trips into a guided tour inside the museum of unnecessary bureaucracy and for confusing saline solution for contact lenses with a liquid bomb.

Chapter 35
Que Sera Sera

Getting toward the end of this autobiography and returning to its proper chronology, I have only to tell about my most recent years.

2006 saw the opening of *The Omen* all over the world on June 6 (6-6-6 the devil's number!) and a new theater engagement in *Road to Mecca* by Athol Fugard, once again directed by Emanuela Giordano and starring Isa Barsizza, an enchanting actress and wonderful person who had a long career, from being an beautiful showgirl in variety revues in the 1950s to achieving an intense acting maturity that she showed fully in the play in which I appeared with her. I was Marius, a Protestant minister in rural South Africa, fighting against the unbecoming behavior and the artistic urgency of his friend Helen (played by Isa), a character inspired by a real artist, Helen Martins, who found out about her "gift" only in old age. Maurizia Grossi, a young talented actress, played the only other role and the three of us had a great time both on and off stage.

In 2007 Pupi Avati called me for his horror comeback after many years. The movie was *The Hideout*; it was shot in English and the story took place in Iowa, in a town where Avati made another movie and that, for apparently no visible reason, he liked to the point of buying a house there.

With due respect for Iowa residents, their state is not exactly the holiday pinnacle of one's life, and when I was at the Chicago airport I told the passport agent that I was going there on vacation (because I had been instructed to say so by the producer, Pupi's brother Antonio). The policewoman stared at me in disbelief and cried, "In Iowa?!" To make it believable I was forced to say that I had friends there, which was indeed a lie, because the only person I knew in the movie was Laura Morante, but she had the lead role and, being very professional and not too assured about her English, was spending her free time just studying her dialogue. As for Pupi Avati, I felt he intensely disliked me. (I guess out of an old-fashioned Catholic repulsion for sodomy.)

I stayed there for quite a while, just busy learning the few scenes with my character, who lacked logic (which the entire plot lacked, in my opinion) and I got bored to death because there was absolutely nothing to do apart from watching cornfields and thinking about committing suicide by eating it raw and green.

But, even if in a cameo role in 2007, I had a much more intense filming experience when I worked with young English director, Darren Ward, on his *A Day of Violence*.

I had recently got on MySpace and that's where Darren wrote me, saying he was a fan and asking if he could send me a script. When I read it I found it unbelievably violent, as the title promised, but also it was extremely well written and ultimately moved me to tears, not an experience I often had in reading a genre script.

I liked very much the villainous role of the head gangster, but Darren explained to me that he was shooting with a small crew of friends during weekends,

and it was of course impossible to fly me back and forth every week.

So I accepted the cameo role of Hopper, a disgusting old drug-dealer who was savagely killed by Nick Rendell (the lucky charm in all of Darren's movies), in the leading role of a debt collector. I was to be slaughtered, and Darren and his special effect guys came to the Manchester convention to make the cast of my neck.

Considering the amount of blood and tortures in the movie, I was expecting to meet a tough macho man director in motorcycle leather, and I was very surprised when I saw in front of me the perfect incarnation of "Mr. Nice," soberly dressed, blue-eyed and with a little French nose augmented with spectacles. Getting to know him better I found out that he was indeed very nice, not only for his looks, but for his wonderful wife, his amazingly beautiful little daughters and most of all for his kind and warm temperament, which anyway didn't prevent him from being a skilled and matter of fact director.

But I didn't know this when I sat on the chair in my hotel room to get the cast done, which is akin to being imprisoned, and having spoken with him only on the phone, I said: "This is where you turn out to be serial killers and post my death online." I had forgotten about this incident but Darren reminded me a few days ago.

If my passionate description of Darren might suggest to readers that I fell in love with him, I gave the wrong impression, because that passion erupted instead with Nick Rendell, who proved to be equally unobtainable but, being a giant with a lot of flesh and muscles on him, won my personal Academy Award for best partner to take naps on in between takes.

Shooting went smoothly on a December weekend and I participated in transforming the room lent us by a friend of Darren's into Hopper's dirty lair; removable paper sheets were applied on the walls and I happily filled them with dirty drawings, something I had always wanted to do on a real wall but never did out of my count Gherardini good conscience. Smoking stage pot from a bong was the only difficult part of the scene, because as much as I had led a wild life, it was my first time using a bong and I was horribly unskilled at it, but I got a knife gently poked in my arm from Nick to force me to stop my fussing and the perfectly realized neck appliance did wonders in spilling a fountain of blood when he cut my throat.

When the movie was released on DVD I could hardly watch some scenes (among them the most realistic and detailed castration ever realized in a movie), but I was very pleased with it and with my Hopper character. It won many awards all over the world (mostly for the first-rate special effects) and Darren started thinking about a new project, this time with me in a major role.

In 2008 I was to play an important character in an Italian indie movie, and once again it was posted on MySpace and this is where director Domiziano Cristopharo found me. The movie was called *House of Flesh Mannequins* and it was a very bizarre but interesting dark story that mixed actors with body art performers. There was a lot of sex and violence in it, but my character was for once blood free, because Mr. Roeg was the blind father of the female protagonist, played by the exquisite Irena A. Hoffman, and he didn't kill anybody and wasn't himself killed, but he just witnessed and commented about all the mysterious goings-on of the plot from a throne-shaped chair. I had never played a blind man before and the idea fascinated me. The movie was to be shot in Los Angeles and in English and Domiziano Arcangeli, an Italian actor who had been living in the U.S.A. for a long time, financed it and starred as the male lead, an ambiguous photographer with a difficult past.

Los Angeles is the archetype town where I could never live, because it's huge and you just have three options: drive a car, have a chauffeur because you are a Hollywood star or be screwed; and it was the third option I was forced to select when, after the perfect business class flight I had asked for, I got stuck in a lousy hotel for a week, because the local production managers had proved totally inefficient and the whole schedule was in a mess.

When I finally got on set, I knew my lines not only in the right order, but also from top to bottom, because I hadn't had anything else to do but study them.

Shooting went well, but I understood that nothing would have worked without the patient care of Daniele Panizza, a friend of Domiziano Cristopharo who had generously stepped into the production and had a practical mind, while our director was as talented as he was vague. He is a very interesting person with many skills (too many maybe), because he is a director, an actor, a singer, a tattoo artist and something else that I might not remember, but, different from Darren Ward, he is totally incapable and not interested in promoting a movie after it's finished, and that's what happened with *House of Flesh Mannequins*. He immediately started working on another project and kept doing so, backed by less and less money and became more and more bitter about not being acknowledged. He should have been born in the happy days when Italy had a flourishing movie industry and talent sufficed; not so in the currently sad days of struggling artists often being defeated, no matter how good they might be. If Federico Fellini lived long enough to see the sad moment when not even he would stand a chance, what chance do Domiziano Cristopharo and the many filmmakers like him have 20 years after Fellini's death?

In 2010, after many years, I directed a play. It was Neil Simon's *The Dinner Party* and it was a very sad experience, because the leading actor, Giancarlo Zanetti, owned the company and he proved to be a hard nut to crack, continuously bullying me and demanding his word on artistic choices. I had been spoiled by the happy years with the Actors Company and being a hired director and bowing my head wasn't my scene. The only good thing about it was that Zanetti had some T.V. work to do and smartly profited from having a director who was also an actor and I substituted for him for the two seasons the play was performed, whenever he was otherwise engaged. On each occasion it was sadly announced that he was ill (so not to arouse the protests of theater patrons paying for his name) and I acted in his very funny role, a cynical and heartless man with some fantastic wisecracks from a comedy genius like Simon in his dialogue.

My next movie was shot in two parts, one in 2010 and the other in 2011, and it was *The Inflicted* by director-actor Matthan Harris, who contacted me on Facebook, which had by this time replaced MySpace as the best social network to meet people. Even if I have a website with my agent's email and phone number clearly written in capital letters, indie directors prefer the personal approach and it is okay by me, because I always desire to read the script before getting into the business talk.

The Inflicted was a solid thriller about a serial killer, played by Matthan himself, and I was for once the good guy as good-hearted Lieutenant Lorenzo of the Dallas police, a Clint Eastwood/Humphrey Bogart role that was an absolute first in my career and one that I was eager to play. Being only 24, Matthan was the youngest director I ever worked with, but there was nothing boyish neither in his acting nor in his assured way of directing. The crew was a small one but they were very good and enlightened by the presence of the director of photography, Cira Felina Bolla, a young girl of Italian heritage, who could create wonders with reduced financing. Her photographic quality reminded me of 1940s and 1950s film noir, and this was one of its stronger points.

In 2012, Matthan came to Rome to present the movie at a Festival and I got his All-American Rugby Player athletic tall body on the back of my moped and guided him through the beauties of Rome. We are now friends and I look forward to working with him again.

In between the two parts of Matthan's movie, I got to the top of my ecclesiastical movie career; I had been a priest in more than one movie, a Cardinal in *The Pasquino Night*, the Pope in *Padre Pio*, Jesus in the theater adaptation of *Paradise Lost* … what was left? … Are you guessing? …. Yes! English director Neil Jones offered me the role of all roles, playing the Almighty in his movie *The Reverend*. It was just one scene at the beginning in which God and the Devil (played by Rutger Hauer) were betting on the soul of a pious man, similar to the story of Job in the Bible.

When Emperor Franz Joseph of Austria asked for the hand of his cousin Elizabeth, age 15, her mother sighed and said, "You can't say no to the Emperor"

Good-hearted Lieutenant Lorenzo (Johnny) in *The Inflicted*

and I quoted her in answering Neil Jones that I was accepting his offer. Can you say "no" to be the Almighty? And being with Rutger Hauer, who had starred in a favorite movie of mine, *Blade Runner*, was indeed a plus. We shot the scene in just one night in Wales, in a wonderful Georgian building full of marble statues and I was all dressed in white, while Rutger was of course wearing black. He was very kind and ironic and I would have liked to have more time to get to know him better.

I then went to visit Darren Ward in Southampton and spent some pleasant days with him and his family. We visited a beautiful castle and I had the idea of being photographed coming out from an ancient tombstone with a "I'll come and get you" zombie expression. And I cooked Italian ragù (tomato and meat sauce) in Darren's kitchen with him filming the proceedings; it appears as an extra on the newly released German DVD/Blu-ray edition of *A Day Of Violence*.

I wrote these lines in 2013, so now, facing imminent publication, I must give a short account of my most recent activities.

I did a cameo role in a very good Italian movie, *Viva la libertà* (*Hooray to Freedom*) by Roberto Andò, another short appearance in an indie Irish production (*Three Sisters* by Daire McNab, who intrigued me very much with his idea of not using written dialogue but improvising my monologue of a father on his deathbed), and *The Invitation*, a short directed by iconic special effects genius Sergio Stivaletti, who proved to be an excellent director and gave me a great over-the-top role in a nice little horror story that will be part of a series for T.V.

The Almighty (Johnny) as he appeared in *The Reverend*

I had two excellent young partners in Rosario Petix and Giulia Di Quilio and we had a great time.

Three Sisters was just very recently released on DVD and I greatly appreciated the quality of its cinematography.

I then had a leading role in *Violent Shit: The Movie* directed by Luigi Pastore (a spin-off from an old German horror trilogy that became a trash/cult favorite), and I participated in a very nice and refreshing Italian movie *Una Gita a Roma* (An Outing in Rome), directed by the very talented actress and director Karin Proia.

As for stage work, I appeared as a bigot reverend in *Road to Mecca* by Athol Fugard, as Sigmund Freud in *The Visitor* by Eric-Emmanuel Schmitt and I directed, for the second time, *Macbeth* and also played the cameo role of King Duncan.

My work with Pietro Ingrao ended in 2014, not because of his death (which happened in 2017 at the remarkable age of 100), but because the Italian economic crisis called for some cuts in public administration and his life benefits fell under the axe.

After 10 years with a monthly salary and some financial security, I am left with just occasional money coming from movies (if they arrive), translations (if somebody asks me for one) and royalties for things I wrote or acted in on T.V. To make it short, I am poor and struggling to get by.

The Duchess of Windsor used to say, "Never too rich, never too thin." If I won't hit the first aim I am pretty sure I'll excel in the second, and begging in front of a church might prove an interesting experience. There's a first time for everything.

Chapter 36
The Alphabet Game

Even the life of any one-year-old baby, if recounted in every detail, day by day, would fill a book of some 1,000 pages, and as I will turn 63 in September 2017, I realize what an adventurous life I led. Many events and many issues I am interested in were left out of this book and, before saying goodbye, I will share with you a few of them, going through the alphabet.

A: As Anorexia—Once you get it you'll never get rid of it. It might be silent for years, and you can even add some fat to your frame and become slightly overweight, but at the first major inconvenience, at the next dangerous corner, at the first spell of depression, your lifelong friend will be by your side and, over the years, will not manifest itself with a conscious refusal of food. You would like to eat, but you can't. You prepare yourself a nice salad, but only two mouthfuls in you stop, because your stomach just closes. For the millionth time it's happening to me right now, so I know. (Smile)

B: As *Beyond Fury*—It's the title of Darren Ward's next project and it will be the third and last part of a trilogy that started with "Sudden Fury" (with David Warbeck) and continued with *A Day of Violence*. I have a wonderful role in it as a gangster boss named Lenzivitch (guess why?). I want to portray him outrageously and over the top, with tacky bright-colored suits, tons of golden chains and rings and the strongest Eastern European accent you ever heard. Zo if you vant to zee me in it just put some blood-fucking money into the financing campaign zat vill zoon start. Got it, you azzholes?

C: as Casting, or to better say, Type-Casting—It's the nightmare of every good actor and it occurs all over the world, but especially in Italy, where Neo-realism mixes up playing a character vs. being the character in real life. In Italy, if you audition for a role in a Western, you'd better go with hat, spurs and possibly appear on a horse. When I auditioned for the role of the Bishop in *Ladyhawke*, set in the middle ages, the casting agent recommended to me to go dressed "suitably" and I had to answer that unfortunately I was short of full suits of armor at the moment.

I was type-cast as weak, frail and crazy, then as cruel and sadist, then as aristocratic and lately as gay and, even if I don't care much about Italy, because I'm not working here anyway, I fear that my open writing in this book about my sex life could make things worse in trying to get roles in other countries. Come on, guys, don't be narrow-minded! I played macho-idiot Mike Logan and Trevor the womanizer on stage. I can't play coarse and vulgar because it's not inside me and I can't play hot blooded Latino-Banderas roles, but not because I have sex with men, but because I am not Latino.

Young Johnny sits on a hill

But I would like very much to play a drag queen as Terence Stamp did in *Priscilla* (oh ... I didn't talk about Terence Stamp ... well, another time). I never wore women's clothes and I would like to have a go at it because one of my theater dreams is playing Lady Bracknell (from *The Importance of Being Earnest*) in drag. English stage directors, if you hire me for that, I will work on an upper class British accent 12 hours a day!

D: As Death—Smoking 40 to 50 cigarettes a day and driving a moped in Rome, it's hard not to think about it. I am not afraid of it and never was, only, I think differently about it than many people. I hope it won't be sudden; it might be better for the one who dies, but it's terrible for those left behind and I experienced that horrible sensation with my father and my brother, so I know. I hope for a death that will give me time to put things in order, to say goodbye to the ones I love and to call "T" by my side. I have a very high pain threshold, but of course I don't want to suffer too much and a long time ago I made a deal with Lisa: She for me and I for her, at the right moment ... as in *The Barbarian Invasions*. I hope you've seen the movie, and if you haven't, just watch it: it's worthwhile.

E: as Evil—I played many evil characters, even if I think I am basically a good person. But, aside from fiction, evil does exist and not as a character with hoofs and horns, but as the bad aspect in our nature. Evil for me is egoism, ingratitude and violence in any form. It would suffice to follow the Gospel word: "Don't do unto others what you don't want others to do unto you," but it's not always that easy.

F: as Facebook—I spend quite a long time on Facebook. It's a great way to promote yourself and get work, but I also like very much to have friends there, and if they are fans I hope for them to become just friends as soon as possible. I patiently answer questions about my horror movies, but what interests me are people's ideas on politics, art and life in general. I also love to watch animal pictures and videos posted by the many pet-devoted friends I have. When my dog Tommy had to go under surgery for a hernia, I hadn't the money to pay the bills; I launched a subscription on Facebook to fund the operation and whoever helped me with whatever sum was getting an autographed picture (if interested). My friends were extremely generous and I will forever be grateful to them.

G: as Gay—The expression is so widely used that I started using it myself, but I never liked it because of its frivolous sound and I agree with a great friend of mine who, when asked if he is gay, answers, "No, I am a faggot."

I couldn't answer in the same way because I am actually bisexual, but even this label is not of my liking (as is any label on human behaviors) as I consider myself just "sexual" and my passions extend beyond to include animals and children. I deeply respect the gay movement for the fight against repression in some parts of the world (what's now happening in Russia makes me shiver) and for gay rights in general, but I do not go to the Gay Pride parades as I don't go into gay bars, gay discos or gay whatever, with the only exception of places that are intended to provide a healthy fuck on the spot.

H: As Hess—David Hess was my first partner and a great friend and his death was a terrible blow. Ruggero Deodato and I had planned to have him back in the sequel of *House at the Edge of the Park*, even if his character died in the first movie; he would have come back in my disturbed mind as a ghost and David was excited about it. I met him shortly before his death when we both attended a Festival in Scotland and we had the time of our life, him singing and conducting a great Q&A with fans. When a fan asked a question about the homosexual attraction between Alex and Ricky, I very seriously said that after 30 years we were ready to say the truth: David and I had been lovers ever since and we were planning on getting soon married in Barcelona. A discussion followed between David and me on who was to get dressed as the bride and people were literally rolling on the floor with laughter.

On the wall in back of the desk where the computer is, I hang pictures of people I love, both dead and alive. There's my aunt Laura, my brother Marco, my father, myself as a little boy, "T," Tommy with Christian (who was my last love story of importance), Alan, Giacomo (at age one and right after his birth with Alessandra), my aunt Viv in a painting made when she was a girl and David with me, in a signed photo from *House* that he gave me. Every morning I have a ritual, which consists in giving a finger kiss to every face. David is the last and, I don't know why, when I kiss him I always ask him to help me make money with the five euros scratch-off lottery card that I buy every morning. Two years ago I won 10,000 euros, so that proves that he is in Heaven and listens to me.

I: as I—I was educated with the principle that talking about oneself is bad manners and you have to say "I" as little as possible. Considering I wrote an autobiography, when it is published I am pretty sure there will be an earthquake on my family grave, because of my dead relatives revolting in their coffins.

J: as Jeremy—Along with Daniel Day-Lewis, Jeremy Irons is, in my opinion, the best living actor, and when he wasn't even nominated for his amazing performance in Cronenberg's *Dead Ringers*, I could have gone to Hollywood

A photoshoot with Johnny from 1987 ... photographed by Donatella Rimoldi

and strangled each Academy Award-voting member with my bare hands. Working with him would be one of the best gifts life could present me with.

K: as Key—I hate doors and I hate keys. If I am in a play, I would prefer to recite, "To be or not to be" walking on my hands than deal with a door (which often happens in modern plays); it takes me ages to remember in which way it opens and it never closes properly (with me, my colleagues close it in a flash). As for keys, they just rebel in my hands; if I am not used to a new one it doesn't open, if it is an electronic one it immediately demagnetizes, and unlocking the chain of my moped is a daily adventure.

L: as Ladylike—It's a quality getting more and more rare by the day. The most ladylike woman I met was Rossella Falk (1926-2013), who was one of the greatest actresses of the Italian stage, an icon of fashion and elegance and was considered the Italian Garbo. She also appeared in a few quality movies such as Fellini's *8 ½* and horror fans might remember her in her last film appearance in Dario Argento's *Sleepless*. She honored me with her friendship, and when the Italian embassy organized a gala for her in New York, I translated her monologue into English, one about Maria Callas that she wanted to perform on that occasion. She was amazingly beautiful even in old age, witty, cultivated and very rich because of her marriage to a multimillionaire, who died before their divorce was finalized. She lived luxuriously but she was also incredibly generous; less fortunate actors could be cured from cancer because of her help, the fatherless children of a friend of hers had their studies paid until graduation, and whoever served in her house was helped when getting married, finding a better job or supporting older relatives. I loved her dearly and I miss her terribly. I was a frequent guest both in her house in Rome and in her country place, where, when we were around the pool with other guests, she would command me to walk around with her saying: "Walk! Show these people how to do it!" She kindly thought I had the best possible gait because of my ballet studies. Hi Rossella, when I get there I'll walk for you as much as you want.

M: as Money—It notoriously "makes the world go around" and I always had the worst possible relationship with it. As in any love story, you can't expect to be loved if you don't love yourself and my problem with money is exactly that

I don't love it. I need some to survive and I use it willingly for pleasing others more than myself, not because I am some sort of saint, but just because, after a short hedonistic phase in my youth, I don't care about clothes or shoes, I don't lust after a yacht, I don't like being a tourist and I travel only for work. I am not interested in technological gadgets and I don't even buy too many books, because I already don't know where to put the ones I have. Once in a while I like to go to a warm place. When I am into eating there are a few expensive foods I like (salmon, seafood, filet) and I like buying things for the kitchen, because I cook pretty well and … not much else.

I would be perfectly happy with honest working fees, but apparently money doesn't like half-ways and either you elbow like mad to have it or you will always risk being poor, which I don't mind up to a certain extent. But when I can't pay home bills, buy cigarettes, feed the dogs and possibly help my son who's still at university, I could kick myself not to have profited from my beauty when I had it and accepted the many offers of steady relationships from very rich men. Some of them were awful, but some were acceptable and the whore in me wouldn't have minded living with someone out of financial interest (with a man, because with a woman I can't accept her paying for a coffee). Too late, but if among you readers there's a millionaire who is into middle-aged bald men, just ring me up or find me on Facebook.

N: as No—I am far from being a yes-man in the current sense of the word, but in my life I very rarely said "no." At times this was out of being lazy, at times because of curiosity and many times because I am basically docile and resilient. If someone really wants something from me, he or she usually gets it, provided my freedom is not put in danger. If anybody tries suffocating me with jealousy or wants to get into my thoughts and my silence mediations, a harsh "no" will always be the answer. I can be used but not possessed.

O: as Obama—Apart from waiting on a riverbank for the dead body of Silvio Berlusconi to pass by, I am not very interested in politics. I am a leftist, I fight for civil rights and for exploited people all over the world, but the quibbles of economy and political strategies are beyond me. I go by instinct and I instinctively liked former President Barack Obama very much. The fact that he is black is symbolically important but not influential and what I like about him are his defenses of minorities, his open and warm way of speaking and his calm and peaceful way of acting even when he calls for a war to be fought, as the current one against terrorism. He is also good looking, he has a nice wife and two pretty daughters, but it's just a plus.

P: As Politically Correct—I hate the expression and I'm sure that if the idea were to be universally accepted, we could attend the funeral of both wit and sense of humor. I use foul language and I call things by their name, because I know that vulgarity exists inside the individual and not in his words. There are comedians who can be coarse and inappropriate saying "handicapped" instead of "crippled," "Afro-American" instead of "black" and "anal intercourse" instead of "butt fucking," while others are light and seldom offensive when calling a blowjob a blowjob and fatso for an overweight person. And I think and hope I am in the latter category. Remember, I am bald but not "follicle changed."

Q: As Queen—If being a Head of State means having decisional power, I am a Republican, but if it means to symbolically represent a country, I am a Monarchist. Needless to say if the royal dynasty in question is not the cowardly and provincial Italian Savoia, who were kicked out after the second World War, then I am referring to the royal families of the United Kingdom, Sweden, Norway, Netherlands, Belgium, Denmark and Spain (I leave out the folkloristic Grimaldi of Monaco, but I think Prince Albert is a very interesting person). The Windsors had very bad moments and some disgraceful marriages (but I think William and Kate are just great) and Juan Carlos, King of Spain, had a great start and then dabbled in elephant hunting and cheating on his wife, but Prince Felipe will surely be a great king. Anyway the monarch I really worship is Queen Elizabeth and I hope to have a British passport in my pocket and be a faithful subject of Her Majesty before she dies; hopefully she will live to be 120.

R: As Ruggero—Ruggero Deodato was not only my first director, but, over the years, he became a great friend and a man I hold in high esteem. He is my opposite. I am lazy and he is fidgety; he is commanding and I am resilient; he is realistic and I am dreamy, but exactly for this reason we work well as a team and we proved it when we conceived in a mad week of brainstorming a sequel to *House at the Edge of the Park*. We wrote a very good and detailed treatment that was developed into a great screenplay by an English writer-director-producer, who gave us the idea. But financing never followed and the project stalled. However, Ruggero has as many ideas as hair on his head (perhaps not millions by now but, anyway, more than me) and I am sure I'll work with him again. Can't wait.

S: As Stefanini—Massimo Stefanini is a friend of mine and a great fashion designer of *haute couture*. When I was young he was madly in love with me, but when I met him back a few years ago, he was just desperately in need of someone who spoke good English because he had a show room at the Hotel De Russie (where Madonna stays when in Rome, to give you an idea of its expense). The three sisters of the king of Saudi Arabia were there and he wanted by all means to have them see his dresses. He hired me and I went into the maddest day of my life (which could be turned into a great movie comedy). It started at 10 in the morning with my writing a letter in over-stated prose to the Royal Highnesses, with the consent of the Hotel Manager for Arabian Affairs (I swear it's true) and I ended up the day at eight in the evening, following one of the Princesses with a notebook and writing down her royal wishes ("this mantle, but in black; this dress, but with a trail—we always wear trails at receptions in the palace—this jacket, but longer, this red gown but in blue…"). She then took out 20,000 euros in cash from her purse, not without first bargaining on prices; she put the money on the table and left. A tailor had taken her measurements and everything would be sent to Saudi Arabia when ready.

Another portrait from the Donatella Rimoldi photosheet in 1987

Massimo was very pleased with my work, my bowings, my saluting with "Salam Alaikum" and, of course, my English. I was in a difficult period after I no longer wrote for T.V., so I was hired part-time and, for a few months, I was working as a waiter in the morning and selling clothes in the afternoon to duchesses, countesses and millionaires, who didn't speak Italian. It was fun on one hand, but on the other I was just horrified and disgusted by the whims and fussing of those women over a button or the length of a glove, and when I was off work I ended up singing Communist songs in the luxury shopping area in the center Rome at the top of my lungs. But Massimo is a great person, I love him dearly, and some of his creations are just as much a form of art as a painting or a statue.

T: As "T"—What else? After the Dramatic breaking up in the late 1990s, we didn't meet for 10 years and only quite recently resumed a very distanced form of relationship with no sex in it. But:

> *He was my North, my South, my East and West,*
> *My working week and my Sunday rest,*

He didn't die as W.H. Auden's friend in *Funeral Blues*, he just doesn't want me anymore. But, as the Romans said, "Hope is the last Goddess" and we might end up holding hands in a rest home for the elderly. And if it doesn't happen I hope I'll die before him, because he solemnly promised to be by me in that moment, and if he will take me in his arms, playing with me the last scene of Verdi's *La Traviata*, I'll think I'll once again be on his red motorcycle, leaving for Paradise.

U: as Universe—I know nothing about astronomy, but the immensity of the universe fascinates me and I would like very much to witness the arrival of extra-terrestrials (possibly not green and naughty as in *Mars Attacks!*). This will

The only commercial Johnny did for Sanbitter, here playing the Counselor of a Roman Emperor

lessen the impact of many stupid issues we currently worry about on the planet Earth.

V: as Vice—I had many vices and the only one left is now smoking. I smoked since I was 13 and I have no intention of quitting and I hope to die as my mother did, her last conscious act being smoking a cigarette. I love the gestures, the taste but not the smell, so I basically live with my windows open, even in full winter.

I never smoke in the same room with a child and I respect people who don't allow smoking in their houses, but if they invite me to dinner, I am bound to spend half of the evening on a terrace or leaning out of a window. As for public places, I avoid restaurants without a smoking area and I am very pissed about the recent restrictions all over the world against lighting up. Smokers are still in the millions, so it's beyond my comprehension why hotels (most especially in the U.S.A.) don't have smoking rooms anymore (and of course never a fucking window that opens; God forbid we should waste healthy air conditioning!). And the very idea that you can't smoke in a park in over-polluted Los Angeles makes me laugh to tears.

W: as William—I worship William Shakespeare as a divinity and I don't think I have to explain why. I unfortunately only directed two of his plays and acted in one, but I translated half of his sonnets into Italian and six of his plays, with equal respect for the alternating prose, blank verse and rhyme (*Othello* is midway). None of them has been published and only *Antony and Cleopatra* was staged once by a small company. Italian directors don't care about wonderful verses being translated into plain prose, most especially if they do it themselves or commission the translations to a wife or a sister to receive the royalties. And Italian publishers are equally uninterested in good Shakespeare translations and settle for disgraceful ones. The same is true for novels or detective stories, with mistakes so apparent that you can spot them even without knowing the original version. As Roberto Faenza told me … what the fuck am I doing here?

X: as X Rated—Theoretically I agree with the fact that kids under a certain age shouldn't be allowed to watch some movies (more the violent ones than the ones with sex), but the web revolution made the issue preposterous, because young people, if they want, can watch whatever whenever and only their parents' care, sensibility and supervision can make the difference. As for adults, I think they should watch what they want and I am strongly against censorship and the editing of movies (based upon morality). When I went online for the first time and read comments about *Cannibal Ferox*, people said such things as: "I love watching a woman tortured" or "the bitch deserved it," I was shocked. I hated the movie even more and I was ashamed that I had appeared in it, but I don't actually think that those assholes would go out and rape a woman, because they saw the movie. In my opinion, the only useful censorship should be the one applied before shooting and not after, fining or incarcerationg whoever tortures animals or employs minors for unsuitable scenes.

Y: as Young People—I am very good with little children (from one day to five or six years old), but I have very little patience with kids from seven to 11 (too physical and restless the boys, and too doll-ish and whimsical the girls). I am extremely good with teenagers. I am better with boys than with girls, but not for sexual reasons—luckily I am not into minors—but just because I understand them better since I am a male myself. I had many difficulties during my teenage years and I didn't forget about it, so I easily identify with their problems and anxieties. If I were to be born again I'd probably become a psychologist for young people, as my brother Marco was.

Z: as Zoo—I spent a long time in them watching animals for my acting training, but I hate them and I would like to see the day when they will be all closed by law or the day when *Planet of The Apes* will come true and we humans will be caged instead of animals. We surely deserve that fate more so than they do.

    And that's all, folks.
    I thank you for reading this tome and I leave you with one final little poem that I wrote a few years ago, and one that expresses very much what I feel about myself these days.
    As my witty and cruel mother used to say: "Considering you are useless, try at least to be agreeable."
    I hope I have been.

JOHNNY JOHNNY

Rome 2005 (completed in October 2007)

You drink too much
You smoke too much
You say too many
Funny things.
And people laugh
And people say
That you still have
Wonderful eyes.
And you yourself
You know so well
The icon mask
Your face became:
The Egyptian skull
The Roman nose
Marlene's cheekbones.
And then the eyes
Oh yes, the eyes,
Who've been compared
To sapphire stars,
To turquoise wings
To seas and skies,
To every flower blue.

And conversation
Keeps flowing witty
Through my promising lips
And I do flirt
And I do smile,
Playing a melancholy trick.
I always know
Which light is better
Which is the best profile
And with my eyes
And with my voice,
With all my slender self
I can create
A world apart
For others to live in.

If you are young
If you are old

If, rich or poor,
Your heart is cold,
Do come to Johnny,
Answer his smile.
He will take care of you.
And if you want
All he can give,
Do come for a massage
And all your troubles
And all your sorrows
Are gone …
Gone with the wind.
For 50 minutes
And just some money
He'll sing you Tara's theme.

For sure I'm Scarlett
At times I'm Ashley,
If needed I'm Melanie,
But when it's over
And the audience left,
No Rhett is there for me.

Not my blue eyes
Not my cheekbones
Will make him come and stay.
No sexy smile,
No golden hands
Will win his strong embrace.

So, Johnny Johnny,
The one and only,
Just close the heavy door.
Switch off the lights,
Drop your sweet smile,
Prepare to go to bed.
The "Johnny, Johnny"
Of all your fans
Will be your lullaby.
And if the tune
Doesn't suit you,
Just use your sleeping pills.

Johnny extends Easter well wishes to all his fans, colleagues and friends throughout the world. The photo above, taken on Easter Sunday 2017, shows Johnny seated, surrounded by stepsisters Francesca and Susanna and their families.

Acknowledgments

The first bigger than life thank-you goes to my friend, director Darren Ward, who patiently, chapter by chapter, corrected my grammar (which tends to be problematic in all the languages that I know, starting with Italian), improved my phrasings and encouraged me all the way by liking what I was writing. God bless him.

While editing my manuscript, the American publisher (Midnight Marquee Press, Inc.) decided to make changes, turning my writing into standard American English. It was entirely the company's decision and I hope my Brit friends will not be offended. I stick with you guys.

A huge thanks goes to my Facebook friends, who were enthusiastic about this book since I announced I was writing it, and they often helped me by chatting with their amazing memory about my horror movies (avoiding me having to watch them all when I didn't remember details). People, you are just great.

And a big hug and a kiss on the nose to my beloved Tommy and Audrey, who understood perfectly I was doing something important and didn't walk on the computer but stayed by my side on the bed and occasionally licked my feet. I love you, dogs.

If you enjoyed this book, send $2.00 for a catalog of
Midnight Marquee Press titles or visit our website at http://www.midmar.com
Midnight Marquee Press, Inc.
9721 Britinay Lane
Parkville, MD 21234
410-665-1198
mmarquee@aol.com

www.ingramcontent.com/pod-product-compliance
Lightning Source LLC
Chambersburg PA
CBHW071307110526
44591CB00010B/806